EDGE OF CHAOS

ALSO BY DAMBISA MOYO

Winner Take All

How the West Was Lost

Dead Aid

EDGE
OF
CHAOS

**Why Democracy Is Failing to Deliver
Economic Growth—and How to Fix It**

DAMBISA MOYO

Little, Brown

LITTLE, BROWN

First published in the United States in 2018 by Basic Books
First published in Great Britain in 2018 by Little, Brown

13 5 7 9 10 8 6 4 2

A CIP catalogue record for this book
is available from the British Library.

Hardback ISBN 978-1-4087-1089-0
Trade paperback ISBN 978-1-4087-1091-3

Printed and bound in Great Britain by
Clays Ltd, St Ives plc

Papers used by Little, Brown are from well-managed forests
and other responsible sources.

Little, Brown
An imprint of
Little, Brown Book Group
Carmelite House
50 Victoria Embankment
London EC4Y 0DZ

An Hachette UK Company
www.hachette.co.uk

www.littlebrown.co.uk

CONTENTS

We all know what to do; we just don't know how to get re-elected after we've done it.

JEAN-CLAUDE JUNCKER,
President of the European Commission

ACKNOWLEDGMENTS

How right was Winston Churchill to observe, "Writing a book is an adventure. To begin with it is a toy and an amusement. Then it becomes a mistress, then it becomes a master, then it becomes a tyrant. The last phase is that just as you are about to be reconciled to your servitude, you kill the monster and fling him to the public."

Writing this book has been all these things and more.

I completed my PhD at Oxford University in economics, not in politics. And while I continue to be fascinated by economic questions—including growth, inequality, and development—it is increasingly evident to me that politics, and not economics, will be the key driver of human progress and prosperity in years to come.

People (like myself) who have been educated or live in the West tend to have a lot of advice for countries that are blatantly, patently nondemocratic. However, we are less effusive when it comes to how we might improve liberal democracy—even at a time when this political construct appears to be under challenge and the need to reform for the better is urgent.

In this book I seek to motivate a debate on how to upgrade and improve the democratic system. While I spent the majority of my formative adolescent years in a nondemocratic, one-party state, I have spent much of my adult life living and working in established democracies. These lived experiences have afforded me a priceless opportunity to observe, examine, and reflect on the benefits and weaknesses of comparative political systems. In this regard, what I offer here are points for discussion and debate, rather than engraved prescriptions.

As always, I have written a book that I would want to read, recognizing that it may be naturally flawed in ways that many political scientists and politicians will readily identify.

No book project is a solo venture, and without the focus and commitment of many people this book would not have been written.

The team at the Wylie agency—Andrew Wylie, Kristina Moore, and James Pullen—have, as usual, been superb. Over the years I have had the support of great researchers who have each left their imprimatur on the book—Rohan Beesla, Chen Liu, and Kim Shechtman—thank you so very much for your diligence and hard work.

A heartfelt thank-you for the herculean efforts of the team at Hachette (Basic Books) who magically transformed a kernel of an idea into the book you see today. Led by the exceptional and indomitable Lara Heimert, Brian Distelberg, Betsy DeJesu, Courtney Nobile, Kelsey Ororczyk, Alia Massoud, Thomas Kelleher, Allie Finkel, and Connie Capone were all supportive at crucial times of the book's writing, editing, and production process. In the UK, Tim Whiting and the Little, Brown team have been equally encouraging and immensely supportive—thank you so very much. I owe a great debt of gratitude to each of them.

Three people have been pillars of this book project, and although their names do not appear on the front cover, this book is as much theirs as mine: Jeremy Adams, Brandon Proia, and Geordie Young spent countless hours helping me road test the ideas and structure of this book. To them I am eternally grateful, while recognizing that all errors are mine alone.

Kristi Brusa is my backbone, and without her, every aspect of this project, and possibly even my life, would fall apart! Her unwavering dedication, efficiency, and affability make my life's pursuits that much more seamless and enjoyable. You are so much appreciated.

I cannot adequately thank my family—my parents, Steven and Orlean Moyo, and siblings Mdolole Steven, Leah, and Seki—who through thick and thin remain unwavering and steadfast in their love, support, and encouragement.

During the last phase of this book my immediate younger sister, Marsha Irene Hlekiwe, passed away, devastating our family. In life she was eternally irreverent, passionate, and determined.

This book is dedicated to her.

Dambisa Moyo

INTRODUCTION

ALMOST THREE DECADES AGO, THE Berlin Wall fell. A period of barely restrained chaos, turmoil, and stagnation across the Soviet bloc had come to an end, and new market capitalist democracies began to emerge not only in the former Soviet sphere but also throughout the developing world, promising economic prosperity and peace for their citizens. Analysts and economists believed the end of communism portended a new era of stability and growth. Yet less than thirty years later, all signs point toward a world once again on the edge of chaos.

Expressions of discontent with the post–Cold War order have been on the rise, particularly since the 2008 financial crisis. The crisis catalyzed a climate of dissent in the West—the source of the financial crisis—and beyond, in which populist movements challenged leaders and elites, from the Occupy Wall Street protests against inequality and corruption in the United States to anti-austerity marches in Europe and uprisings in the Middle East.

In December 2010, a poor Tunisian fruit vendor named Mohamed Bouazizi lit himself on fire to protest the arbitrary expropriation of his goods and his economic future. Within weeks Bouazizi's act of self-immolation precipitated the Arab

Spring revolutions, as under the slogan of *"Ash-shab yurid isqat an-nizam"* ("People demand removal of the regime") protests spread throughout the Middle East and North Africa, from Tunisia to Bahrain, Egypt, Jordan, Libya, Sudan, and Yemen. Today, that region is in the midst of what some are likening to a modern Thirty Years War.[1]

Protests have also shaken South America, Asia, Eastern Europe, and Southern Africa, to the extent that by the beginning of 2014 nearly half of the world's economies (65 out of 150) were expected to be at a "high" or "very high" risk of social unrest—the highest rate of risk registered over the past decade.[2] Meanwhile, angry citizens—from Buenos Aires to Kiev and Sofia, from Bangkok to Cape Town and Ouagadougou—were rapidly confirming those predictions. Three million people protested in Istanbul's Taksim Square and elsewhere throughout Turkey, demanding a voice in their political and economic futures; in Bangkok, two years of protests ended in a military coup; and massive demonstrations broke out in Brazilian cities, denouncing the billions spent staging the World Cup soccer matches in a country where one out of fifteen people is poor.[3]

This wave of rising political anxiety has not been confined to developing nations, as campaigns against austerity, migration, income inequality, and globalization have also gripped developed countries. In November 2014, 100,000 people rioted in the streets, setting fire to vehicles in a march against EU-sanctioned austerity—in Brussels! Around the same time, 50,000 demonstrators organized by the Campaign Against a Europe of Capitalism and War swarmed Barcelona in a demonstration against globalization. In July 2016, Berlin crowds protested Germany's open-door policy to refugees, which had reached 1.1 million in twelve months. In September 2016, around 200,000 rallied in Germany, Austria, and Sweden against the Transatlantic Trade and Investment Partnership (TTIP) between the European Union and the United States. In the United States, where workers at McDonald's and Walmart have demonstrated against low wages, polls reveal widespread concern about "income inequality," formerly a topic of interest mainly to economists and other academics.[4] The United States now has the highest level of income inequality in the industrialized world, a fact that some regard as "a threat to American democracy."[5] Meanwhile, the public's revolt against globalization, which many blame for the loss of jobs and the hollowing out of the middle class, culminated in the British vote to exit the European Union and the election of political neophyte and outsider Donald Trump as US president in 2016. Trump's ascendancy, in particular, represented a rebuke of the deeply entrenched political establishment that had dominated US politics for decades.

At a glance all of this global unrest appears disparate; however, these movements are united by a common thread: average citizens expressing anger at the impotence and corruption of the ruling political elites. It is a rebuke of political decisions to embrace trade and internationalism, policies that did not in fact "lift all boats" as the proponents of globalization promised, but actually harmed the livelihoods of so many. And it is a rebuke of government's failure to create economic growth.

No matter what government does, it seems to fail. This failure is perhaps most worrying in the United States—the world's leading economy for most of the past century. Not only does much of the world rely on the US economy (which accounts for a greater share of global gross domestic product (GDP) than any other country's, totaling approximately one quarter), but the United States is also an economic and political model that many other countries have viewed as a path to prosperity, and have thus sought to mimic.[6]

The failure is evident across many measures of living standards: in deteriorating real wages, rising poverty rates and worsening poverty statistics, as well as stagnating employment numbers. In terms of income, between 1979 and 2014 the top 10 percent in the United States saw their wages rise by a third, while the median wage rose by just 8 percent and the bottom 10 percent flatlined. Today, twenty million Americans live in extreme poverty, members of one in twelve American households go hungry, and, according to the US Census Bureau, the proportion of US citizens living below the poverty line increased from 11 percent in 2000 to almost 16 percent in 2012.[7] Joblessness, in terms of both unemployment and underemployment, has systematically worsened over the past decades. As an example, Charles Murray reported in 2016, "for white working class men in their 30s and 40s . . . participation in the labor force dropped from 96 percent in 1968 to 79 percent in 2015," meaning that, in essence, since the 1960s, one in six men of prime working age in this group has dropped out of the workforce.[8] Manufacturing employment accounted for about a third of the American labor force in 1970; as of 2010, that share had dropped to a tenth.[9] The European Union has not been spared from similar employment trends, with youth unemployment topping 40 percent in Spain and Greece and 37 percent in Italy, and nearly one in four youths in France unemployed.[10]

Worse still, not only are US living standards declining, but also the prospects of achieving social mobility and escaping economic destitution have fallen over time. In the last thirty years the probability has more than halved that an individual born into the bottom 25 percent of the income distribution in the United States will end his life in the top 25 percent. Meanwhile, according to the Pew Research Center, "the middle class made up 50 percent of the US adult population in 2015, down from 61 percent in 1971."[11]

Furthermore, American households continue to live a precarious financial existence, making it hard to plan or invest in a more prosperous future. According to US Federal Reserve data, Americans now owe $1 trillion in credit card debt, the highest level since the 2008 financial crisis, and US households owe a roughly equivalent amount in student debt and auto loans. A US Federal Reserve report notes that 47 percent of respondents said they either wouldn't be able to cover an unexpected $400 expense through savings or their credit card, or would have to cover it by selling something or borrowing money. Furthermore, life expectancy—a barometer of economic and social success—has remained flat for all groups combined from 2013 to 2014, and has actually declined for white American men and women according to a 2016 report.[12]

The confluence of these factors has contributed to the weakening of social cohesion (with rising rates of suicide, drug use, divorce rates, and violence in Middle America), culminating in the erosion of the middle class. It is the disaffected middle class that is at the heart of the rebellion against the political establishment in the United States and beyond.

Against this backdrop, angry voters' rebellion against the establishment should have come as no surprise. In the UK referendum, seventeen million voters gave the government the mandate and instruction to leave the European Union after its membership of over four decades. Meanwhile, in the United States, Trump's election was decidedly clear: not only did he win the presidency, but the Republicans held on to majorities in the Senate and the House of Representatives and won many gubernatorial races—an emphatic rebuke of the Democratic status quo. For its part, the US establishment has stressed that while Trump won the Electoral College, Hillary Clinton won the popular vote by nearly three million votes over Trump. However, these aggregated data mask the true disaffection of America's Rust Belt and the South. After all, if wealthier New York and California are removed from the calculation, it is actually Trump who wins the popular vote by nearly three million votes.

In rich countries as well as poor, people want change. They demand policies that will improve their lives: better education, improved health care, more jobs—and quickly. Danger signs abound that policymakers are no longer able to deliver strong and sustainable growth—at least not under current political and economic thinking.

Growth is imperative for fulfilling human demands and improving lives. Economically, growth promises to reduce poverty and raise living standards; politically, growth is the sine qua non for free markets, free people, and the rule of law; individually, growth is essential to allowing people to maximize their potential.

But today, economic growth across the global economy is patchy and anemic. Most of the world's largest and most strategically vital emerging nations—including Argentina, Brazil, Colombia, India, Indonesia, Mexico, South Africa, and Turkey—are only growing at 3 percent or less a year. This is far below the roughly 7 percent minimum needed to double per capita incomes from one generation to the next and consign poverty to history. Although there is some evidence that Europe emerged from recession in early 2017, the growth forecasts remain stalled at around 1 percent, hampered by the structural challenges of high unemployment and political uncertainty. The Japanese economy continues a twenty-five-year period of malaise and tenuous prospects. And in the United States, despite recent GDP and job growth, and in spite of the initial positive reaction of financial markets to Trump's election, the continued erosion of infrastructure and education dampens prospects for long-term growth. Most alarming, the International Monetary Fund has almost consistently cut its global growth forecasts over the past half decade after the 2008 financial crisis, warning in 2014 that the world economy may never regain its pre-2008 pace of expansion. This evidence of economic decline signals a more serious and deleterious corrosion of the global economy as it faces extreme long-term structural impediments or headwinds.

Three key drivers of growth—capital, labor, and productivity—have eroded under unprecedented headwinds. We face massive demographic shifts yielding too many young, unskilled, and disaffected workers in emerging economies, and aging populations already draining pension and health systems in developed economies. Widening income inequality, diminishing social mobility, commodity scarcity, and technological advances that enhance productivity at the cost of putting more people out of work all threaten to further dampen growth worldwide. The result of leaving these headwinds unanswered will be economic depression—a catastrophe for which existing policy tools are "impotent," as the economists Lawrence Summers and Paul Krugman have both argued.[13]

As much as the US economy will struggle to overcome these headwinds, other economies will likely struggle even more, particularly those that have depended on the United States for trade and foreign direct investment and as the largest bill payer of public goods and police of international sea-lanes. Moreover, at roughly 22 percent of the budget, the United States is the largest contributor to the North Atlantic Treaty Organization (NATO), a group of twenty-nine countries committed to mutual defense in the event of an external attack.[14]

In the face of these economic headwinds, liberal democratic capitalism is in retreat. After the fall of the Berlin Wall, this political and economic model—characterized by universal suffrage, civil rights and personal freedoms, and the individual control of capital and labor—had seemed ascendant. But now alternative models, such as authoritarianism, state capitalism, and illiberal democracies, have proliferated, offering formidable challenges to liberal democratic capitalism's model of achieving growth. Meanwhile, liberal democratic capitalism itself has become weak, corrupt, and oblivious to its own ailments.

As they confront these challenges, leaders of liberal democratic capitalist nations are hobbled by the quirks of their own political systems. Needing to satisfy the electorate in order to remain in political office, policymakers tend to favor short-term policy responses. In focusing only on the gains that can be won today, they ignore the costs and consequences borne tomorrow. The short-termism that clouds policymaking leads politicians to embrace inferior policies.

Protectionism, for example, is now on the rise. According to Global Trade Alert, the G20 imposed 644 discriminatory trade measures on other countries in 2015. And as a result of increased capital controls on banks, cross-border capital flows have declined—with international loans having decreased 9 percent from 2014 to 2016, according to the Bank for International Settlements. State intervention in the economy is increasing even in traditionally capitalist societies. This is evident in the growth of welfare states, the expansion of the public sector, and the rise of governments as employers and allocators of capital. In the long term, such policies are likely to exacerbate military as well as economic conflict over scarce resources—pressuring politicians to make even worse decisions and fomenting a vicious downward cycle.[15] Most importantly, such policies will only produce lower global growth.

The defining challenge of our time is to create solid and sustained economic growth that continues to meaningfully improve people's lives. This is true in the United States, the Eurozone (countries using the euro), and other industrialized economies that are creaking under mounting debt, challenging demographics, and stagnating productivity. It is just as true in the developing world—home to 82.5 percent of the world's people, 70 percent of them, on average, less than twenty-five years old. A period of unprecedented economic expansion has slowed in some places and has ended in others, and there can be no substitute for restoring growth everywhere.[16]

Edge of Chaos argues that liberal democracies of the sort prevalent in the West simply cannot deliver this growth without substantial reform. Without fundamental changes, democratic politicians will struggle to address the numerous headwinds the global economy faces today. Indeed, the myopia within democracy leads to the misallocation of scarce resources, such as capital and labor, and shortsighted investment decisions by politicians and business. Ultimately, the myriad economic challenges are a manifestation of a corrosive problem in the democratic political process.

This book proposes ten far-reaching reforms to democracy that are designed to combat this myopia, overcome the headwinds challenging the global economy, and galvanize economic growth. The proposals transform the way elections are held, alter how politicians are judged, and ensure that both voters and politicians take a long-term view. To this end the proposals include lengthening political terms to better match long-term economic challenges, imposing minimum standards on both politicians and voters, and many more.

Stagnant growth, entrenched poverty, high unemployment, unwinding globalization, and geopolitical unrest have become the new normal. The skepticism among policymakers, politicians, and ordinary people about the capacity of democratic capitalism to deliver growth and reduce poverty over the long term is in fact very rational. The state capitalism of China, Lee Kuan Yew's Singapore, and Chile under General Augusto Pinochet have all moved hundreds of millions of people out of poverty and in some cases delivered impressive advances. The formidable economic performance over recent decades of such nations and others that are not liberal democracies—64 percent of the world's elected governments in all—seems to suggest that democracy is not a prerequisite of economic growth.

Yet *Edge of Chaos* insists on the promise of liberal democracy. After all, per capita incomes in liberal democracies continue to rise, albeit sluggishly. Meanwhile, the problems of growth are not confined to market capitalism—and real problems such as corruption infect state capitalist and other competing systems. Rather than turning away from liberal democracy, nascent democracies need to prioritize creating growth over the immediate devotion of some paradigm of democratic perfection. And established democracies must put their own houses in order by passing aggressive constitutional reforms.

Above all, policymakers must face up to the facts of the twenty-first century. In an interconnected world of anemic growth, other countries' crises will become our crises, whether they take the form of terrorism, income inequality, refugees, the resurgence of infectious diseases, or illegal immigration, and governments will grow ever more fragmented and weak, further undermining an already fragile international community. For Americans, and policymakers in the world at large, protectionism and isolationism are no remedy. Historical evidence makes clear that protectionism will be accompanied by higher unemployment, lower economic performance, and stagnating living standards in the United States and elsewhere. An economically weakened and isolationist America will call into question the Pax Americana, whereby the United States oversees international peace and security, and thus expose the world to the unpredictable whims and values of nondemocratic powers. These are not the solutions the world needs.

Creating sustainable economic growth in the twenty-first century requires no less than aggressively retooling history's greatest engine of growth, democratic capitalism itself. This requires a clear-eyed assessment of how ineffective the system is in its current state, politically as well as economically—and then implementing the repairs that will yield better outcomes. Too much is at stake for us to remain wedded to the status quo. The ominous rise of protectionism and nationalism throughout the world portend that the global economy and community are eroding already. The only way forward is to preserve the best of liberal democratic capitalism and to repair the worst. We cannot cling to past practices and old ideologies simply for their own sake.

Doing nothing is no choice at all.

1

THE IMPERATIVE IS GROWTH

FOR THREE SUN-DRENCHED DAYS IN April 1994, millions of South Africans formed lines that stretched for miles to participate in the first truly democratic election in the nation's history. Children cheered from the tops of billboards that featured a picture of Nelson Mandela and his call to action: "Vote for jobs, peace, and freedom."

Today, more than twenty years since the end of apartheid, South Africa has changed profoundly. All citizens, regardless of race, now have the right to vote and thus help shape the country's future. But living standards remain dreadful. Unemployment still fluctuates around the 1994 rate of 20 percent, and nearly half the population lives below the poverty line. Average life expectancy has gone from 62 to 57.4, mainly as a result of South Africa's dubious distinction of having the world's highest incidence of HIV and AIDS. Meanwhile, the income gap is widening. According to the Gini coefficient,

1

a measurement of inequality in which 0 represents perfect equality and 100 perfect inequality, South Africa measures 63.38—a massive gap between rich and poor. (For comparison, Brazil and Colombia have coefficients around 53, the United States and China are at 41 and 42, respectively, and Norway and Denmark are both at 27.) Two decades after its first democratic election, South Africa ranks as the most unequal country on Earth.[1] A host of policy tools could patch each of South Africa's ills in piecemeal fashion, yet one force would unquestionably improve them all: economic growth.[2]

Diminished growth lowers living standards. With 5 percent annual growth, it takes just fourteen years to double a country's GDP; with 3 percent growth, it takes twenty-four years. In general, emerging economies with a low asset base need to grow faster and accumulate a stock of assets more quickly than more developed economies in which basic living standards are already largely met. Meaningfully increasing per capita income is a critical way to lift people's living standards and take them out of poverty, thereby truly changing the developmental trajectory of the country. South Africa has managed to push growth above a mere 3 percent only four times since the transition from apartheid, and it has remained all but stalled under 5 percent since 2008. And the forecast for growth in years to come hovers around a paltry 1 percent. Because South Africa's population has been growing around 1.5 percent per year since 2008, the country's per capita income has been stagnant over the period.

The slow-growth story we see in South Africa is common among developing countries. Even the largest and most strategically important of these economies (by population size and economic influence) are generating a meager annual growth rate of 2–3 percent a year.[3] At the time of this writing, Brazil, Russia, India, and China (grouped together by the moniker BRICs) all have growth forecasts far below the "magic" 7 percent number. Brazil and Russia are expected to struggle and possibly contract, with some forecasts projecting negative economic growth.

The virus of slow growth has spread across borders, with even the world's richest economies falling victim. For instance, between 1970 and 1990 average growth rates in the OECD (Organisation for Economic Co-operation and Development) were consistently around 3.4 percent per annum, compared to around 2 percent today, with the Eurozone emerging from a minor recession in 2012. Moreover, in the first quarter of 2017, larger developed economies such as France and Italy posted annual growth rates around 1 percent. While economists and analysts assert that the United States may be back on a path of stable growth, for instance, as GDP has ranged between 1.5 and 2.5 percent since 2010, US GDP growth has never exceeded 2.5 percent since the financial crisis. The last time the country recorded a GDP above 5 percent was in 1984.

Even so, the benefits of this limited growth are spread unevenly across the population. From poorly educated workers to a glaring lack of infrastructure, many of the variables that have dimmed American prospects for decades still remain unaddressed and will continue to drag growth downward in the years to come.

This chapter reveals why the growth forecasts of many developing countries and developed economies alike are so dire. It explains why growth matters so much for living standards and human progress, and why permanently diminished growth threatens to translate into permanently lower living standards. And because we cannot understand the importance of growth without discussing how we measure it, the chapter explains GDP, its shortcomings, and why it remains the definitive tool by which economists, politicians, and policymakers gauge a country's progress, establish new public policy, and set benchmarks for comparison and improvement.

GROWTH MATTERS—POWERFULLY—TO ORDINARY people. When economic growth wanes, everyone suffers. Stagnation exacerbates numerous social, health, environmental, and political problems. The very essence of culture, community, and people's individual expectations about the kinds of lives they can lead become dimmer, coarser, and smaller in the absence of growth.

Economic growth is about satisfying the most basic of individual human needs. On the micro level, for the individual, the accumulation of money itself is pointless unless one uses it to improve one's own station or else improve society in general. Likewise, economic growth at the macro level should translate to improvements in access to and quality of such basic needs as food, shelter, security, and health care. Stagnation at either level means these individual and societal needs go unfulfilled, often with dire results.

The linkages among deteriorating economic growth, worsening living standards, and increasing poverty and instability are well established. A classic historical example is the 1789 French Revolution, which was touched off by rioting prompted by a decade of deteriorating living conditions, including tax hikes and food shortages. The lack of progress and ensuing economic crisis ultimately led to a political revolution.

In the present day, Greece has experienced a similar pattern. Between 2008 and 2016, the Greek economy contracted by 45 percent in GDP terms, leading to a concomitant rise in poverty. Job losses, wage cuts, and reductions in workers' compensation and social benefits all led to Greek households becoming on average 40 percent poorer. By 2014, disposable household income had sunk to below 2003 levels. Major riots in 2010, with over a hundred thousand people marching in Athens, culminated in the election of a new far left government led by the Syriza Party in 2015.

Growth enhances the living standards of both individuals and society as a whole in three main ways. First and most straightforwardly, growth offers the individual an opportunity to improve their own livelihood. For example, a worker who earns a bonus or extra income can use that money to obtain better health care, education, transportation, and food. Because of the growth in their income, they are able to secure goods and services that enhance their life. Conversely, if an individual loses their job or receives a reduced income, they can be forced to cut back on health care, food, and education. Growth can make an individual's life better or worse in this simple way.

Second, growth in income can allow an individual to have an impact on the wider community. They can hire others or invest their windfall. Through everyday purchases, the individual has the opportunity to support other businesses and individuals, and help others increase their own standards of living. By investing or making their capital available to be borrowed, they enable others to grow their incomes, improve their lives, and better society. Many small and medium enterprises in particular rely heavily on this type of individual investment. Given that over 90 percent of businesses in the OECD are small and medium-sized enterprises of fewer than 250 employees (and 60–70 percent of employment), and that in developed countries a large percentage of a nation's overall economic growth comes from such companies, an individual's investments can meaningfully affect the economy.[4]

Conversely, the absence of growth in the wider community can have a profound effect on the individual. Economic contraction can foster political and social unrest and a breakdown in social cohesion. The town of Gary, Indiana, symbolizes this kind of industrial decline. Once a thriving steel town, it has seen its population tumble to less than 80,000 from 180,000 in the 1960s. The town's steelworks employed 5,000 people in 2015, a fraction of the 30,000 who worked there forty years earlier.[5] Gary has a poverty rate of 38 percent, high crime, and poor levels of education attainment. The lack of growth in the city's overall economy has had meaningful negative effects on individual quality of life.

The relationship between growth in income and human progress (or conversely between a growth slump and a reduction in living standards) is explained by the multiplier effect. Additional income earned by an individual will be transmitted across the economy in multiples of its original value. This theory was originally devised by the British economist John Maynard Keynes to show that increases in government spending would result in increased income for the population. However, the original source of new capital need not be the government.

Say that a factory worker receives a $2,000 bonus after a successful year and that he spends it all in a lump sum. When he does so, perhaps on upgrading his home, the $2,000 becomes the income of multiple traders in his town, who in turn go on to spend it elsewhere. The worker's $2,000 can quickly become $3,000, or $4,000, and so forth. In essence, the $2,000 enables not just one transaction (the original payment to the general contractor), but many subsequent ones, so that rather than being saved, the money is spent.

There is a third, more complex way that growth can enhance (or by its absence diminish) the quality of life: through its role in preserving transparent political structures. Personal rights and freedoms can only exist if a society is able to hold government accountable. Growth allows society to sustain itself and to ensure accountability, but in the absence of growth, society weakens. In this way, economic stress creates the conditions for political upheaval and, at the extreme, the breakdown of liberal democratic institutions.

Germany in the 1920s and 1930s offers the classic example of this sort of breakdown. Germany faced an enormous reparations bill from the First World War, high levels of debt, hyperinflation, surging unemployment, and the 1929 cratering of world financial markets. The country's subsequent economic collapse enabled the rise of Nazi extremism. More recently, in the aftermath of the 2008 financial crisis, Spain's economy faced a growth contraction of approximately 6 percent, while unemployment soared to 26 percent by 2013.

Amid these conditions, momentum grew for the breakup of the country through Catalonian independence. The clamor for Catalonian secession has intensified since the end of the financial crisis and aggravated ill feelings among Catalans, who are concerned that they are being forced to pay more into Spain's coffers than they should. An unofficial poll held by the Catalonian regional government in 2014 revealed that 80 percent of voters backed independence. The breakaway of Catalonia from Spain would be costly, as the region contributes 19 percent to Spain's GDP, produces 45 percent of Spain's high-tech exports, and is the gateway for 70 percent of the country's exports. The consequences of a Catalonian secession for government revenue, jobs, and the broader Spanish economy would be considerable.

When growth is strong, it sets in motion a virtuous cycle of economic opportunity, upward mobility, and rising standards of living. Without it, society contracts and atrophies in ways evident not merely in economic indices but more meaningfully in the lived experiences of people and their communities. Although growth alone cannot end disease pandemics, address environmental and climate concerns, improve educational outcomes, or blunt the threat of radicalized terrorism, without growth solving these problems becomes much harder.

How does economic growth help in resolving these seemingly intractable challenges? First, it enables a government to fund and enhance public goods—education, health care, national security, and physical infrastructure. In a climate of rising economic growth, governments (and businesses through increased sales and revenues) gain marginal dollars that they can earmark for these purposes. Without economic growth, governments are forced to reduce resources in one area in order to fund budgetary needs in another.

Second, strong economic success is a precursor to private investment and innovation that act as a springboard for improved living standards and progress. Economic growth helped drive US living standards throughout the twentieth century. Incomes rose thirty times, and hundreds of thousands of Americans were moved out of poverty. In a similar vein, China's legendary economic expansion consisted of double-digit growth rates over three decades, helping move over three hundred million Chinese out of indigence.

Without economic growth, the public purse faces reduced tax revenues and is unable to fund and deliver on basic human needs in the form of public goods. Essentially, a lack of success is a precursor of worsening living conditions and unrest. In periods of collapsing growth—the 2008 financial crisis is a stark example—all manner and marks of human progress, including real wages, job opportunities, life expectancy, and social mobility, suffer. A lack of economic success does far more than just diminish living standards; it promotes disaffected and destitute populations. While economic failure fuels destabilizing angst, strong economic progress should dissuade radicalization and rebellion.

Certainly there are limits to what growth can do. It is inescapably true that certain phenomena are immune to being solved by growth. Even if economic growth can meaningfully undermine the ability to recruit for extremist movements, there will always be ideologues immune to any economic success. Terrorism thus represents one phenomenon beyond the reach of growth alone. Economic improvement can ameliorate the situation but not eradicate it in its entirety. Likewise, economic growth alone cannot solve income inequality. After all, we have seen countries where income inequality worsens even as they grow. Growth can even become a problem in its own right, as poorly managed economic growth spurts can leave a damaging legacy of debt and inflation. Economic growth alone is no panacea, but without it long-term societal progress is impossible.

Quite clearly economic growth is utterly vital to the survival, success, and stability of a nation. The challenge of economics since its inception has been to pinpoint the key elements of growth and to navigate the maze of individuals and businesses to determine how these contribute to real, sustained growth. Before delving into the measurement of economic growth, it is important to understand the engines of growth. To that end, it is worth examining what drives growth and considering how best growth should be measured.

Viewed through the prism of economics, growth is a function of three key factors: capital (how much money an economy has invested minus deficits and debts); labor (measurable in terms of both quality and quantity); and total factor productivity (a catchall of other factors that affect economic growth beyond capital and labor, including innovation, technology, political systems, laws, and regulations).

Productivity is thought to account for more than 50 percent of why one country grows and another does not. Transparent and reliable laws, clearly defined property rights, and advances in technology all contribute to higher productivity and thus catalyze economic growth.[6] Drags on productivity, such as debt and demographics, can limit growth. In the aftermath of the 2008 financial crisis, many developed countries have suffered under the weight of mounting debts and deficits. Demographic shifts have also proven taxing, as they have taken the form of a decline in the working-age, economically active population and a rise in an aging, economically inactive, increasingly expensive population. Subsequent chapters will analyze these factors in greater detail, but for now, suffice it to say that these levers act to dampen economic growth.

Evaluating the true health of an economy is complex. The presence of debt can complicate the picture. A neighbor who appears to be wealthy with a large house and new car might just as easily be heavily in debt, one unexpected bill away from bankruptcy, as he might be debt free, but neither scenario is obvious to the naked eye. At the macroeconomic level of an economy, debt similarly complicates the growth picture. As we shall examine in detail, debt can have deleterious effects on economic growth.

To be sure, high-level growth statistics can be misleading. Over the past three decades, aggregate growth numbers in the United States (and elsewhere) increased, suggesting that living standards were increasing. However, these growth gains accrued more to the owners of capital rather than to the ordinary working populace who depend on labor for their income. This disparity can be seen in a comparison between capital's record returns—between 1970 and 2017 the Dow Jones stock index has risen by more than 4.5 times in value, and S&P 500 annual average real returns have been around 8.7 percent—and the performance of real wages, which have flatlined over the same period. Moreover, American workers have found themselves much more in hock to lenders, having amassed burdensome debt in mortgages and student and car loans, further eroding their living standards. The split between gains to capital holders and losses to labor providers is echoed in the 2016 US electoral map. It is no coincidence that the two states—New York and California—that are home to the great pools of American capital, Wall Street, Hollywood, and Silicon Valley, saw voters heavily endorse the status quo, whereas the voters in America's industrial heartland overwhelmingly voted for change.

Evaluating growth on the scale of a national economy, or globally, is complex. Before we can trace the engines of growth, along with the most common barriers to it, we must go back to the beginning to understand how economists calculate the wealth of nations in the first place.

In 1085, William the Conqueror, the reigning monarch of England, commissioned the Domesday Book to estimate the value of his domain. It was among the earliest attempts to measure the economic standing of a country. William's surveyors calculated that the total value of England's land was approximately £73,000. A formidable undertaking, the survey relied on subjective individual judgment. The bulk of the survey was devoted to calculating the value of rural estates, the primary sources of national wealth. The tally also included arable land, the number of plough teams, river meadows, woodland, watermills, and fisheries. Observers at the time marveled at how comprehensive the survey was, noting that "there was no single hide nor yard of land, nor indeed . . . one ox or cow or pig which was left out and not put down in his record."

The Domesday Book was the gold standard for estimating economic data for a millennium, although it would not be the last attempt to calculate national wealth. In the 1660s, English economist and philosopher William Petty tabulated national income and wealth across England. His calculation included land, ships, personal estates, and housing, and it captured both the stocks—that is, the value of existing holdings of property—and flow aspects—the growth of those values over time. Petty ultimately assessed England's total wealth at the time at approximately £667 million. But what was missing from both his estimate and the Domesday Book was a means of looking across borders to compare national wealth. It was not until the twentieth century that a more harmonized, globally accepted means of comparing the economic standings of different nations would emerge.

It ultimately took the Great Depression to expose how badly such comparisons were needed. Lacking comparative economic data, policymakers were hard-pressed to design policies that would steer the United States out of crisis. The solution finally came in the form of the National Income and Product Accounts produced in the early 1930s by the Russian-American Nobel laureate Simon Kuznets. Kuznets collated and analyzed statistical indicators of economic growth across fourteen European countries, the United States, and Japan over sixty years. This provided the basis for cross-country comparison of national wealth. First presented in a report to the Senate in 1934, "National Income, 1929–32," and then further developed during and after World War II, Kuznets's work laid the groundwork for calculating gross domestic product (GDP)—defined as the value of all goods and services produced within an economy over a specified time period. It is the sum of private consumption and investment, government spending, and net exports—that is, the value of what the country exports less what it imports. Applying consistent measurement standards of these variables allows economists to compare economies across the world. Whereas GDP measures the value of income created, say, in a year, the Domesday Book captured the full value of the inventory of assets, or the wealth of England at that moment in time. For policymakers to this day, GDP remains the definitive yardstick for economic performance, permitting them to assess the health and progress of a nation's economy and, by extension, people's lives.[7]

Yet GDP's dominance has brought criticism. It fails to capture changes to an economy's structure, such as the shifts to a service-led or technology-based economy. Some have protested that it fails to capture the unofficial or black market economy. Others have asserted that any purely economic indicator by itself may be inadequate to truly measure society's progress. It is therefore no surprise that over the last several decades, economists, sociologists, and other academics have devised other metrics for tracking happiness, well-being, and social progress, some of which have garnered a substantial following.

Implicit in these metrics is a challenge to GDP as the dominant measure of human progress—despite the fact that these measures sometimes themselves rely on GDP or some variance of GDP and come with limitations of their own. Even so, GDP remains a compelling measure of economic as well as social progress inasmuch as improvements in economic GDP translate into social progress. Policymakers have nevertheless become interested in these alternative measures, which, even if they do not displace GDP as the most prominent measure of economic growth, have value in complementing GDP in future assessments for economic and living standard progress. Furthermore, these proposed additions to GDP remind us that the endgame for public policy is progress and improved living standards rather than GDP growth for growth's sake. Nonetheless, these rankings reveal that consistently richer countries (in terms of GDP) rank at the top of the indices and poorer ones at the bottom.

For example, happiness indices reflect a demand that happiness be recognized as a criterion for government policy. First published in 2012, the *World Happiness Report* measures happiness by indexing GDP per capita alongside social support, life expectancy, freedom, generosity, and the absence of corruption. Of the 155 countries collated in the 2017 *World Happiness Report*, the ten happiest countries, in descending order, are Norway, Denmark, Iceland, Switzerland, Finland, the Netherlands, Canada, New Zealand, Australia, and Sweden. The ten least happy countries, beginning with the least happy, are the Central African Republic, Burundi, Tanzania, Syria, Rwanda, Togo, Guinea, Liberia, South Sudan, and Yemen. While the United States is the largest country in GDP terms, it ranks fourteenth on the 2017 happiness index.[8]

A more traditional measure that goes beyond GDP alone is the United Nations' Human Development Index (HDI). First published in 1990, the HDI assesses longevity, education, and income across each nation's population, on the premise "that people and their capabilities should be the ultimate criteria for assessing the development of a country, not economic growth alone."[9] The HDI reveals how two countries with the same level of gross national income (GNI)—that is, the total domestic output (GDP) plus foreign GDP generated by citizens abroad, minus domestic output created by foreigners—can end up with such different outcomes. In this way, it allows observers to compare the relative effectiveness of different policy choices and capital investments. In this index, Norway, Australia, and Switzerland rank at the top, with GNIs above US$40,000, and the Central African Republic, Niger, and Chad are at the bottom of the index, all with GNIs of less than US$2,000 per capita.

Some of these measures move beyond individuals and attempt a holistic assessment of the health of society. Since its founding in 2012, the Social Progress Imperative has offered a Social Progress Index that examines a range of social and environmental indicators beyond GDP, from access to electricity to religious tolerance, to measure three distinct dimensions of social progress: Basic Human Needs, Foundations of Wellbeing, and Opportunity.

The 2017 Social Progress Index covers 133 countries and 94 percent of the world's population. The world as a whole would score 64.85 in Social Progress based on an average of all countries. On average, the top cluster of fourteen countries ranked as having "very high social progress"—including Denmark, Finland, Iceland, Norway, and Switzerland among others—scores 94.92 on Basic Human Needs, Foundations of Wellbeing at 89.68, and Opportunity at 84.04. The cluster of seven countries described as having "very low social progress" include the Central African Republic, Afghanistan, Chad, Angola, Niger, Guinea, and Yemen. For this cluster the average dimension scores of Basic Human Needs, Foundations of Wellbeing, and Opportunity are 42.67, 45.42, and 27.74.[10]

The Legatum Prosperity Index is distinctive in that it is the only global measurement of prosperity that combines objective and subjective data to measure both wealth and wellbeing. Countries are ranked according to their performance across eight equally weighted subindices, with New Zealand, Norway, and Finland ranked the top three, and Yemen, Afghanistan, and Central African Republic as the bottom three in the 2016 rankings. These include Economic Quality, Business Environment, Governance, Education, Health, Safety & Security, Personal Freedom, and Natural Environment.

What can we learn from these various indices? While noneconomic factors such as health, well-being, and quality of life matter to humanity, economic measures such as GDP generally correlate to success in the other areas, with a small amount of variation among those who are awarded the top spot. In a nutshell, economic growth underpins all else; a country needs economic growth to achieve happiness, wellbeing, and ultimately human progress.

To be sure, GDP estimates provide a snapshot of GDP at a single point in time, but nothing more. A large GDP can indicate that a country is rich yet mask that its economy might be struggling and scarcely growing. For example, in the aftermath of the financial crisis, France has barely grown—with 2016 GDP growth of a paltry 0.8 percent. The fact that French GDP in 2015 was US$2.4 trillion may suggest that the country is ranked among the richest in the world, yet the economy has declined from US$2.9 trillion in 2008 and has seen a 20 percent decline in the country's per capita income in the same period.

In contrast, a very poor country with low GDP can celebrate a rapid GDP growth rate of 10 percent per year, yet the economy overall remains poor. This is often true of poor countries that have high GDP growth rates but are starting from a low GDP base. For example, Côte d'Ivoire grew by 8.4 percent in 2015 but remains among the poorest countries in the world, with a GDP per capita of US$1,398.69. Another limitation of GDP is its inability to capture nonmonetary forms of economic progress. The living standard in a country would certainly improve if technical innovations allowed, for instance, a day's worth of food to be produced in less working time.

The *Economist*'s Big Mac index attempts to capture just this. It offers a lighthearted yet nevertheless intriguing estimate of the number of minutes of work needed to afford a McDonald's Big Mac sandwich. At the low end, in Copenhagen a worker needs to work just 20 minutes to afford the hamburger. Someone in Mexico City requires 280 minutes, making Mexico among the most work-intensive of the countries in the index. This metric can quickly capture the impact of policy changes. In the United Kingdom, new minimum wage legislation came into effect in April 2016, with the result that the amount of work required to afford a Big Mac shrunk from 26 minutes to 18 minutes.[11]

Beyond these limitations, GDP and GDP per capita are vulnerable to the critique that they are imprecise. GDP measures also fail to show distributional effects of income or wealth and therefore mask inequality. In essence, they say nothing about who the winners are when GDP is rising and conversely do not say who the losers are when GDP is falling.

Most of us know growth when we experience it. An individual's sense of economic progress is captured most simply in Ronald Reagan's question: "Ask yourself, are you better off now than you were four years ago?" Nevertheless, money has become the yardstick by which individuals, governments, and societies as a whole are judged.

THE AMOUNT OF MONEY PRODUCED by an economy—its GDP—has become the most revealing and relevant measure of goods and services produced that year. In spite of its limitations, there is no better modern-day method for aggregating and comparing a country's economic progress against other countries than GDP. This is why policymakers continue to rely on it. Furthermore, because new measures of societal progress have not yet gained traction, GDP reigns. However, GDP ultimately remains an abstraction. Growth is not.

Growth, most visible in the form of rising living standards, is the key to a stable, successful society. Having established why economic growth is so important and how best to measure it, we must now contend with the range of factors that are holding back growth and thus challenging human progress. One way to better understand these factors is to compare how different nations have grown historically.

2

A BRIEF HISTORY OF GROWTH

UNDERSTANDING WHY SOME NATIONS GROW and others don't holds the key to creating growth in the future. Simon Kuznets, the godfather of GDP measurement, opined that there are four kinds of countries in the world: developed countries, underdeveloped countries, Japan, and Argentina. What lay behind Kuznets's categorization of countries in the middle of the twentieth century was at least in part an inability to explain Japan—nobody knows why it grows—and Argentina—nobody knows why it doesn't.

Kuznets's historical framing remains broadly relevant in explaining many countries today. His list sums up the categories most worthy of our attention: countries that have successfully grown, countries that have not grown enough to become wealthy, countries that defy growth expectations and succeed against all odds, and countries that should grow but end up squandering their rich resources and endowments.

Despite the rapid evolution of economic thinking since the 1930s, the same growth questions continue to confound economists. Even for such an authority as Kuznets, economic growth was a puzzle and remains so for today's policymakers. Crafting solutions for slow growth requires an understanding of history and the paths trodden by the economic winners and losers of the past.

Attempts to explain economic growth have not been confined to the field of economics. Explanations span geography, history, culture, institutions, and policy. While each approach provides useful and even compelling insights for deciphering the puzzle of economic success and failure, no single one encompasses the whole story.

Geographical determinists, for instance, believe that a country's environment and terrain drive its wealth. In *Guns, Germs, and Steel*, Jared Diamond argues that the ability of nations to feed themselves (and export surplus) lays the foundation for prosperity.[1]

On its face, this is an appealing theory. As a practical matter, however, natural resource endowments are not an unambiguous blessing when it comes to economic growth. In many cases, they can be a curse. Economies based on exploiting natural resources—from oil, gold, copper, and iron ore to cotton, sugar, and other agricultural products—have long struggled with managing the windfalls they earn from selling their commodities into the international marketplace. For example, during the 1970s commodity boom, many countries (particularly across the developing world in Africa and South America) lost their newfound wealth through poor investment decisions and corruption.

There are also more insidious effects of bountiful resources. One of these is a phenomenon known as Dutch Disease. This term was coined by the *Economist* in 1977, when the Netherlands enjoyed a boom in foreign currency revenues from its natural gas reserves. The effect of this windfall was to devastate the Dutch export, manufacturing, and industrial sectors and to increase joblessness, which more than quadrupled in the 1970s. By selling commodities on the international marketplace, countries earn vast sums of foreign currency, generally in US dollars. As the dollars flood in, local currency becomes relatively scarce. Because shopkeepers and tradespeople can only take local legal tender, those with US dollars convert them to the local currency. The local currency becomes more valuable relative to US dollars; as a result, export prices rise on the international market, making the traded-goods sector uncompetitive. The only way to stay competitive is to cut wages and jobs.[2]

Dutch Disease effects can be seen even in countries where the exchange rate remains fixed by policy diktat. In these cases, the surfeit of foreign money flowing into the country expands domestic demand, raising the prices of goods and services. Foreign currency inflows push up the prices of local goods and services, fueling broader inflation and making local industries less competitive.

Given that poorer countries depend on exports to kickstart growth, anything that harms exports can harm the overall economy as well. Moreover, because the export sector is so crucial to productivity gains (such as on-the-job learning) anything that hurts it will hold back economic growth and the economy as a whole.

Worse still, policy interventions to tackle the adverse effects of Dutch Disease can themselves compound the problem and further damage economic growth. For example, raising interest rates to combat inflation or "sterilizing" foreign currency inflows (a practice in which the government absorbs excess cash from the economy by issuing bonds or IOUs) makes investment less attractive, and therefore growth becomes harder to achieve.

In short, resources alone will not lead to economic success. It is impossible to determine a country's economic growth path solely by looking at its terrain, at whether or not it has easy access to waterways, or at the extent to which it is resource endowed. After all, the average summer temperature hovers around 45 degrees Celsius (113 degrees Fahrenheit) in Saudi Arabia, and Switzerland is landlocked, but these factors have not stopped either country from achieving marked economic success.

Quite clearly, numerous factors matter for economic growth, and looking to the divergent histories of different sorts of countries helps us see how those multiple factors manifest.

Delving into the growth stories of developing countries, developed countries, and Kuznets's enigmas of Argentina and Japan can help us better understand the complex combination of ingredients that is critical for economic growth and success. Why, for instance, did China, the largest economy in GDP terms in the early 1800s, come to be among the poorest countries in the world in terms of both GDP and GDP per capita, only to bounce back over the last forty years? How did Japan go from economic oblivion to an advanced industrialized economy? How did Argentina, an economic powerhouse a hundred years ago, fall into cycles of economic despair within a generation? And how did the industrial revolution catapult Western economies to the economic dominance they retain today?

CHINA HAD GONE FROM BEING the richest economy in the world in the nineteenth century to one of the poorest by 1950, only to reemerge over the last four decades as an economic powerhouse while shifting the balance of global power toward the East. No one was more vital to tracing China's rise, fall, and rise than Angus Maddison, who in 1995 published an economic database calculating growth, population, and breadth of infrastructure dating back to 1820 and comparing Europe, China, India, and the United States. In that year, China's share of world GDP exceeded all other regions combined, standing at 32.9 percent, thanks to Western demand for its exports. India, too, held a remarkably strong position in the 1800s, with a 23 percent share of GDP, likewise thanks to a strong export base.[3]

Yet the subsequent decades witnessed a dramatic shift in the balance of world economic power. By 1890 the West had taken over. The industrial revolution pushed Europe to the lead, with a 40 percent share of world GDP. Meanwhile, China experienced a rapid decline, while America was ascending; the two countries briefly held the same share of 13 percent.

By 1950, the transition seemed to be all but over. The United States and Europe were booming, together representing a massive 60 percent of world GDP—America alone at close to 30 percent. After falling to 5.2 percent, China would spend the following twenty-five years treading water around the same share of approximately 5 percent of world GDP. From the vantage point of 1950, China's future economic rebound seemed very unlikely. Indeed, following the victory of Mao Tse Tung's People's Liberation Army in 1949, US secretary of state Dean Acheson saw little cause for concern. In his view, China was "not a modern centralized state," and he saw no sign that Mao and the communists would find a way to turn the corner.

As of 1978, Maddison's log appears to confirm Acheson's analysis. At 3.4 percent, China had fallen further behind the dominant West than ever before. Yet changes were afoot. Japan was already beginning to reap the rewards of industrialization, and as America deindustrialized, its consumers began to feed Japanese growth by purchasing products from abroad. Now, just forty years later, China is the second largest economy in the world. As of December 2014, when adjusting for purchasing power parity (how much you can buy for your money in different countries), the Chinese economy was worth US$17.6 trillion—just ahead of the US$17.4 trillion estimate for the United States.[4]

China has emerged to dominate the economic landscape over the last four decades, becoming deeply involved in trade, foreign direct investment, and capital markets across the globe. According to the International Monetary Fund, China contributed about one-third of the world's total growth in 2013, and even with slower growth it will continue to add at least 1 percentage point to world growth in the coming years. Trade, exports, and more recently an explicit policy pledge to move to a consumption-led economy are at the heart of China's success. Chinese overseas investment is expected to reach over US$3 trillion worldwide by 2025.[5]

Much has changed since the 1800s, when China was the world's largest economy. The intervening years saw the economy crater through to the middle of the 1900s, then rise to a position of relative strength today. China's economic success was interrupted by a spate of natural disasters and plagues, political fragmentation, and rebellion, which together weakened its ability to enact policies that promoted growth and development. The country was effectively sidelined while other regions such as the United States and Europe were making rapid progress. For example, the Taiping Rebellion, which lasted fourteen years, from 1850 to 1864, was enormously disruptive, destroying over six hundred cities and leaving over twenty million people dead. It did so much damage that the government of the Chinese Qing Dynasty had to rely on aid from Britain and France to defeat it.

More recently, China masterfully executed a carefully choreographed plan for achieving long-term growth. Many aspects of how the Chinese political class manages its economy are antithetical to the Western values of democracy and free markets. But this stance has not put off foreign investors, who are attracted to the government's willingness to prioritize physical infrastructure, political security, and stability over the health of the population, transparency in decision making, and transparency in the rule of law (if not necessarily the system of governance). In essence, the pursuit of economic growth overrides any views on the political system they invest in.

Currently China's political class has a strategy to evolve from an investment-led exporting economy to one more in line with Western economies, relying on domestic consumption. The transition to this new economic equilibrium will not be linear. China will likely experience significant economic volatility and market gyrations as the structure of its economy shifts. There is also mounting skepticism about China's ability to manage its debt levels, and the country's lack of individual political freedoms will continue to hamper its growth prospects. But Chinese policymakers will, no doubt, be focused on continuing to show economic progress in advance of two target dates: 2021—one hundred years after the formation of the Communist Party—and 2049, one hundred years after the formation of the People's Republic of China.

While China's economic path in the late 1800s was marred by political unrest, around the same time Japan embarked on a clear, deliberate, and explicit plan that would set in place (until recently) its prolonged economic success. Japan's Meiji Restoration (1868–1912) brought about enormous political and social changes that are widely credited for Japan's emergence as a modern nation in the early twentieth century. Under Emperor Meiji, the key pillars of the restoration period were administrative reforms that replaced a feudal system with a modern cabinet system of government, an opening up to Western trade, and a buildup of military strength.

Japan's program of reform was built on the modernization of all elements of government and society. Education, administration, and the military were all profoundly changed in the process, as were economic, social, and legal policies.

Economically, the country transformed from an agrarian feudal system to an industrial economy. Taxation and land reform contributed to modernization and industrialization. The government also funded an infrastructure rollout of railroads, shipping lines, ports, spinning mills, munitions, textiles, chemical plants, and iron smelters, later transferring ownership to the private sector. The Meiji period was also a period of financial development marked by the emergence of the banking sector. Together, these reforms and expenditures jump-started capitalism in Japan.

The Meiji transformation may have formed the basis for growth and success across much of the twentieth century, but Japan has more recently experienced an economic stagnation like no other. Suffering a growth rate that has averaged a paltry 0.85 percent a year over the past quarter century, it has only in the last year shown any semblance of an economic turnaround. Policymakers have done virtually everything canonical models and economics textbooks would suggest they should do under such dire economic conditions—from fiscal policy and expanding government spending to implementing negative interest rates to encourage more borrowing by business and households.

In a search for a path back to economic growth, Japan's demographic trajectory offers little help. If the country's fertility rate continues to remain low—it was 1.4 in 2016—the population will fall to approximately 87 million by 2065 and dip as low as 50.5 million by 2115, causing a shortage of labor and declining living standards resulting from reduced economies of scale. As the economic gap narrows between Japan and potential sources of migration—such as China, where the largest share of Japan's guest workers come from—it will become ever more difficult for the Japanese workforce to sustain even current levels of labor. Experts have referred to Japan's demographic prospects as a "time bomb crippling Japan's economy," noting that it currently averages "less than three people of working age for each retiree. By 2030, it will have less than two."[6]

Optimists hold out hope for a more aggressive structural reform agenda that would, for example, coalesce around greater agricultural reform and further land liberalization. Such a shift could jump-start Japan's renewal and place the economy on a path toward resurgent growth. For now, and until Japan develops a credible growth plan, the risks grow that its population will disengage from the economy—choosing to hoard money and reduce spending on economic and social activities. Naturally, these trends have even further dire consequences for the country's prospects for economic growth.

It is difficult to pinpoint the precise origins of Japan's recent decline. Nevertheless, we have seen in Japan's economic rise the unquestionable importance of political stability and credible institutions, and in China's rise the necessity of executing wise public policy decisions with an eye toward the long term. In contrast, the case of the Argentine economy reveals the dangers of political instability, short-term thinking, and a growth-harming agenda, including inconsistent trade policy.

Argentina's is a story of political and economic starts and stops, peaks and troughs. In 1913, Argentina was the world's tenth wealthiest nation per capita. The following year it ranked among the richest countries, behind Australia, the United States, and the United Kingdom, but ahead of France, Germany, and Italy. Yet by the 1930s the economy was on a path of steep decline; today it is among the slowest-growing economies on Earth. Over a fifty-year period, between 1930 and the mid-1970s, Argentina had six military coups; three periods of hyperinflation in which inflation exceeded 500 percent per year between 1975 and 1992 (peaking in March 1990 at over 20,000 percent); numerous debt defaults; and an economic growth rate that has, since 1970, dropped below zero (that is, regressed) on seven different occasions. Through it all, protectionism has remained a central feature of Argentine trade policy, rendering many of the nation's industries globally uncompetitive.

Argentina is endowed with abundant resources. Not only is the portion of Argentina alongside the Andes among the most metal-rich areas in the world, but it is also estimated that the country may contain four-fifths of the world's reserve of lithium brine. In addition, Argentina is ranked third in the world as an exporter of biofuel, producing more than any other country.[7] Yet, even with its natural resource endowments of fertile and arable land and a coast linking to global trade, policy ineptitude and political instability have prevailed, squandering the opportunity for economic success.[8]

Among the biggest policy errors occurred when Argentina failed in 1944 to align itself with the United States, which was beginning its economic ascendancy. Instead, its leaders chose to align with Britain, just then commencing its economic decline. Argentina's wealthy landowners also neglected investment in manufacturing and industrialization, favoring a cheap, uneducated agricultural labor force. That attitude prevailed throughout the 1940s, when Argentina failed to invest in education, suffering one of the lowest rates of secondary-school attendance internationally. Lacking an educated population, Argentina would struggle to innovate and be competitive. Argentina's elites were also reluctant to upend their economic status quo, preferring instead to protect and defend safe monopolies rather than take risks in competitive enterprise. So when industrialization did come, it was limited and late.

Between 1975 and 1990, Argentina's real per capita income declined sharply by more than 20 percent. Rising public expenditures, increasing wages, and inefficient production fueled inflation, which escalated through the 1980s, exceeding an annual rate of 1,000 percent. Argentina's economic and political crisis between 1998 and 2002 was catastrophic. Over that four-year period, Argentina's economy contracted by 20 percent. In just two years, output collapsed by more than 15 percent, unemployment jumped to over 25 percent, the currency lost three-quarters of its value, and poverty grew from 35 percent in 2001 to reach a high of 54.3 percent in 2002.

If China, Japan, and Argentina offer a narrative of economic booms and prolonged busts, the countries of the industrialized West—the United States and Europe—present a virtually uninterrupted trajectory of economic progress. Over the past fifty years, income levels in the United States have risen thirty times, and poverty levels have fallen by 40 percent. Between 1950 and 2000, Europe's per capita GDP tripled. For over a century, the combination of liberal democracy and market capitalism has created economic growth, reduced poverty, expanded infrastructure, extended life expectancy, and buttressed innovation. Unfettered political freedoms, strong, trusted institutions such as the British and French parliaments, as well as the continual shifts toward private ownership and tradable property rights, the backbone of market capitalism, all drove the economic success whose fruits we witness today.

Almost all of these countries seamlessly traversed the arc of economic development from agrarian state to manufacturing, to services, and then finally research and development, seeing increases in economic growth all along the way, in both GDP and GDP per capita terms. This evolution has not been linear or without its tensions. Nevertheless, it was driven by a constant and growing recognition that liberalization of the political and economic systems would best catalyze economic growth. This combination of political and economic liberalism in Europe and the United States would serve as the foundation for their emergence as the undisputed economic champions of the world between the industrial revolution and the post–World War II period.

Yet in the wake of the 2008 crisis, and for the first time in living memory, the West's growth path is in doubt. As we shall see in the next chapter, the key drivers of economic success over the last several decades—such as demographic shifts and productivity gains linked to technological advancements that improved efficiency—are now becoming barriers to further economic growth. Policymakers struggle to create sustained economic growth in developed countries that, in the aftermath of the financial crisis, continue to suffer under the weight of high debts and deficits, eroding quantity and quality of labor, and declining productivity.

What lessons can we glean from this brief history of growth? A common thread running through the stories of Japan, China, Argentina, the United States, and Europe is the importance of strong and trustworthy institutions. Over an expansive body of scholarship, historians, political scientists, and economists have concluded there is a correlation between a country's economic growth and the strength of its institutions. Without a civil service, police, and judiciary that can be relied on, poor economic outcomes will almost certainly ensue. As David Landes has argued, strong political institutions that protect the rule of law, individual freedom, and private property underpin development and economic growth.[9]

The United Kingdom presents one such example. Niall Ferguson has stressed how the British common-law legal system and civil service were central to economic development across the regions it colonized. Like Landes, Ferguson highlights the central importance of political institutions, the enforcement of the rule of law, constraints on the executive, and avoiding excessive government expenditure. These provide a vital foundation for investment, innovation, and ultimately growth.[10]

The absence of these features can impede growth. *In Search of Prosperity*, edited by Dani Rodrik, cites Indonesia and Pakistan as countries that have over time struggled to achieve sustained economic growth owing to ineffective public institutions. For Pakistan since its inception in 1947 and for Indonesia since 1997, economic progress has been inconsistent, and both countries have found it difficult to deliver high levels of good schooling and health care.[11]

In keeping with this analysis, China's contemporary economic success is largely attributable to its political system, which has been capable of defending and enforcing property rights. China's law explicitly allows owners to reap economic benefits from property ownership, including the right to make a profit. Furthermore, the owner has the right to possess, utilize, and obtain profits from the real properties owned by others. China's example shows that what is important for investment and, ultimately, economic growth is policy predictability and institutions that preserve and defend property rights—not necessarily democratic institutions per se.

China's political institutions may not be completely transparent or even democratic, but they are unquestionably strong. China's governing Communist Party controls the National People's Congress and State Council, which as the legislature and executive, respectively, have formed the institutional bedrock of China's economic success. Through these structures, the political leadership is able to roll out the country's public policy agenda across an extensive network of local government.

Institutional strength is not simply about the ability to deliver sound policy in peacetime and normal economic conditions. It is also about the adaptability of these institutions and their capacity to stand firm even under the pressure of exogenous economic volatility and political upheaval. Poorly fashioned bureaucracies and inherited institutions that fail to keep up with current population makeup and a modern economic and political construct leave themselves vulnerable. History is littered with examples of this path to political downfall—from the French Revolution to the end of the Soviet bloc to the 2016 populist discord threatening the existence and future of the European Union, catalyzed by the referendum vote by Britain to exit the community.

IN ADDITION TO NATURAL RESOURCES and strong political institutions, other factors that shape growth include colonialism, war, and cultural norms.

Colonial powers partitioned continents to establish national boundaries that forced traditionally rival ethnic groups to live together; colonialist bureaucracies were also incompatible with the lives of indigenous populations. Nation building proved virtually impossible, as tribal and ethnic clashes continually undermined economic success and sometimes led to outright war.

Civil war can be an economically destructive event to a country as well as to its neighbors. Paul Collier and Anke Hoeffler estimate that the typical civil war costs a country around four years of its annual GDP.[12] In Rwanda's case, it suffered a 63 percent drop in GDP per capita as a result of its 1990 conflict.[13] Furthermore, Collier and Hoeffler estimate that countries on the border of a dispute can lose as much as 50 percent of their own GDP, and clusters of smaller states are particularly vulnerable to this phenomenon.

War can destroy the institutions, capital, and frameworks that provide the support necessary for society and the economy to function. In 2014, violence cost the global economy US $14.3 trillion—or 13.4 percent of world GDP. If violence were to decrease by 10 percent globally, an additional US$1.43 trillion would effectively be added to the world economy each year. To put this in perspective, this number is roughly eight times the US federal expenditure on education and more than six times the total cost of the Greek bailout to date.[14]

Culture itself has also been posited as a factor in the rise or decline of nations. The work of German political economist and sociologist Max Weber explored cultural norms, social conventions, and religious beliefs as the reasons for differences in economic development. In particular, Weber argued that a Protestant work ethic and advancement through hard work fostered innovation that would drive productivity and buttress economic success in nineteenth-century Britain and Europe.

THUS THE ECONOMIC IMPACT OF factors ranging from geography to colonialism to culture must be acknowledged. However, tracing Kuznets's four growth scenarios through the rise and fall of economies makes it clear that economic and political decisions are the primary drivers that accelerate or decelerate economic success. This is not to say that creating growth is simple. The economic advance and stagnation of Japan over the past century, the rise and fall and rise of China, Argentina's faltering progress, and the steady growth and recent slowdown in the United States and other advanced economies all reveal that there is no off-the-shelf recipe for growth. Moreover, given that historical, geographic, and cultural factors can also influence the trajectory of an economy, policymakers need to be both vigilant and open-minded in designing growth-enhancing policy strategies.

One clear lesson from the past two hundred and fifty years, however, is that political and social stability plays a vital role in long-term economic success, as do free peoples and free markets. Yet even if freedom is necessary for long-term economic success, the current growth malaise (particularly in the freest nation-states) and the startling economic success of politically stable but nonfree nations like China together suggest that freedom of markets and citizens alone is not sufficient. History shows that winners in the growth race were led by long-term thinkers with an appetite for risk taking and investment. The policies of the losers in this race were easily swayed by short-termism, complacent in the belief that the prevailing conditions today would continue well into the future. This stance has proved foolhardy in the past and risks tomorrow's economic future, particularly given the sheer breadth and scale of the headwinds the global economy faces today.

3

HURRICANE HEADWINDS

IN *THE GREATEST GENERATION*, AMERICAN journalist Tom Brokaw describes the emergence of the United States from a period of destitution in the 1930s. The book tells of those born in the early twentieth century who weathered the Great Depression, won the Second World War, established America as the number one global power, and moved the United States from a path of economic decline and depression toward one of mass prosperity. The story of America's remarkable economic trajectory during those years holds many lessons for us today.[1]

During this period of strong and transformational economic growth, the United States operated full throttle on the three key factors of growth: capital, labor, and productivity. Major capital investments included the creation of the expansive interstate highway system beginning in 1956, which by 2017 had reached nearly forty-seven thousand miles, as well as the massive investment in equipment and machines in the agricultural sector, which constituted a significant part of America's economy. In terms of labor, the G.I. Bill, passed in June 1944 by President Franklin Roosevelt, offered education and other benefits such as business loans to World War II veterans, thereby upgrading the quality of the workforce. Within little over a decade, more than two million veterans had attended college and more than five and a half million had received training thanks to the bill. The quantity of labor increased as well, with the absorption of women into the formal workforce on the home front beginning during the war. These years also saw a marked growth in productivity, prompted in part by technological advancements, including fertilizer, pesticides, and machinery such as combine harvesters, mainframe computing, and manufacturing. Between 1945 and 1975, output per hour of labor (a measure of productivity) increased 127 percent. This tripartite surge in capital, labor, and productivity propelled the US economy forward through the postwar years.

Just a few decades later, however, each of these factors now faces severe headwinds. We are living in a period of low growth and even economic stagnation. While it is becoming increasingly difficult to determine where growth will come from, there is ever more clarity on the factors likeliest to derail global growth. This chapter seeks to shed new light on seven hurricane-strength forces barreling down on the global economy. When it comes to capital, these headwinds include high levels of debt, natural resource scarcity, and misallocation of capital. Affecting labor are the declining quality and quantity of the global workforce as a result of demographic shifts and worsening effects of widening income inequality. Finally, total factor productivity (the share of output that comes from variables that are not labor or capital) is sapped by the counterintuitive effects of technological advancement, as well as a decline in the efficiency through which capital and labor can be converted into economic growth.

Paradoxically a number of the factors explored here once supported economic growth. New technologies, for instance, once powered industrialization and increased production efficiency. Even though workers lost jobs in the transition, they found new work in new regions and new industries. Today, however, jobs are disappearing at an increasing rate as a result of new technologies without any clear alternatives to absorb the workforce.

And while the demographic forces of the past supported economic growth, the population shifts of today pose a challenge. The baby boom of the 1950s was positive when that cohort was of working age, but it is now a drag on growth and contributing to ballooning pension and health care costs, since many of that age group are older and retired.

Understanding the seven headwinds described in this chapter is crucial to understanding why the current economic malaise is different from previous economic challenges. Our current crisis is nothing like the 1973 oil spike that was followed by stagflation, out-of-control inflation, and a global debt crisis in the early 1980s, which policymakers sought to combat with interest rate changes. It is likewise entirely unlike the 1930s, when policymakers were at least able to draw on monetary tools (lowering interest rates) and fiscal tools (larger government spending) to ameliorate the crisis. These old solutions of monetary and fiscal policy are proving impotent to resolve the current distress. So are the policies of protectionism in trade and restriction of immigration, which despite their growing popularity dampen economic growth rather than encourage it.

The global economy will only succeed if policymakers can more efficiently allocate resources over the long term, and grappling with the gale-force headwinds against growth is a necessary first step.

LOOMING OMINOUSLY OVER TIMES SQUARE in New York, a debt clock measures the second-by-second change in the gross national debt as well as families' share in that debt. In 2000, the clock stood at nearly $5.7 trillion. By mid-2005, that figure had grown to approximately $8 trillion, and in 2015, it reached more than $18 trillion. America's growing national debt has risen to the forefront of political debate. So great was the concern about the level of debt (as well as a lack of agreement in Congress to raise the debt ceiling) that on August 5, 2011, Standard & Poor's, the credit rating agency that grades debt issuers' ability and willingness to repay what they owe, downgraded the US government for the first time in history.

The United States is not alone in its debt spiral. As McKinsey Global Institute has reported, since the financial crisis, "global debt has grown by USD $57 trillion . . . raising the ratio of debt to GDP by 17 percentage points."[2] Globally, debt to GDP is now at a staggering 350 percent. In the aftermath of the financial crisis many countries, particularly the United Kingdom, France, and the countries described with the acronym PIIGS—Portugal, Ireland, Italy, Greece, and Spain—saw their debt burdens rise rapidly; for these seven countries government debt rose from 5.6 trillion euros around 2009 to 8.2 trillion euros in 2016. This steep increase reflected, in part, the growing use of debt as a tool to address the financial crisis. At the time of this writing, global public debt stood at an estimated US$71.5 trillion, compared to a world GDP of roughly US$60 trillion (although according to some estimates global GDP is as high as US$78 trillion).[3]

At relatively low levels, nations and companies alike can benefit from taking on some debt obligations. Borrowing money for investment in the present can lead to future economic gains, especially if borrowing makes the difference between investing and not investing. A modest and manageable amount of borrowing is better than not investing at all. Taking on debt can help pay for important public investments in education, health care, and infrastructure. Debt of this sort has been crucial to US growth over the past century. The approximately $3.8 trillion municipal bond market in the United States allows for the funding of infrastructure and the construction of schools, hospitals, and highways. In the postwar years, municipal borrowing more than tripled from $20 billion in 1945 to $66 billion in 1960, as governments and states invested heavily in building infrastructure.[4] In this way, debt can serve as a catalyst for future economic growth.

But there is a limit to debt's efficacy, as demonstrated in the experience of commodity-driven economies. In periods of rapid economic growth, politicians often borrow from the international capital markets to fund investments, hoping that commodity prices will remain high over the foreseeable future. However, if global commodity prices collapse, or when growth inevitably slows, debt repayments become a larger share of public spending, reducing money earmarked for such needs as education and health care. Worse still, the debt, if priced in foreign currency (for example, in US dollars), becomes much more expensive, as slow growth is often accompanied by a reduction in the value of the home currency versus the US dollar. This mounting debt burden from the greater expense of debt further harms economic growth. In the United Kingdom, interest payments on public debt stood at 8 percent of total tax revenue in 2015, and the payments of £43 billion were equal to half of the UK government's education budget that year. In the wake of the global financial crisis, Greece, Italy, and Ireland saw their interest payments on public debt rise to 10 percent or more of tax revenue; cash was essentially redirected to debt repayments when it could have been used to enhance investment and economic growth.

The relationship between debt and growth is not linear. Taking on more and more debt does not translate into higher future growth ad infinitum. In fact, the combination of slow growth and fast-rising debt can prove lethal. Today, with global growth relatively stagnant, countries are piling up debt at a faster rate than their economies can expand.

Policymakers continue to grapple with the complex relationship between debt and growth, and at what point debt becomes a hindrance rather than a help to economic progress. In *Growth in a Time of Debt*, an extensive study covering over two hundred years of history, Harvard University professors Carmen Reinhart and Kenneth Rogoff concluded:

"When external debt reaches 60 percent of GDP, annual growth declines by about two percent." Reinhart and Rogoff describe a mixed record of sovereign borrowing leading to high debt levels; they highlight how, in extreme circumstances, defaults have had deleterious consequences on economic growth. Lenders are ultimately reluctant to deal with any counterparty for whom they have reason to worry about repayment risk—or at least, they will demand high costs for doing so. And debt crises not only crush existing debt holders by rendering their bond holdings worthless but also discourage new capital from flowing in.[5]

Even if economists can define a threshold above which debt becomes a problem for economic growth, policymakers struggle to enforce it, particularly during times of economic stress such as the 2008 financial crisis. The 1992 Maastricht Treaty bound signatories to a debt-to-GDP ratio of no more than 60 percent and an annual government deficit of no more than 3 percent. In the wake of the stresses of the financial crisis these rules were generally ignored, as the average debt-to-GDP levels across all European Union member states soared to over 92 percent in 2014.

In 2014, the International Monetary Fund concluded that there was no definitive relationship between absolute levels of debt and economic growth, but nevertheless stressed that higher debt leads to more volatility in GDP growth. Moreover, the trajectory of debt—that is, whether it was rising or falling—did have notable effects on the path of economic growth.[6] As countries around the world have assumed more debt, the debt debate has moved from the periphery of policymaking to the fore. Even in the case of a country like the

United States, which has a global reserve currency, reasonable people agree that amassing unsustainable debt constrains a nation's economic growth.

Ultimately, there is a short list of prescriptions for escaping the precarious situation of unsustainable debt. The majority of those prescriptions, which include outright default, fiscal austerity, and bailouts, all further contract the economy and worsen prospects for economic growth. Only growth itself, including debt-financed growth if managed in a sustainable way, can lift countries out of high indebtedness in a manner supportive of (or at least not harmful to) a country's prospects for long-term prosperity. The risk to global debt today is that few of the world's important economies are pursuing a path of sustainable debt.

NATURAL RESOURCES ARE PART OF the assets or capital endowment of a country. Abundant natural resources can position a nation's economy for strong growth, especially in a world in which those resources are becoming scarce and more valuable. However, the combination of greater global demand and a shrinking supply of commodities poses a dire threat to global economic growth. Ultimately the global forces will influence the fortune of individual nations: a world of depleting natural resources cannot support long-term economic growth.

The key commodity inputs to economic growth are arable land, potable water, energy, and minerals. Today, the greatest amount of untilled, arable land is in Africa, yet this land is often hard to access because of untraversable terrain. In comparison, China, with 1.3 billion people, has only an estimated 11.3 percent arable land. This shortage has served as an impetus for China to go outside its borders in search of commodities and land on which to grow food. China's systematic and aggressive approach has made it the "go-to" power buyer for commodities and resources. China invested nearly $200 billion globally in 2015, with about a third of the total invested in the energy sector.[7]

Potable water is also in increasingly short supply. Although 70 percent of Earth is covered by water, about 97 percent of this water is too salty even to be used to clean toilets. Water is essential not only for drinking but also for manufacturing and food production. For example, it takes 20 gallons of water to make one egg and 150 gallons of water to make a quarter-pound hamburger (113 grams).[8] The risk of shortage is why such countries as China and Saudi Arabia are investing the most in desalination and are at the forefront of efforts seeking a resolution to water scarcity.

Water will soon become scarce for many other countries as well. According to a report from the Office of the Director of National Intelligence (ODNI), "between now and 2040, fresh water availability will not keep up with demand absent more effective management of water resources." Water shortages "will hinder the ability of key countries to produce food and generate energy, posing a risk to global food markets and hobbling economic growth." Furthermore, while the problem may be manageable for wealthier developed countries, the water shortage is a "destabilizing factor" in poorer ones. In addition to outright water wars, the ODNI suggests that water will become a form of political leverage for countries that possess it, with states using "their inherent ability to construct and support major water projects to obtain regional influence." In the next ten years, water shortages will contribute to social disruptions and political instability, which in turn can fuel conflict.[9]

Beyond land and water, resources like minerals and energy are becoming ever harder and more expensive to acquire. In the quest for mining and energy resources, producers are seeking out more politically unstable and difficult terrain. For example, in 2014, Rio Tinto's US$5.4 billion underground expansion of the Oyu Tolgoi mine in Mongolia experienced severe delays after a dispute over investment terms with the government. This contributed to the ousting of Mongolian prime minister Norov Altankhuyag and further delays and financial costs to Rio Tinto. (As of 2017, the Mongolian parliament voted to nationalize the mine.)[10]

These supply-side constraints of arable land, potable water, energy, and minerals are only half of the equation; demand for natural resources is the other half. Numerous factors influence the demand for commodities. The weather can play a role, as hot summer months can increase energy demand to support air-conditioning. Commodity substitutes are also a factor, as innovation adds alternatives, such as solar and nuclear power, to the traditional suite of resources. Economic theory suggests that as scarcity takes effect, prices will rise, and demand will fall. Government policy, however, has interfered with market forces. Subsidies, taxes, and price restrictions can allow demand for products such as energy and fuel to hold up or even continue rising. But ultimately what places the most pressure on resources is population growth.

Over the past fifty years global population growth has been uniquely rapid. As demographers attest, this is a phenomenon never seen in history or prehistory, and one never to be seen again once, by some forecasts, the population plateaus over the course of the next century. This population trend may, in some respects, seem counterintuitive. A swelling global population means more people, more workers, more consumption, and a boost for growth. However, the current population dynamics could entail a much darker future, especially in a world of finite resources.

The Worldometers website displays, moment by moment, the number of births and deaths around the world on a daily and annual basis.[11] In total, there are approximately 7.5 billion people on the planet today, representing roughly 7 percent of the approximately 108 billion people who, according to the Population Reference Bureau, have ever lived on Earth. According to United Nations estimates, the global population will plateau only after reaching a number between 9.6 and 12.3 billion people on Earth in 2100.[12]

A January 1960 *Time* cover story entitled "That Population Explosion" heralded the fact that the world's population had reached 3 billion. But even more so, the milestone underscored the unprecedented rate of population growth in just one generation. Whereas it took until about 1800 for the human race to reach 1 billion people, and around 125 years to increase from 1 billion to 2 billion, the increase to 3 billion took only thirty-five years. In just sixty years the global population has exploded—from around 2.5 billion in 1950 to 7 billion in 2011. Today, India alone is adding 1.3 million people a month to its population, and the global populace is rising by 80 million each year—equivalent to adding more than a whole United Kingdom annually.

By current forecasts the world population will top 9 billion people by 2050, expanding by an additional 1.2 billion over the next twenty years—an almost 30 percent increase in the world population in a mere forty years.

The pace at which the world population is growing will gradually slow. The United Nations projects women almost everywhere to bear fewer children by the middle of the twenty-first century. Currently the global average is 2.5 children per woman, down from 4.3 in the 1970s. This is expected to decline to just 2 by 2100. Nevertheless, in the near term the pressures exerted on the limited supply of global resources by rising global population are meaningful. The resource imbalance will put pressure on commodity prices to rise, and this inflationary pressure could have negative consequences on longer-term economic growth and living standards.

In addition to growing rapidly, the global population in its entirety has gotten wealthier over recent decades. This newfound wealth is creating further demand for resources. Rapid economic growth across the emerging world—on the back of both population growth and increasing wealth—has been a catalyst for greater demand for commodities like food, mobile phones, indoor plumbing, and cars.

Although the slowdown that has followed the 2008 financial crisis has provided something of a reprieve, the structural effects of a large and growing population portend greater natural resource demand in the future.

Urbanization, too, promises to create even greater demand for resources. By 2030 an estimated 60 percent of the world's population will live in cities. The number of cities of five hundred inhabitants or more is projected to grow by 30 percent in Asia and 80 percent in Africa.[13] Across emerging markets, explicit and managed urbanization policies are under way. For example, the Chinese government has publicly stated policy targets that will increase the number of cities with at least one million people from the current total of around 80 to 221 cities, and over 20 cities with at least ten million people each. To put this in context, Europe and the United States together have 10 cities with at least one million people each.

Urbanization has generally been seen as more efficient for the delivery of goods and services. Larger numbers of people congregating in dense cities are regarded as good for growth, considering the demand for commodities rises as population density increases. Essentially, not only do cities deliver goods and services more efficiently to their inhabitants, but they also demand more natural resources than less densely populated areas, as a city of one million people requires more commodities than a town a thousand. Furthermore, urban areas are generally associated with higher per capita incomes (urban per capita incomes in India are at least twice as high as in its rural areas), which lead to higher consumption of white goods (such as refrigerators and washing machines), food, energy, telecommunications, and water. Consequently, urbanization can place upward pressure on resource prices and in turn become a drag on economic growth.

There is a long history of concerns about how natural resources will be unable to keep pace with population demand. This clamor dates as far back as 1798, when Thomas Malthus worried about how the global population growth would outstrip commodity supply. Since then the Club of Rome in the 1970s and "peak oil" proponents have joined this chorus, even as the world has been bailed out of crises, often by technological advancements, every step of the way. Even so, potential new sources of resource supply, for example, shale oil, are subject to volatility. Such innovations may mitigate the risk of commodity scarcity over the longer term but are unlikely to eliminate real concerns in their entirety, which presents the increasing risk of greater conflict in the future. A report by the US National Intelligence Council warns that more resource-based conflicts may be on the horizon.[14] The US director of national intelligence has warned of water shortages in a number of countries—particularly those that rely on the Nile, Tigris-Euphrates, Mekong, Jordan, Indus, Brahmaputra, and Amu Darya. Over the next decade many large and significant countries with close ties to the United States (such as in the Middle East) will experience severe water shortages, deteriorating quality, or floods, and this could fuel political instability and even state failure.

The effort to manage scarce natural resources and address the challenge of climate change creates pressures to restrict growth and has created international disputes over what kind of growth is appropriate and sustainable. After all, according to many environmentalists, economic growth itself is degrading the planet. Meanwhile, economists on the other side of the debate worry that growth will be damaged by overprioritization of environmental concerns. There exist compelling arguments for "green growth"—the idea that economic growth can be enhanced by addressing climate change, CO_2 emissions, and water scarcity—yet the debate between environmentalists and economists still rages.

In some sense, this clash of environmental versus economic viewpoints reflects the tension between the industrialized developed West and the rest. Western policymakers tend to caution emerging countries that, without advocating "green growth" and pursuing a growth agenda that takes environmental concerns into greater consideration, they risk lower quality and worsening economic growth. Emerging market countries are quick to point out that a reckless environmental agenda was the backbone of Western development, and that advanced countries remain among the greatest polluters on the planet. Resolving this tension is key to addressing the natural resource headwind and setting the global economy on a trajectory of higher economic growth.

TODAY, CAPITAL IS CONSTRAINED BY high, unsustainable indebtedness and scarce natural resources. One of the three pillars of growth is thus undermined in two different pernicious ways. Simultaneously, the labor market, the second key driver of GDP growth, faces its own headwinds.

In 1997 a ninety-year-old Alec Holden placed a bet with the bookmaker William Hill that he would reach the age of 100. William Hill gave him odds of 250 to 1. In April 2007 he won the bet. When Holden picked up the check, William Hill announced that they would no longer offer such generous odds—raising the target for such wagers to 105. Said a spokesman, "If you're prepared to bet you'll live to 105, you'll probably be offered odds of 150 to 1; to get the full 250 to 1 offered to Mr Holden, you've now got to get to 110, and you can only wager up to £100."

Particularly in the West, many like Alec Holden are living longer and spending decades of their lives in retirement. A big question facing economists today is how we pay for the increasing numbers of Alec Holdens across the world. By 2050, one in six of the global population will be age sixty-five or older, compared to one in twelve in 2015. The aging of the world population is raising the dependency ratio—that is, the ratio of retirees to workers. This surfeit of expensive non-workers alongside a paucity of productive workers constitutes a major headwind for economic growth.

We are moving into a world inhabited by fewer and fewer workers who can actively and productively contribute to economic growth. By 2050 there will be sixty-four countries in which more than 30 percent of the population will be over sixty years old. In fact, over 50 percent of the populations of Germany, Spain, Italy, and Japan will be over sixty. Without a young workforce, economic progress will stall. Meanwhile, China risks getting old before getting rich, with some estimates suggesting that half of China's population will be fifty years old or older by 2050. Japan is already combating a negative population growth rate. Forecasts estimate that 40 percent of Japan's population will be over sixty-five by 2060. There were six thousand fewer births in 2013 than in 2012. These trends suggest that the country will lose a third of its population over the course of the next fifty years, with negative consequences for its labor market and economic prospects. More generally it has been reported that "some 48% of the world's people live in a country where birthrates are not sufficient to sustain existing populations: All of Europe except Iceland, BRIC mainstays Brazil, Russia, and China, and even some emerging markets like Vietnam."[15] Fertility in all European countries (that is, EU members) is below the level required for maintaining population levels over the long run.

As the economically active population shrinks, the population of economically inactive people grows. And all the while, the life expectancy of the aging cohort of baby boomers is increasing. Global life expectancy is expected to rise to seventy-seven years by 2045. This trend brings mounting health care and unfunded pension costs that act as a drag on economic growth. The United Nations forecasts that by 2050 one in three persons living in a rich country will be a pensioner, and nearly one in ten will be over eighty years old. In the United States, the Social Security bill was close to $900 billion in 2015, making it the largest single item in the annual federal government budget, and representing approximately 25 percent of federal expenditures (up from 0.22 percent during World War II). These numbers are, if anything, conservative, as they do not include additional public pension commitments at the state and city levels. According to the UK Office for Budgetary Responsibility, "spending on pensioners is the largest category of social spending, with gross public spending at 6.1 percent of GDP in 2010 (slightly below the OECD average of 7.3 percent)."[16]

All of this is to say that the West is getting older. The less productive and more expensive to maintain this growing aging population becomes, the greater the burden it will place on already stretched fiscal balances and on the economy overall. A country populated by fewer and fewer young and able-bodied workers will inevitably face the prospect of labor shortages, lower productivity, and slowed economic growth.

Of course, the challenge of aging populations is not just the bailiwick of the rich, industrialized world. The UN's latest population forecast estimates that the world median age is due to rise from twenty-nine to thirty-eight by 2050. And the fact that, as we have seen, women worldwide are having fewer children means the balance will certainly tip in favor of the aged before too long.[17] According to the UN's Research Institute for Social Development, "currently, Europe has the greatest percentage of its population aged 60 or over (24 percent) but rapid ageing will occur in other parts of the world as well, so that by 2050, all major areas of the world except Africa will have nearly a quarter or more of their populations aged 60 or over."[18] Between 2015 and 2050, 66 percent of that growth will be in Asia, 13 percent in Africa, 11 percent in Latin America and the Caribbean, and the remaining 10 percent in other areas.[19]

IT'S NOT JUST THAT THE workforce is dwindling in quantity. An issue of quality is also emerging as a further drag on global growth. Decades of underinvestment in quality education have churned out a working-age population ill-equipped to work or contribute effectively to the modern economy.

The global cohort of unemployed youth between the ages of eighteen and twenty-four has now surpassed 71 million.[20] This represents a constant threat to political stability and hampers prospects for economic growth across the world. In the United Kingdom alone, approximately 826,000 people are deemed to be "not in education, employment, or training" (NEETs). These individuals are largely unskilled, unemployable, and increasingly disaffected.

In the United States, the threat of declining workforce quality was clear at least as long ago as 1983. In that year a report produced by the US Department of Education entitled *A Nation at Risk* clearly stated the problem. "Our once unchallenged pre-eminence in commerce, industry, science and technological innovation is being overtaken by competitors throughout the world," the report read. "The educational foundations of our society are presently being eroded by a rising tide of mediocrity that threatens our very nature as a nation and a people."

Yet save for relatively small efforts such as the No Child Left Behind legislation, little has been done to address the concerns of *A Nation at Risk*. The Programme for International Student Assessment (PISA) is a test administered to fifteen-year-olds throughout the world to compare reading, science, math, and other skills. As of 2015, US students rank thirtieth among the thirty-five OECD members in math skills.[21] Without a dramatic course change, a generation of US students will enter the workplace unequipped to compete.

Behind these striking macro statistics are signs of inequality in educational outcomes—and these are disturbing in their implications. The global consulting firm McKinsey summed it up best: "The persistence of these educational achievement gaps imposes on the United States the economic equivalent of a permanent national recession." The report goes on to note that narrowing the gap between black and Latino student performance and white student performance could have resulted in 2008 GDP rising by up to $525 billion, or 4 percent of GDP. Given demographic shifts, the magnitude of this impact will only grow. For the first time in America's history, its next generation of workers will be less educated than its last.

However, far more urgent than the problem of rich nations' aging populations and undereducated workers is the mounting concern about emerging countries' demographics. Essentially, the young and increasingly educated workforce is underutilized in developing economies that have too little economic growth to create job opportunities for them. The burgeoning population across the emerging markets is generally skewed young—with upwards of 60 percent of the population under twenty-five. Meanwhile, students in emerging market countries have outperformed in the PISA tests, moving to the very top of the global league tables. While a young, well-educated workforce should be an asset to a developing nation, stalled economic growth makes them a burden on society and a further drag on economic growth.

ALONGSIDE CAPITAL AND LABOR, A third factor that drives economic growth is encapsulated by the term "total factor productivity" (TFP). Three economic headwinds holding back TFP are the role of new technology in the creation of an unemployed underclass, growing income inequality, and declining "pure" productivity, which is to say declining output per worker.

In 1930, the British economist John Maynard Keynes predicted that economic growth and "technical improvements" would lead to a fifteen-hour workweek by 2030. Today, less than fifteen years from that date, technological innovations continue to increase productivity—and to increase the possibility that production may be able to take place without requiring human workers at all.

Throughout history transformational technological innovations have tended to cause disruption while also creating wealth. The speed and scale of today's revolutionary technologies could have a greater impact on our daily lives than previous technological shifts. Rapid advances in digital computation, telecommunication, robotics, and artificial intelligence make it increasingly practical for blue-collar and manual-labor jobs, from autoworkers and car mechanics to firefighters and packagers at Amazon, to be filled by robots immune to human error, who never get tired or injured on the job. According to a 2016 *Economic Report of the President*, workers earning less than $20 an hour face an 83 percent probability of losing their job to automation. Even white-collar workers like doctors, lawyers, and securities traders have watched some of their work go to machines. In due course, smarter computers are bound to assume many of these jobs.

Technological advances are, of course, not unambiguously bad. They can have positive effects on economic growth and living standards. At a macro level, innovation transforms the way we communicate, travel, borrow and lend financial capital, and obtain health care and education. Automation ensures faster and better delivery of public goods and can yield considerable economic benefits. Moreover, at a micro level technology can help a company increase its revenue by enhancing delivery of goods and services to its customers.

Technology can also help enhance the manner in which a business functions and survives, cutting its operating costs and thus increasing the company's profitability.

Companies tend to assess technology with a profit lens, examining how innovations can help them create financial value. For example, according to Elena Kvochko at the World Economic Forum, "the Internet accounts for 3.4% of overall GDP in some economies. Most of this effect is driven by e-commerce—people advertising and selling goods online." Findings from various countries confirm the positive contribution to GDP growth of Information and Communication Technologies (ICT). In Kvochko's words, "a 10 percent increase in broadband penetration is associated with a 1.4 percent increase in GDP growth in emerging markets. In China, this number can reach 2.5 percent. The doubling of mobile data use caused by the increase in 3G connections boosts GDP per capita growth rate by 0.5 percent globally."[22]

But for every gadget that enables us to process data and information faster and more cheaply, there is a burgeoning social and public policy challenge of rising unemployment that has dire consequences for growth. Over time and for the foreseeable future the downside risks of technology outweigh the benefits it brings.

There is a real concern that automation and technology will produce a jobless underclass across the global economy. For example, a 2013 report from Oxford Martin School estimates that a startling 47 percent of jobs in the United States are at risk from technological change.[23] One sector of the US economy particularly vulnerable to automation, in the form of driverless vehicles, is the trucking sector (alone estimated to have 3.4–4.5 million drivers[24]), including long-haul truckers, bus drivers, and cab drivers. Some current estimates suggest that for the majority of states, trucking is the most common job (though others argue that retail and services make up a much larger share of the labor force).[25] Losing those jobs to automation would be a massive blow to those states' economies.

As technological capabilities expand and costs fall, robotics can be expected to gradually replace human workers across low-wage service occupations. Japan's workforce already includes over a quarter million robots. And, as I have previously reported in *How the West Was Lost*, at some clinics and hospitals in the United States, robots are already at work. For a fraction of the cost of human wages, robots change linens, move surgical equipment, bring patients food, and remove garbage. What's more, these low-wage service occupations are the ones that have seen the most US job growth over the past decades. If these trends continue, US employment may be severely affected by automation in the coming years.

China's automation trajectory is similarly daunting in its implications. Reports have suggested that computerization puts more than three-quarters of jobs in China at "high risk" of automation.[26] A report in a *Financial Times* report notes that "China had 260,000 industrial robots" in 2015, and quotes Rahul Chadha, an executive at Mirae: "Using the rule of thumb that one industrial robot replaces four to five workers, this suggests that robots have rendered more than one million people jobless."[27]

Across the world, rising salaries and worker demands for better pensions, health care, and other conditions of labor will likely serve only to encourage greater and more rapid automation across all sectors of the economy—from agriculture and manufacturing to services and ultimately the R&D sector. In their 2015 report on automation, Carl Benedikt Frey and Michael Osborne report that "the three leading companies of Silicon Valley employed some 137,000 workers in 2014 with a combined market capitalisation of $1.09 trillion. By contrast, in 1990 the three largest companies in Detroit had a market capitalisation of $36 billion while collectively employing about 1.2 million workers."[28] Silicon Valley is generating multiples of value using a fraction of the number of human workers that Detroit has—a hub that was once a manufacturing engine of America's progress.

At a potentially higher risk for disruption in the coming years than other sectors is the financial sector. The change in banking and how we conduct financial transactions will likely be seismic. Through robo advisors and electronic market-making, numerous workers are already being replaced in favor of automated platforms. British bank RBS shed 550 employees with the introduction of one automation of their fund management services. A 2016 report by Citigroup, the fourth biggest US bank, said that 40 to 50 percent of US and European bank workers could lose their jobs within ten years, mainly as a result of retail banking automation.[29]

The diminution of labor's contribution to the economy is being felt worldwide. Loukas Karabarbounis and Brent Neiman of the Universities of Minnesota and Chicago put the global decline in labor's share since the early 1980s at roughly 5 percentage points, so that labor is contributing just over half of national income on average. Their 2013 study finds that forty-two out of fifty-nine countries experienced a fall in the share of labor accruing to GDP. Moreover, much of the recent global decline in labor's share of GDP "can be explained by the decrease in the relative price of investment goods," which in turn is driven by advances in computer-driven technologies, leading companies to substitute labor for capital in production.[30]

Technologists themselves are not safe from technological disruption. In 2011, Nokia's chief executive Stephen Elop warned that his staff were on a "burning platform" and that technology was eating the company alive. Three years later Nokia was subsumed into Microsoft. Other research finds that "the labor cost of performing a standardized computational task has fallen by at least 1.7 trillion fold between 1850 and 2006, with the bulk of this decline occurring in the last three decades."[31] At a time when seventy-one million young adults under age twenty-five are unemployed worldwide, it is clear that for all of its improvements to efficiency, technology could markedly worsen the growth picture by capping job creation.

Even so, technology is hard for companies to resist, considering how much it promises to reduce the costs of doing business. Logistics, staffing, and routine tasks all promise to become cheaper and more efficient as they are automated. This is not to say that these jobs are not valid, nor is it an argument against technological advancement—it is simply a recognition that if technology is taking away jobs at a faster rate than it is creating them, this poses a problem for economic growth.

Automation and new digital technologies not only threaten job deterioration but also create new risks of cyber-terrorism and bioterrorism that could hamper economic growth. The Government Accountability Office reported that federal data were compromised in "information security incidents" 77,183 times in 2015, compared to 5,503 in 2006.[32] In June 2015, as a result of technological failure in the biometric data storage system used by the State Department, embassies were unable to issue visas for three weeks. This prevented farm laborers from entering the United States, resulting in significant crop losses (whose value is yet to be determined), and forced companies to increase costs as they were required to pay for lodging and food for stranded laborers. Clearly businesses face the risk of fraud and cyber security concerns, especially as automation proceeds; they must aggressively regulate, monitor, and pursue bad actors, be they states or rogue employees.

Historically, technology advances have on balance created economic growth and improved living standards. Human progress proceeded despite monumental shocks from the agricultural and industrial revolutions. For example, the diminution of the US agricultural sector was correlated with the dramatic improvements in living standards in the United States in the twentieth century. In the early 1900s approximately 50 percent of the US population was employed in some aspect of the agricultural sector.[33] Over the century, technology and machine advancements replaced the agricultural labor workforce, and today less than 2 percent of Americans work in farming. Technology represented both a pull and a push factor—it may have pushed workers out of a shrinking sector, but it pulled workers into a higher-paying manufacturing sector. And as explained in Dani Rodrik's "The Past, Present, and Future of Economic Growth," as countries move from an agricultural economy to manufacturing and industrial products to services and then R&D, per capita incomes rise in tandem.[34]

With the benefit of hindsight, we now know that the majority of farming labor was deployed into manufacturing and industry jobs. But today, the policymakers charged with avoiding destabilizing levels of job losses in the economy are frustrated that they cannot predict which new sector can absorb millions of low-skilled workers who are displaced by automation. Nor can they reasonably assess how quickly technology's full impact might make itself felt. Although the technology sector promises new jobs in biomedicine, data analytics, and coding, many of these opportunities are not yet tangible. Accurately understanding technology's economic impact is complicated by significant measurement issues. Civil servants and businesses are not adequately capturing the economic impact of hardware, software, and digital technology in advance, leaving policymakers unable to assess how technology is fully affecting the modern global economy.

A question exists as to whether measurement of productivity is fundamentally flawed. US productivity growth has been measured at around 1.5 percent on average per year from 2005 to 2015 (for the sake of comparison, median global productivity growth averaged 1.9 percent yearly from 1950 to 1970). The recent rate of productivity is so low that it represents a slowdown from the previous decade, but that slowdown seems to defy high profits and company valuations within the technology sector over that period.

Some tech leaders believe that many of the promised benefits of recent technological advances, such as mobile robotics, will become evident in the near future. A 2007 study reports that "productivity follows investment in digital technologies with lags of between 5 and 15 years," which could mean we will see a boost in productivity and economic growth in the future as autonomous vehicles and medical advancements are realized.[35] A 2015 report by Citi research states, "The extensive type of growth that relies on adding more capital or workers in production—a process that is subject to diminishing returns—has come to an end."[36] The simple proposition here is that tech may indeed be slowing economic growth, but living standards could still improve as goods and services become cheaper to acquire. Ultimately, technological innovation offers positives and negatives. It could reduce the need for workers in both the manufacturing and service sectors in a way that creates a rising jobless class. However, technology could also drive down the costs of household consumption.

On the surface, a world of less work and cheaper goods and services certainly seems appealing. However, it would also create a number of new problems. In such a world, what would people actually do? Would they, as Keynes postulated, stop pursuing the accumulation of riches and contemplate God, culture, and immortality? Would they enjoy their newfound free time, or would they start wars?

For all the promise of technology, it undermines all the old assumptions about productivity and growth. And today and for the foreseeable future, the reality is that technology is putting workers, particularly the low-skilled, out of work. The most tangible effects of technology are joblessness and cost cutting rather than revenue generation and growth. And the fact that those most exposed to the threat of technology are at the lower-income ranks fuels another headwind that is undermining economic growth: income inequality.

A 2015 Oxfam report proclaimed that the richest 1 percent in the world owns nearly half of the world's wealth, and their 2017 report announced that the eight richest people are worth more than the world's poorest 50 percent. Behind the widening gap in wealth is an increase in income inequality between the richest and the poorest. As income inequality has increased (so that the incomes of the poor have substantially fallen behind those of the rich), it has become more difficult for the poor to increase their wealth.[37] The key reason that income inequality has climbed to the top of the international policy agenda over the past decade is its ever increasing impact on economic growth. Once considered largely neutral in its effect, there are now good reasons to believe that income inequality is indeed a headwind.

According to the OECD the relationship between growing income inequality and slowing economic growth is one not just of correlation but of causation. The world's leading industrialized economies have lost a combined 8.5 percent of GDP over the last twenty-five years because of worsening income inequality. By the OECD's estimates, income inequality has accounted for a decline in economic growth on the order of approximately 6 percent for the United States and 9 percent for the United Kingdom and Norway.

To be clear, over the past few decades inequality between countries' incomes has actually improved, as poorer economies have posted significant economic growth, converging toward average income levels in wealthier countries. However, within these countries, income inequality has worsened considerably. In the United States, for example, the average income of the top 1 percent is fourteen times higher than the average income of the rest of the population.[38] In 1978, it was just ten times higher. *Forbes* annually lists the four hundred wealthiest people in the United States. According to the Institute for Policy Studies, "With a combined worth of US$2.34 trillion, the Forbes 400 own more wealth than the bottom 61 percent of the country combined, a staggering 194 million people." This amounts to owning "more wealth than 36 million of these typical American families. That's as many households in the United States that own cats."[39]

Worsening income inequality has pernicious effects. Not to be conflated with the negative effects of outright declining wages, which lower living standards for the individual, the deleterious effects of widening income inequality are felt by a society as a whole. In particular, the fact that some in society are unable to escape economic hardship and poverty, face falling educational attainment, and feel left behind by fellow citizens who appear to be progressing economically leads to disaffection, mistrust in the system, loss of faith in leadership, and potential social and political instability. It is these aspects of worsening income inequality that hinder growth.

The income inequality trends identified by the OECD have significant implications for living standards and ultimately economic growth. Research from the University College of London, for example, postulates that there is a difference in life expectancy of twenty years between those born in central London near Oxford Circus and others born further out on the rail line. Newborns around Star Lane have a life expectancy of 75.3 years—a dramatic contrast to the 96.4 years projected for those near Oxford Circus.[40] An *Atlantic* article found a similar disparity on a global basis, as rich men born in 1940 can expect to live ten years longer than poor men born the same year.[41]

Meanwhile, there is also a real risk that income (and subsequently wealth) inequality can manifest as greater political inequality, even in a democratic system. According to the *New York Times*, just 158 families in the United States account for approximately 50 percent of the money fueling political campaigns. And with estimates that there are more than twenty lobbyists for every member of Congress, and campaign costs running into the multiple billions of dollars for a single presidential election, money remains central to how the United States conducts electoral politics. These vast amounts of money skew incentives and, as described by the *Economist*, can "add to the length and complexity of legislation, making it easier to smuggle and extract special privileges."[42] Even at the international level, wealthier countries have a history of using their wealth to buy votes to secure and influence voting decisions.[43]

Despite the rising importance of income inequality, public policymakers continue to struggle to address it. There are at least three key issues that complicate the income inequality debate: first, that inequality appears to plague both capitalist and noncapitalist economies; second, that even within market capitalist countries, neither left-leaning tax-and-spend redistributive policies nor right-leaning low-tax policies have curtailed the trend of worsening inequality; and third, that policymakers do not agree whether to prioritize reducing absolute inequality or relative inequality. Each of these angles warrants consideration in turn.

First, there is a growing acceptance that the "invisible hand" of market capitalism cannot prevent or redress income inequality. Meanwhile the policy choices available to state capitalist societies, such as China, can reduce income inequality. Consider the fact that the United States, the largest economy in the world with a GDP of US$16 trillion, with market capitalism as its economic stance and liberal democracy as its political approach, possesses an income inequality fairly similar to that of China—with the United States estimated at 46.1 (in terms of the Gini coefficient) and China at 42.2. Moreover, while US income inequality has worsened over the last decade, China's has improved, because its political class has deliberately enacted policies targeted at improving income inequality.

Yet even within developed countries, the public policy strategy for confronting inequality is far from settled. In broad terms, left-leaning politicians tend to focus on absolute poverty levels, taking the view that society should have basic minimum living standards for all citizens. As such, they tend to prioritize redistributing income through (higher) tax-and-spend policies that are designed to reduce the gap in incomes and wealth. More generally, left-leaning interventions include raising minimum wages or cash transfers aimed at setting a basic income level in society. Finland, Spain, Canada, and the Netherlands have also adopted this approach of providing transfer payments to citizens. Meanwhile, more right-leaning policies recognize relative incomes in a society and are guided by the premise that society and income inequality can be reduced over time as long as the rich are incentivized to create jobs and invest in the economy. After all, they argue, a society's wealthiest do, and should be encouraged to, invest and create opportunities that enhance the living standards of all in society, including the poor. Therefore, their supply-side policies include keeping tax rates low.

Despite attempts to combat income inequality by both left-leaning and right-leaning policies, the income debate continues unresolved, and income inequality has continued to widen in many countries.

There are compelling arguments to suggest that absolute levels of income and basic, minimum living standards matter much more for societal progress than relative income inequality in and of itself. As real wages have declined over the past several decades across much of the developed world, and many metrics that measure living standards have worsened (for example, health care and education outcomes, quality, and access), the case for focusing on the absolute rather than the relative has mounted.

Yet social mobility is perhaps even more important. Social mobility has historically been key to improving income inequality, but over the past decades it too has worsened. For example in the United States, over the past thirty years the probability that someone born into the bottom quarter (25 percent) can make it to the top quarter has halved. Moreover, if born into the lowest 20 percent, you only have a

5 percent chance of making it into the top 20 percent without a college degree. Without addressing social mobility, resolving income inequality is impossible.

TOTAL FACTOR PRODUCTIVITY EXPLAINS ROUGHLY 50 percent of why one country grows and another one stalls. Yet TFP is a "kitchen sink" concept that encompasses everything from a country's prevailing rule of law and transparency to technical measures of how efficiently a country converts its key factors of production—capital and labor—into economic growth. For ease of measurement, "pure" productivity is equal to a unit of output per worker—that is, output divided by the number of workers. So if one country can generate the same amount of unit GDP output as another can by employing fewer workers, it is regarded as having a relatively higher rate of pure productivity.

Globally, productivity has been on the decline over the past decade. Global labor productivity of 2.1 percent in 2014 was below the pre–financial crisis levels of 2.6 percent, and well below the average among emerging economies of 4.4 percent.[44] And the declining productivity is affirmed across disaggregated data by country over time. As *Foreign Affairs* has reported, "in the 1960s and 1970s, the G-7 economies saw, on average, a 4.4 percent increase in output per hour worked every year." In the two decades leading up to the financial crisis, it slumped to 1.8 percent, and by 2015, it had fallen to 0.4 percent.[45] Meanwhile, productivity levels in developing economies remain considerably lower than in developed economies. Developed countries have seen marked declines in the last quarter century, while many rapidly developing countries have registered notable productivity gains by innovating and adopting new technologies. In fact, virtually all the gains in global productivity have come from China over the past decades. But even in the Chinese economy productivity has begun to stall—productivity growth in China has slowed to 7 percent in 2014 from an average of 9.5 percent from 2007 to 2012.[46] Similarly, Brazil saw a dramatic decline in productivity growth at 0.3 percent in 2014, down from 1.8 percent in 2013; labor productivity growth in Russia weakened to 0.4 percent in 2014, down from 1.5 percent in 2013. This trend has defied expectations that emerging economies would experience an enormous uptick in productivity by simply absorbing and adopting the technologies and innovations of the industrialized West.

Productivity declined in virtually every sector in the United Kingdom in the aftermath of the 2008 financial crisis. Since the start of the Great Recession in early 2008, UK labor productivity growth has remained very low—15 percent below a precrisis trend. In the postwar period, UK labor productivity growth was averaging roughly 2 to 3 percent a year.[47] The *Financial Times* concludes that "lawyers, accountants and management consultants lie at the heart of the UK's productivity problem." A quarter of the decline in productivity since 2008 can apparently be attributed to these "professional services." Just four sectors—"professional services, telecommunications and computing, banking and finance and manufacturing"—account for the majority of the stagnation.[48]

Highlighting the importance of productivity, Bank of England chief economist Andy Haldane has said that the United Kingdom is twenty times richer than it was in 1850, and that 90 percent of its growth in wealth results from improved productivity. Yet, cognizant that UK productivity has been flatlining, he has also noted that as many as seventeen million adults possess math skills on par with those of a child in elementary school. Such a deficiency could cost the economy as much as £20 billion (US$30 billion) a year and could only be improved through a focus on training and skills.[49]

Reversing the productivity decline is central to resolving the economic malaise currently witnessed around the world, as well as to turning the stagnation story around. However, fixing the dramatic and persistent collapse in productivity is a puzzle for the economic profession, particularly as there seems to be disagreement as to whether productivity is actually in decline.

There are at least two bearish arguments for the position that the decline in productivity is real; two more sanguine, bullish arguments (mainly around measurement) state that productivity is not declining and may in fact be increasing. First, on the bearish side, analysts suggest that fundamental changes in the structure of developed economies, such as the evolution from manufacturing to services, are forcing productivity lower. The sheer number of people working in the service sector as opposed to manufacturing has risen considerably. Given that the service sector is the largest proportion of the US economy, the "mix-shift" problem—the shift of workers from manufacturing to services—is a notable factor. In essence, because advanced economies have moved from being predominantly manufacturing-based to services (a field that has yet to be fully disrupted by technology and in which there remain many more workers per unit of output) this shift is forcing productivity lower.

The service industry accounted for nearly 80 percent of US private-sector GDP, or \$9.81 trillion in 2009. Service jobs accounted for 84 percent of US private-sector employment in 2010. The share of service jobs has grown steadily, from 64 percent (46.1 million jobs) in 1970 to 76 percent (85.77 million jobs) in the mid-1990s to 84 percent (112.12 million jobs) by 2010. Conversely, the manufacturing and agriculture economy shrunk from 33 percent of total employment in the postwar period to 12 percent in 2009, down to 8.8 percent in 2013. As of June 2015, 63.5 percent of total global wealth comes from the services sector.[50] According to Adam Szirmai, a scholar of technology studies, "since the late 18th century, the manufacturing sector has been the main engine of growth"; however, as of 2009, the value added by the service sector "accounts for over 70 percent of GDP in advanced economies."[51] This differs from emerging markets, in which agriculture (as well as manufacturing in larger, more advanced emerging countries, such as China) makes up the most sizable contributor to GDP.

Viewing productivity as a question of mathematics, where productivity equals output divided by workers, we see that today's manufacturing sector has relatively few employees. As the denominator has shrunk, the productivity ratio has increased. In contrast, the service sector, which is yet to be fully affected by technology disruption, has a growing denominator. This large number of employees drags down productivity estimates. Even the simple act of going to a restaurant to enjoy a meal means the average guest will be met by a host, coat-check staff, and at least one server. This is not counting the manager, chefs, busboys, and others operating behind the scenes. Clearly, this makes for a far cry from the shop floor in a modern, largely automated factory. Not only is today's manufacturing sector arguably more automated than the service sector, but the less productive service sector is a greater contributor to the economy, thereby dragging down productivity overall.

Apart from this mix-shift argument, demographic shifts also explain declining productivity. The cohort that is aging out of the workforce has more skills and experience than younger generations, leaving the workforce lower-skilled, less experienced, and underqualified. As a result, greater numbers of employees are necessary to yield the same quantum of unit output, pushing productivity downward and hurting growth.

This view comports with the OECD report that the next US generation will be less educated than the preceding generation for the first time in American history, as well as worsening performance in the OECD PISA statistics in mathematics, reading, and science. Indeed, Robert Gordon of Northwestern University forecasts that global productivity will trend downward. Gordon considers a range of factors that will affect productivity, including demographics and technology, and concludes that productivity peaked in the mid-twentieth century. He goes on to say that the last time the world actually saw real productivity gains was with the advent of electricity in the 1800s and the subsequent innovations that led to its delivery for conventional commercial and residential use.

Gordon explains that periods of slow and rapid growth are linked to the timing of the three industrial revolutions: the first led by rail and steam; the second by electricity, petroleum, telecommunications, and sanitation; and the third by computers and mobile telephony. Gordon argues that the second revolution was the most important of the three and underpinned the rapid productivity growth between 1890 and 1972. He contends that productivity growth slowed for the next quarter century, before a brief revival from 1996 to 2004 fueled by digital technologies.[52]

Despite the persuasive evidence that productivity is falling, others put forward two *bullish* arguments, suggesting that productivity is not falling and could in fact rise. Both of these views tend to revolve around claims that productivity is being mismeasured in the first place. In particular, as we saw in Chapter 1, some argue that GDP measures do not adequately reflect gains in quality and quantity from technology that would be reflected in enhanced productivity.

One might look to the technology enhancements that have occurred across sectors that are not visible in GDP calculations. Many argue that technology has enhanced living standards without actually affecting GDP. For instance, Wikipedia, whose contributors are not paid, certainly raises productive output for its users. As a consequence, the numerator in productivity calculations is lower than it ought to be.

There is also a question of timing. Those who believe that output per unit worker is rising make the point that current GDP has a built-in time lag that ignores or at least does not fully appreciate the positive impact of technology. Much in the way that it would have taken industrial factories and, for that matter, society as a whole some time to adopt and absorb the scale and reach of the benefits of electricity, the global economy has yet to appropriately absorb the dollar-value benefits of such technological innovations as social media, which could be considerable. For now this means that the "bulls" believe that productivity numbers, and by extension GDP estimates, are artificially low.

Of course, were the service sector to adopt automation at the scale already experienced in the manufacturing sector, and undergo diminution of jobs in a similar way—an outcome that is not only expected but by many accounts already under way—the erosion of workers would actually raise productivity. But the overall impact would, paradoxically, be worse for long-term growth, because the costs of the increase in unemployment would outweigh the productivity gains. What is becoming increasingly clear is that policymakers may face a tradeoff between employment and higher productivity.

For all of the debate surrounding productivity, it is apparent that productivity has meaningfully declined over the past decade. Even if there is some truth to the notion of mismeasured and underestimated productivity, the difference would not be enough to alter the overall picture of declining productivity.

The implications for economic growth of slow and slowing productivity are severely negative. According to a McKinsey report on global growth:

> Even if productivity were to grow at the (rapid) 1.8 percent annual rate of the past 50 years, the rate of GDP growth would decline by 40 percent over the next 50—slower than

in the past five years of recovery from recession. The global economy expanded six fold in the 50 years after 1964 but would grow only threefold between 2014 and 2064 making it more difficult to meet social and debt obligations. To compensate fully for slower employment growth, productivity growth would need to be at least 80 percent faster than it is currently, at 3.3 percent a year.[53]

CREATING AND MAINTAINING ECONOMIC GROWTH are the defining challenge of our time. But from crushing debt to misallocated capital, demographic shifts to rapid technological advancements, widening income inequality and falling productivity to natural resource scarcity with concomitant environmental degradation, growth faces headwinds of historic proportions. Until we set forth a sturdy and sustainable strategy for accelerating growth, we will be unable to address the most intractable problems of our world today, be they in health, education, climate change, or development.

Each headwind is a major challenge in itself; together, they threaten to unravel globalization, raising rates of poverty while reducing living standards—creating a global army of hundreds of millions of unemployed and underemployed people clamoring for government help. The severity and confluence of all these headwinds—in capital, labor, and total factor productivity—are unprecedented in their ferocity and potential deleterious impact on global economic growth. Overcoming them requires a farsighted approach that more efficiently allocates resources over a long-term horizon, rather than our current short-term approach to political decision making.

Instead, policymaking today is moving in the opposite direction—becoming ever more oriented toward the short-term. At a time of flatlining, lower-for-longer growth, public policy appears to be pushing us further toward economic instability.

One example is the wave of protectionism that has taken hold in the wake of the financial crisis. Globalization and its central tenets—global trade in goods and services, cross-border flows, and the private sector at the forefront of economic progress—have been a major source of economic growth in the postwar period. As the next chapter shows, an isolationist world portends a dangerous future.

4

THE FALSE PROMISE OF PROTECTIONISM

NEARLY SIXTY YEARS AGO, A mechanical engineer named Keith Tantlinger left his job as vice president of a company in Spokane, Washington, that manufactured trailers for trucks. He set out to improve the shipping container, which was then built in a multitude of sizes, could not be lifted by crane or easily transferred to trucks and trains, and could not be stacked too high, for fear that rough waves would knock cargo overboard. He set out to build a better box.

What Tantlinger did was simple enough: he developed a corner mechanism that locked the containers together, making easy stacking possible. But the consequences of his innovation were enormous: millions of ships now carry tens of millions of containers of goods that reach hundreds of millions of consumers around the world, all thanks to

Tantlinger's design. The history of globalization is hung on a timeline of stories like Tantlinger's, reminding us that though today's global economy feels inexorable, it grew out of many events, big and small, each a prerequisite for making our lives more interconnected, globalizing our world.

The principles of globalization are enshrined in the Washington Consensus, codified in 1990 by economist John Williamson.[1] Williamson focused on free trade in goods and services, cross-border capital flows, the movement of people, and the preeminence of the private sector as an engine for economic success. These became the template for economic policy for more than twenty-five years.

Brexit and the election of Donald Trump in 2016 represent a profound challenge to the Washington Consensus. Much of the criticism leveled against globalization today is related to the idea that it enriches the few, leaving the many behind. Those making this argument frequently advocate the wholesale abandonment of globalization, putting the very existence of an international agenda at risk.

This challenge to the Washington Consensus has been a long time coming. Politicians today are paying the price for decades of expedient short-term policymaking that has run counter to the thesis of globalization. While politicians have been advocating open-door trade policies over the last several decades, in reality trade and immigration policies with a more protectionist stance have prevailed over genuinely free trade. This diluted form of globalization failed to create equitable growth, permitted the economy to stagnate, and left politicians vulnerable to the millions of disaffected voters who blame globalization itself for their deteriorating circumstances.

Rather than make the increasingly difficult case for globalization, the leaders of leading nations are pivoting toward greater isolationism. Leaders who once embraced globalization, as well as new leaders standing on a platform of isolationism, are moving toward protecting local industries through higher trade tariffs and their labor markets, along with increased immigration control, in attempts to boost domestic employment. However, this fresh cycle of short-term thinking further undermines long-term economic growth.

History has shown that when developed countries start on a path of protectionist policies that lead to greater isolationism, other countries are forced to follow suit. The risk is a great unraveling of globalization. This chapter seeks to reckon with protectionism's consequences on trade, capital flows, and immigration and to highlight the perils of the deglobalized world that myopic policymakers are constructing.

To UNDERSTAND THE FATES WE potentially face, it's worth exploring what globalization means in practice. Globalization can be seen as a spectrum—at one end of the spectrum is a world with no globalization, where states exist in total isolation from one another, while at the other end is full globalization, characterized by unfettered movement of goods, services, capital, and people. In practice, full isolation and full globalization are abstract ideals; neither exists in pure form in reality. In general, most countries operate in between these extremes, adopting a middle-of-the-road approach to openness and internationalism—a globalization-lite regime, as it were.

Theoretically, under a fully isolationist approach, policies are nakedly protectionist, limiting global trade (through the imposition of higher trade tariffs and quotas, and competitive currency devaluations), capping cross-border capital flows, and curbing immigration. In each case, the goal is to strengthen the domestic economy by protecting jobs and shielding the local economy from the costs of global competitive forces. However, history shows that protectionism causes economic weakness, costs jobs, and slows economic growth. One of the clearest examples can be seen in the almost nine hundred import duties raised by the Smoot-Hawley regime in the 1930s, which led to dire consequences for employment and GDP.[2] Strict and high capital requirements (aimed at making banks stronger) can drastically limit international lending, significantly cap cross-border flows, and thereby constrain investment in the real economy. Ultimately this isolationist stance of higher erected national borders is to the detriment of growth and living standards.

The other extreme is an ideal of complete globalization, in which trade, capital, and even labor flow freely across national borders as if they do not exist. This pure form of globalization rests on the idea of comparative advantage—whereby one country carries out a particular economic activity (such as making a specific product) more efficiently than others. Trade, capital, and labor then flow to where they can derive the greatest economic benefit. As everyone grows and produces the goods and services for which they have the greatest comparative advantage, not only do their wages rise, but by earning more they have more opportunity to buy more and higher-quality goods and services from across the world. The promise of globalization, according to this ideal, is that "everyone wins," with notable economic gains flowing to citizens across the world—whether based in developed or developing countries, or provider of labor or capital. In the view of some globalization advocates, if this has not happened in practice, it is not because the idea of globalization itself is problematic; it is because its implementation has not gone far enough.

What prevails instead is a middle ground of partially implemented globalization. Indeed, it is unclear whether full globalization can ever truly be implemented under current conditions. The real world is characterized by a mishmash of bilateral (as opposed to global) trade agreements that reflect national interests and political expediency. Despite efforts to the contrary, capital flows and immigration decisions are made by national authorities. This middle ground of globalization is a direct product of zero-sum thinking—the idea that in key policy decisions and their implementation, nations are essentially winners or losers. It is also a product of the short-term mentality of policymakers who are oblivious to the true costs and consequences, borne tomorrow, of the policy decisions they make today. In effect, policymakers are paying the price for not pursuing and implementing a purer form of total globalization.

The unavoidable conclusion of the Brexit vote and the election of Donald Trump is that globalization has failed to deliver all things to all people. Instead of benefiting from a globalizing world, many millions of people are instead suffering under worsening living standards and falling real wages, groaning under mounting personal debt and lack of opportunity. Rather than lifting all boats as promised, greater globalization and global integration in trade, capital flows, and immigration have created pockets of losers whose objections to a global world order have seeped into political discourse.

Globalization's success seemed almost inevitable until just a few years ago. As recently as 2014, experts predicted that "trade would grow twice as fast as GDP while international investment and information flows scaled new peaks."[3] Yet according to the *Financial Times* just two years later, "flows of finance, goods and services have slowed—falling from a peak of 53 percent of global output in 2007 to 39 percent in 2014"—evidence that in the aftermath of the global financial crisis, trade and capital flows have been hit hard. While globalization helped to improve living standards and foster growth in a number of developed companies beginning as early as the 1990s, it also created new economic problems. In the case of Mexico, and Latin America more generally, globalization and greater market openness led to greater government indebtedness, recession, and banking-sector stress, and efforts to address these aspects intensified the costs and accentuated cycles of economic booms and busts. The North American Free Trade agreement (NAFTA) opened trade to Mexico, granting the country access to capital investment. As a result, the Mexican government was able to increase its borrowing in US dollars. Political instability led to the devaluation of the Mexican peso in late 1994, precipitating capital flight and a spike in inflation to over 50 percent. Mexico's so-called Tequila Crisis proved to be an early warning of the risks that came with globalization and the opening of free trade. It prompted the International Monetary Fund (IMF) to reexamine its efforts to promote open capital markets and integration. It also prompted other countries to question the benefits of free trade.

With recent declines in trade and reverses in globalization, we have entered an age of ambiguity. Established measurements suggest that globalization is now slowing or, worse, receding. The DHL Global Connectedness Index describes itself as providing "the most comprehensive and timely account of the world's global connectedness . . . covering 140 countries that encompass 99 percent of the world's GDP and 95 percent of its population. It focuses on 12 types of trade, capital, information, and people flows (or stocks cumulated from past flows)." Drawing from more than one million data points that stretch back to 2005, this measurement reveals that some aspects of globalization appear to have gone into reverse. The 2014 DHL Global Connectedness Index reveals "only a very modest increase in the overall level of globalization from 2011 to 2013. While information and capital flows are growing, flows of people remain stable, and trade connectivity is trending downward." What we are seeing may amount to the biggest drop-off in the overall level of globalization since World War II.[4]

In the run-up to the financial crisis, the mantra of many economists and politicians was that globalization was good for growth. But now there is a rising din of concern that globalization might be not only correlated with worsening living standards (declining real wages in the United States and across Europe, widening income inequality) but also a catalyst for these economic ills.

Therefore, as the world settles into a period of low growth, politicians and policymakers are grasping at politically expedient policy measures to attempt to salvage their economies in the short term, such as pulling out of trade deals (such as the United States did with the Trans-Pacific Partnership) and imposing new trade tariffs. Protectionism is on the rise. Led by the United States, the G20 imposed 644 discriminatory trade measures on other countries in 2015, according to Global Trade Alert. In the wake of intensified capital controls on banks, cross-border capital flows have been in decline.

Many of these threaten longer-term economic prospects. Bad policy leads to the misallocation of scarce resources. Not only does this have a negative effect on GDP in the long term, but it kills off economic growth and foments political instability in the short term, further discouraging much-needed investment. As these phenomena worsen economic growth, additional bad policy decisions aimed at short-term gain will only worsen the cycle. As we attempt to overcome the headwinds preventing us from achieving growth, we must avoid misguided solutions that attempt (sometimes in good faith) to save us from chaos but will end up pushing us over the edge instead.

The rising disaffection with globalization cannot be ignored. The concerns are valid; many people have lost out and been left behind as internationalization has gathered momentum. Millions of emerging market farmers have been shut out of trade zones, while many workers, particularly in the manufacturing sector of developing countries, have seen their wages fall as globalization has taken hold. Protectionist, multibillion-dollar programs—such as the European Union's Common

Agricultural Policy (just under 40 billion euros per annum) and farm subsidies in the United States (around US$20 billion a year)—prop up domestic producers at the expense of emerging economies. These unfair trade practices not only are antithetical to the ideals of globalization but also have a devastating impact on the income and living standards of farmers in South America, Africa, and Asia, who are unable to compete with subsidized rivals in the West. The result is a dramatic drop in the amount of proceeds from trade available for much-needed investment in infrastructure in emerging economies. And this has resulted in slower growth across the developing world, home to more than 80 percent of the world's population.

The protectionism around farming in developed countries is an example of how globalization has been compromised. Essentially, as stated above, these shortcomings identified here are not of globalization so much as of globalization's incompleteness. People's concerns around globalization are valid; however, their concerns are not with globalization per se as much as they are about the halfhearted and skewed way globalization has unfolded. Put another way: they think they are objecting to globalization when in fact they are objecting to an incomplete and impure form of globalization that has benefited too few people. To be sure, some in developed and developing economies have benefited from globalization, but it is also true that large pockets of society—such as farmers in the developing world and manufacturing and industrial workers in the West—have suffered in an increasingly integrated international regime.

The results of a University of Chicago study harden the resolve of those who believe globalization has had limited benefit. In a presentation entitled "What Future for Capitalism?" University of Chicago professor Luigi Zingales has compared the economic growth performance of developed and developing nations in what he terms the preglobalization period (1950–1980) versus the globalization period of 1980–2007. As Zingales reveals, developed economies such as France, Italy, Japan, and Sweden all registered declines during the globalization era, and no discernible increase in economic growth. The study shows that at the macro level, only large emerging market economies have benefited. These include India, which nearly doubled from 2 percent to 3.8 percent, and China, which grew from 3.2 percent to 8.8 percent in the preglobalization and globalization periods, respectively.

The last three and a half decades have offered the potential for broad-based wage growth, but the vast majority of people have seen few of these economic gains. Real wages have suffered, hurting living standards for many workers in developed economies and around the world. For example, German real wages declined by 4.5 percent from 2000 to 2009.[5] And, according to the Economic Policy Institute, "ever since 1979, the vast majority of American workers have seen their hourly wages stagnate or decline. This is despite real GDP growth of 149 percent and net productivity growth of 64 percent."[6] A 2015 Pew survey notes that, "after adjusting for inflation, today's average hourly wage has just about the same purchasing power as it did in 1979, following a long slide in the 1980s and early 1990s and bumpy, inconsistent growth since then. In fact, in real terms the average wage peaked more than 40 years ago: The US$4.03-an-hour rate recorded in January 1973 has the same purchasing power as US$22.41 would today."[7] Whatever the cause of these trends—whether jobs moving offshore to lower-cost countries or automation replacing workers—they are serving as a catalyst for protectionism and more aggressive deglobalization.

Although there are real frustrations prompting the rising antiglobalization chorus, these flaws ultimately have less to do with the ideal of globalization itself than with the inferior form of globalization that policymakers have implemented over recent decades—a kind of globalization lite.

Given the unsettling political portents, it is understandable that politicians and policymakers today are responding to the electorate's grievances against globalization. But regrettably, across the world—in emerging and developed economies alike—politicians are pivoting toward inferior political and economic models that offer quick wins but are guaranteed over the long term to reduce economic growth, increase poverty, and spur more political and social unrest. Rather than address globalization's shortcomings, their policy choices will only entrench the inferior model of globalization, guaranteeing a descent into an economic equilibrium of higher barriers and even lower growth.

ON MARCH 4, 1933, IN his first presidential speech, Franklin Roosevelt stated: "Our international trade relations, though vastly important, are in point of time and necessity secondary to the establishment of a sound national economy." Roosevelt's protectionist approach is a common one among politicians when their economies are under pressure and they themselves feel pressed to act. A protectionist stance may be appealing and even understandable in the immediate term.

Such an approach can appear to protect jobs in an economic down cycle. But in the long term, it not only harms the nation's economy but can diminish growth globally as well. Today, dismantling our globalized economy in an uncoordinated and unilateral fashion, nation by nation, is having devastating effects on trade, capital, and labor.

Certainly since the 2008 global financial crisis, trade, a central pillar of globalization, has deteriorated. As nations erect trade barriers and avoid new free trade agreements to try to stop the bleeding in their own economies, billions of dollars are blocked from entering the veins of global commerce. Many nations are employing tariffs and quotas to raise the prices of imported goods and services, in favor of local producers. In the European Union, tariffs, quotas, export bans—from bananas to rare earths—have weighed down global trade. Already there is considerable evidence that global trade is diminishing. In 2013, the World Trade Organization revised its forecast for global trade growth down from 4.5 percent to 3.3 percent—a striking decline from the average 5.3 percent growth of the previous twenty-five years. According to the *Financial Times*, "[2015] saw the biggest collapse in the value of goods traded around the world since 2009, when the impact of the global financial crisis was at its worst."[8]

But it is not just naked protectionism that is driving this trend. Loose monetary policies such as quantitative easing and ultra-low interest rates weaken the home currency, so that a country becomes more trade competitive at the expense of its trading partners. In what are termed "beggar thy neighbor" approaches, other economies follow suit with the view to becoming even more competitive, by increasing global demand for their goods and reducing home demand for imports. Ultimately, such tit-for-tat policy responses, in which one country attempts to fix its economic woes in a way that damages other economies, make the whole global economy suffer.

Of course, this retrenchment in global trade is not new—it is an all-too-common response to economic difficulties. As we have seen, the American Smoot-Hawley Tariff is the classic example of this protectionist sentiment. By imposing an effective tax rate of 60 percent on more than 3,200 products imported into the United States, Smoot-Hawley accomplished the impressive feat of decreasing GDP by more than $47 billion, from $104.6 billion in 1929 to $57.2 billion in 1933 according to the US Bureau of Economic Analysis. Similarly shortsighted policies were common across the West at the time, constricting economic growth in a time of profound uncertainty. Yet they continue to have appeal today. As of 2016, the United States has raised its tariffs on imports of cold rolled steel from China to 522 percent from 266 percent.[9] Other recent examples of goods under US trade protection and associated tariffs are paper clips (at roughly 130 percent), peanuts (at 163.8 percent), and tobacco, facing a staggering 350 percent tariff.[10] Although intended to protect the economic welfare of its own people, a nation's trade tariffs are anathema to liberal market-friendly thinking. As politically appealing as they may be in the short term, they tend to hurt economic growth in the long term.

The turn to protectionism now is merely the latest in a series of shortsighted decisions that began in the early years of globalization and would go on to undermine it. First, leaders squandered the windfall from trade and failed to invest in longer-term, economic growth–enhancing projects. Far-sighted US politicians in the 1980s would have backed a big investment agenda in infrastructure, schools, and skills to usher in a new economic era on the back of the wealth earned from globalization, thereby avoiding declines in wages and employment. However, this did not occur.

Second, rather than end protectionist policies protecting their farmers, Western governments instead kept farm subsidies in place and sought to compensate emerging countries for lost income through billions of dollars of foreign aid flows. However, foreign aid programs have been a catastrophe, fueling corruption, leading to inflation, killing off export sectors, supporting political factions, and fostering dependency. Moreover, the United States has provided low-interest loans to Middle America, especially to support home ownership. These debt programs (particularly through Freddie Mac and Fannie Mae) gave people the illusion that their livelihoods were improving even as their wages were falling and debt obligations were rising. This debt was a direct cause of the financial crisis that many are yet to emerge from. In both instances economic growth has, over the long term, suffered.

Finally, national interests remained paramount, despite the emergence of a global world order. Today's form of globalization is one in which no one is responsible for the global economic interest. To give effective globalization a chance, national governments would need to cede real power and authority to global institutions. Such international agencies do exist: for example, the World Trade Organization is supposed to preside over trade, and the IMF maintains oversight over international capital flows. But even these institutions are answerable and superseded by policy agendas of national governments, and thus struggle to implement a truly global agenda that benefits all.

Politicians, especially those in political systems with short electoral cycles that force them to vie constantly to win the next near-term election, are unlikely to cede power and authority to a supranational agency. Therefore the question becomes whether policymakers can take any action to limit the costs that globalization imposes on the losers without jettisoning the whole globalization agenda and letting nation-states become more protectionist. Put another way: Can public policy mitigate the costs to the losers in a globalization-lite world? Historical evidence to this effect is not encouraging.

This new wave of protectionism in trade builds on a phenomenon that has been entrenched in the developed world for decades. Even at the best of economic times, countries such as the United States (via its farm subsidy program) and those in Europe through the Common Agricultural Policy engage in trade protectionism. This goes some way to explain why the United States, despite touting the virtues of free market economics and capitalism, is ranked by the Fraser Institute's index on economic freedom as only the sixteenth most economically free country in the world.

Nor is it just trade that is under protectionist siege. Capital is also facing new barriers to free movement. Capital is money targeted for investment in physical plant and equipment and in infrastructure, such as roads, railways, ports, and factories—all crucial for increasing growth. All countries, but poorer countries in particular, rely on capital inflows to fund their economic growth and development. For our purposes here, in addition to foreign direct investment (FDI), capital flows encompass short-term payments and cash movements. This refers, for example, to hedge funds trading in stocks across different countries, or global companies needing to shift cash around to pay salaries across borders.

Recently, capital flows to emerging economies have been in decline. In October 2015, the Institute of International Finance reported that for the first time since 1988, the amount of money flowing out of emerging economies would, in 2015, exceed the quantity of money flowing in. Worse still, with only around US$550 billion of foreign investor capital expected to flow to emerging countries (at its peak in 2007 it was closer to US$1.2 trillion), capital flows to the developing region in 2015 would be lower than those registered in 2008 and 2009 in the depths of the global financial crisis.[11]

In recent years, much of the movement of capital away from the developing world occurred in response to tightening monetary policy by the US Federal Reserve after a period of loose policy to stave off the financial crisis. The program of reducing quantitative easing, known as the "Taper Tantrum" of summer 2013, combined with a subsequent fever pitch of speculation over interest rate increases, contributed to the withdrawal of capital. In February 2017, the Institute of International Finance reported that capital flows to emerging markets remained flat, at around US$680 billion, with high downside risks for FDI. Financial market expectations for interest rate hikes in the United States are a contributing factor to weakness in capital flows destined for the emerging markets, as investors look to gain from higher-interest-rate environments. However, the anemic economic growth conditions across the developing world also lower the opportunity for returns and hurt capital inflows. The softness in capital flows to emerging economies could prove more damaging in the long term as the prospects for economic growth continue to wane. Already the world's largest and most strategically vital emerging nations—such as Argentina, Brazil, Colombia, India, Indonesia, Mexico, South Africa, and Turkey—are only growing at 3 percent or less a year. Ever more damning is the implication of the IMF's October 2014 "World Economic Outlook" that the world will never again see the rates of growth witnessed prior to 2007.[12] This weak economic backdrop comports with a weak capital inflow story. According to the Reserve Bank of Australia, the movement of money through the financial system has been stagnant over the past decade. In dollar terms, cross-border capital inflows among the G20 economies have fallen nearly 70 percent since mid-2007.[13] Ultimately, slow economic growth leads to decreased investment, which in turns leads to even slower growth.

Exogenous factors are not the only force driving down capital cross-border flows. Feeding off the fervor for trade protectionism, public policy has turned decidedly protectionist on capital flows too. Capital controls (particularly in developed nations), especially those imposed on banks and other large financial institutions in the wake of the financial crisis, effectively increased the cost of higher-risk lending—which affected emerging economies disproportionately. Deepening the problem has been protectionist tendencies within developing markets. In India, Brazil, Cyprus, and elsewhere, choke points are appearing in cross-border capital flows. For example, in 2013, Cyprus became the first Eurozone country to apply capital controls, limiting credit card transactions, withdrawals, and transfers abroad. All of these policies were intended to prevent an outflow of capital. Although the capital controls were subsequently reversed two years later, many economists see Cyprus's capital control measures (and the tacit endorsement of them by international organizations such as the IMF and the European Union) as a tipping point away from the globalization agenda that had governed the global economy for three decades, and indication of growing support for deglobalization, if even just for short-term rebalancing reasons.

Capital flows serve as the lifeblood of an economy, and they are slowing not just as a result of investment decisions in the wake of worsening global growth prospects but also because of deliberate protectionist policies by governments. As such, it is no surprise that economic growth rates in emerging countries have continued to stall. Protectionist measures on capital flows—although precipitated by policymakers' desire to stabilize and strengthen the financial infrastructure in the wake of the 2008 financial crisis—have inadvertently contributed to lower growth by reducing the capital available for investment. The problem has been made worse by the way countries have reacted to other nations' policies by imposing additional capital controls of their own, further limiting cross-border investment and forcing global growth even lower.

The globalization agenda was designed to integrate countries by easing the trade in goods and services, the flow of capital, and the movement of people across borders. Over the last thirty years, and despite recent retrenchment, globalization has succeed to some extent on the first two scores. But it has done much less with regard to the movement of people. And if anything the 2016 Brexit vote and the election of Donald Trump on an anti-immigration platform have shown that national governments seem to be moving further away from globalization's aspirations. The 2015 European refugee crisis exemplifies how the movement of people has never fully been integrated into a global regime, despite it being a key pillar of the globalization agenda. Because immigration has remained the purview of individual nation-states, rather than coordinated across borders, this backdrop has led to a disorderly movement of people and ultimately moments of crisis, as in 2015.

The over one million refugees who have arrived in Europe since 2015 make up just a small part of the over sixty-five million people displaced by war or persecution—the largest number in recorded history. But the present refugee crisis marks the first time in history that the European Union has been tasked with accommodating so many people from outside the continent, including new arrivals from Libya, Syria, Iraq, and Afghanistan, particularly in such a disruptive and disorderly fashion.

Although labor quality and quantity are key inputs of all canonical economic models of economic growth, there remains no globally integrated approach to migration to correspond to the international frameworks, agencies, rules, and regulations that govern capital, in the form of trade and cross-border flows, and productivity, largely driven by the spread of ideas. Labor policy remains the purview of nation-states, whose approaches often differ dramatically. For example, whereas Canada and Australia make immigration decisions based on a point system (which grants weights to academic achievement, work experience, and so forth), the United States does not have as transparent a grading system for new immigrants.

The lack of a globally integrated immigration approach is a form of protectionism that hurts economic growth. According to the International Labour Organization, there are approximately 73.4 million young people between the ages of eighteen and twenty-four who are out of work around the world. The global labor imbalance is particularly pronounced when you consider the worsening demographic dynamics of an aging population in the "West" (including Japan), versus the skew to the young in the rest, where up to 70 percent of the population is under the age of twenty-five.[14] Deploying labor from countries of surplus to regions of deficit could serve to solve this imbalance. Countries that face a dearth of labor already tap the global talent pool in a unilateral way by attracting labor through guest worker programs and specialized visas. However, these unilateral approaches can be inefficient in that they impose caps on the movement of labor, thereby leaving pools of talent underutilized. A global policy that targeted an optimal migration level could capitalize on the pools of workers around the world.

Such a proposition is contentious. The debate on immigration is complicated by two factors: first, its impact on inequality, and second, its links to state-sponsored welfare systems. Immigration increases the labor pool and thereby reduces labor costs; thus it is seen as attractive to large businesses and wealthier individuals who might wish to employ cheaper labor in jobs ranging from caregiving for children and the elderly to construction. But lower-income workers often see immigration as increasing the competition for finite jobs, forcing their own incomes downward and reducing their living standards. As a general rule, the greater the proportion of lower-skilled workers within an immigrant population, the greater the downward pressure on wages, which in turn worsens income inequality. However, one study in the United States finds that immigration has only marginally affected income inequality over time, by less than half a percentage point change in the Gini coefficient scale. Similarly, UK studies have found only a small impact by immigration on wages—of approximately two pence an hour (or £40 a year). Meanwhile, local citizens worry that open-door migration adds considerable pressure to state provision of welfare and employment prospects. With more people coming into a country than leaving there is a concern that the state welfare system will come under strain, particularly if the newcomers are unable to find work. In an economic environment of slow and slowing growth, and with the mounting ferocity of the economic headwinds—rising population, widening income inequality, and higher (state) debt burdens—concerns about increased immigration become more biting and impossible for politicians to ignore.

Nevertheless, politicians are not immune or protected when public perception of immigration's impact diverges from reality. When disorderly immigration is combined with both worsening income inequality and an unsustainable welfare state that cannot support a growing population, these factors can be a drag on growth.

This chapter has shown how policymakers are erecting new barriers to trade and to capital. While with regard to labor we are starting from a point of much less integration and coordination, backtracking exists there as well, whether with Brexit or Trump's proposals. In essence, the anxieties of the low-global-growth era are leading to a retreat from even the most modest efforts at helping people find work across borders. Within the framework of capital, labor, and productivity—the three key drivers of economic growth—there has been a general acceptance under the rubric of globalization that the movement of capital and ideas (embedded in productivity) is acceptable. In contrast, the free movement of people is fraught with social, cultural, and economic resistance.

IN 2012, THE *New York Times Magazine* featured a report from Greece on how ordinary people were faring amidst a wrenching depression: "A quarter of all Greek companies have gone out of business since 2009, and half of all small businesses in the country say they are unable to meet payroll. The suicide rate increased by 40 percent in the first half of 2011. . . . Nearly half the population under 25 is unemployed."[15] The reporter concluded: "Greece is devolving into something unprecedented in modern Western experience."

At the time feverish Greek demonstrations against its economic collapse, austerity, and globalization were largely seen as a view from the fringe. Riots and protests across the country that started in 2008 were still continuing in 2017. Today, Brexit and Trump tell us these sentiments—once perhaps hidden—are now central to political debate. Whether it was debt or globalization or a combination of both that precipitated Greece's economic woes is almost immaterial; the protests represented an outright rejection of globalization and the international bodies such as the European Union and the IMF that were imposing global policies in the national context. The demonstrations were not just about better public management; the austerity Greece faced was seen as objectionable also because it was deemed necessary by foreign (global) dictate. Meanwhile, at a macro level, Greece's GDP per capita fell from US$32,000 in 2008 to US$18,000 in 2015, and with the exception of some weak growth in 2014, the economy has been contracting ever since it first shrunk in the final quarter of 2008. The country's debt-to-GDP levels has risen to close to 180 percent—among the highest in the region. Living standards have deteriorated considerably, with more than 45 percent of young adults unemployed and more than a third of the country's total population classified as being at risk of indigence or social exclusion.

For many policymakers today the fear of losing control of their economies to outside forces and becoming "another Greece" is tempting them to pivot toward quick-fix protectionist policies that in the long term are likely to inhibit economic growth and spark more turmoil. Trade protectionism, capital flow diminution, and restrictions on migration are all likely to reduce the investment needed to power growth.

First, a decidedly more siloed world—of higher trade barriers and more biting restrictions on capital repatriation—will force businesses to adopt more local and less global business models. In essence, businesses will be more likely to adopt a federal structure, relying on local and regional capital, and will be less likely to be centrally run from leading financial centers. This change will significantly alter how businesses fund themselves, how they structure costs, and how they view the long-term growth proposition.

Second, a world of greater protectionism and more fervent deglobalization has a significant bearing on inflation, which will come in two stages: first as short-term deflation and then as long-term inflation. Deflation is a natural artifact of protectionism as it cools economic activity through reduced trade. Already, a world of slowing economic growth and dragging global demand has lowered prices and subdued inflation in all manner of goods and services. This has been observed perhaps most starkly across the commodity composite from oil, copper, and iron ore; prices have fallen considerably alongside the weakness in global demand. Beyond low energy costs, low and declining wage growth and indeed the price of capital (money) itself—reflected in the decline in the price of money (the interest rate)—are all a reflection of a prevailing deflationary world.

Mounting protectionist trends will only serve to enhance and reinforce the deflationary trends already observed in the aftermath of the 2008 financial crisis. For example, the twelve months leading up to June 2016 had five months of zero or negative inflation. Meanwhile, US inflation stood at just 1 percent in the year up to May 2016. The persistence and stickiness of low inflation—even seven years after historically low interest rates (hovering close to 0 percent) and with vast quantitative easing programs for printing money in Europe and the United States—defy warnings of steep and sharp inflation dating as far back as 2009. Nevertheless, even if the prevailing policy stimulus has not stimulated inflation, protectionism will.

Rising trade tariffs alone will increase the prices of imports. But beyond these trade effects, wages in a relatively closed economy with reduced movement of labor could also force wages higher. This confluence of trends will have an inflationary effect in the longer term. In regard to timing, classical canonical models of economics estimate a roughly five-year boom-to-bust business cycle for the shift from deflation to inflation. However, the fact that aggressive policy interventions have thus far done little to raise prices, and in fact are correlating with deflation, suggests that traditional models and timing expectations are out of kilter with the unpinning of the economy. In essence, although the basic mechanics of prices and the global economy still hold sway, the timing horizons have shifted—perhaps because of the advent of technology that may be forcing prices downward—so that these protectionist forces will still play out, but more slowly than in previous cycles.

Third, as protectionist tendencies mount across the globe, governments will likely favor national champions. These are companies that enjoy regulatory protections, tax breaks, and subsidies that offer an unfair advantage in their home markets against foreign competitors. What results are corporate monopolies rather than competitive markets, where the government becomes a bigger arbiter of who wins and who loses. Ultimately, lower competition grants greater pricing power to favored companies and industries, disadvantaging the consumer, and promoting larger and more inefficient companies.

Already, many countries protect their key industries and companies. In 2013, Russia was ranked as the most protectionist country in the world by Global Trade Alert, an independent trade-monitoring think tank. Russia has a list of forty-five industries, including finance, oil/energy, broadcasting, and publishing, where foreign investment is subject to government approval. In the United States, the Committee on Foreign Investment in the United States (CFIUS) serves a similar function, though the turn toward protectionism may lead it to take a more aggressive role. CFIUS made headlines in late 2016, when then-President Obama blocked the Chinese acquisition of a German computer chip manufacturer with US subsidiaries. Though the Obama administration explained that its actions were motivated by national security concerns, the *Financial Times* reported on calls by members of Congress of both parties to broaden CFIUS's mandate, permitting it to apply a more stringent economic benefits test to prevent foreign acquisitions of US companies.[16]

Greater capital requirements and restrictions to repatriate capital will invariably limit the ability to invest across borders and will thus limit growth for companies, countries, and the global economy as a whole. These trends are inimical to economic development and progress, placing global investment and commerce in grave danger in terms of profits and returns. They threaten to upend equity and bond markets, foreign exchange, commodity prices, corporate investment decisions, and global trade. Left unchecked, the result will be more destruction of the global economy, greater despair and unrest, conflict, corruption, and a sense of utter hopelessness.

ACROSS THE WORLD, CITIZENS ARE angry and chalk their frustrations up to globalization. Although their worsening economic realities justify their angst, in reality globalization is not to blame. Public policy has settled for a globalization lite, rather than allowing full globalization a genuine chance to "lift all boats." Globalization makes markets more efficient, increases competition, and spreads wealth more equally around the world. Such is the promise of full globalization.

But rather than reaching for this goal, global public policymakers who are faced with backlash have been shifting globalization into reverse, away from the globalization ideal. Under pressure to show results, policymakers around the world are pivoting toward inferior political and economic models. The trends discussed in this chapter—the diminution of global trade, the collapse of cross-border capital flows, mounting constraints on the movement of labor, and deglobalization—point to the misallocation of two major factors of production: capital and labor. They lead inexorably to deteriorating living standards and greater geopolitical unrest. Not only do they pose a threat to the future of economic growth, but they have helped to set in motion a global economic death spiral.

5

A CHALLENGE TO DEMOCRACY'S DOMINANCE

IN KENYA, THE CAMPAIGN POSTERS have come down. The polling booths have closed. Following a hard-fought election in 2013, the country's new president, Uhuru Kenyatta, has taken the oath of office and is preparing to leave on his first major foreign trip. For newly elected leaders in emerging countries, this represents a high-profile rite of passage. They visit the country that is, for them, a beacon of progress, a partner in prosperity, and a model to emulate. With a wave from the tarmac, President Kenyatta boards his plane and takes off—not west, toward the White House, but east, toward China's Great Hall of the People.

To billions in the developing world, the value of free peoples and free markets—ascendant in the aftermath of the Cold War—is no longer axiomatic. Instead, under intense pressure to deliver more, better, and faster growth, governments in the developing world are being drawn down an alternative path. Embodied by the meteoric rise of China—though hardly limited to it—this new paradigm of a less democratic, more authoritarian state capitalism promises a sure path to success.

On the surface, this model's embrace of greater state intervention in the economy purports to solve many of the immediate economic and demographic challenges dogging the world's emerging nations. It promises rapid economic growth for disaffected youth, massive reduction of poverty, badly needed infrastructure improvements on an epic scale, and solutions to social problems such as the provision of health care and education. But while this economic and political model holds tantalizing promise in the short term, it places the world on a dangerous path in the longer term. For all of its seductive, immediate appeal, the alternate path to prosperity that is sweeping the developing world is decidedly inferior to Western liberal ideology, liberal democracy, and market capitalism.

When the state eschews a robust private sector in favor of tightly gripping the reins of the national economy, protectionism rises, innovation suffers, and in the long run growth can stagnate. State capitalism encourages just the sort of protectionism and preference for national champions that, as the previous chapter showed, can harm growth. Emphasizing the correlation between trade and economic growth, the IMF's economic advisor Maurice Obstfeld stated that the backlash against globalization "threatens to halt or even reverse the post-war trend of ever-more open trade."[1]

Emerging markets are turning to this new approach to put out the fires of social and political unrest that are smoldering around the world. Paradoxically, this model will only fan the flames. With authoritarian state capitalism, individual rights and freedoms are deprioritized in favor of collectivism, which curtails innovation and in turn damages long-term economic growth. While China's state-centric economic approach is well documented, less well-known is the fact that this tectonic ideological shift toward state capitalism has accelerated across emerging markets in recent years. This alternative path is specifically appealing to emerging economies that are hungry for economic growth.

FOR TWENTY-FIVE YEARS AFTER THE end of the Cold War, democracy flourished and spread across the world. On the back of glasnost, perestroika, and the fall of the Berlin Wall, democracy created nascent liberal states. This trend toward democracy was an undoubted win for liberal ideals and flew in the face of authoritarian values. It seemed to mark the end of the schisms that had divided East and West, and developing and developed countries, since World War II. History had delivered its answer to the question British prime minister Harold Macmillan posed in his seminal 1960 speech, "Wind of Change": "As I see it, the great issue in this second half of the 20th century is whether the uncommitted peoples of Asia and Africa will swing to the East or the West. Will they be drawn into the Communist camp? Or will the great experiments in self-government that are now being made in Asia and Africa, especially in the Commonwealth, prove so successful and by their example so compelling, that the balance will come down in favor of freedom and order and justice?" Free market capitalism and liberal democracy were, it seemed, the only path toward prosperity.

Yet today, for many in the emerging economies, where 85 percent of the world's population lives, the Western insistence on political rights as a prerequisite for economic growth seems misplaced. Hundreds of millions of people in the developing world live on less than a dollar a day. For them, the choice between food and freedom is a debate between the urgent and the merely important—something difficult for many in the richer West to understand. Political freedom may be desirable, but placing food on the table and a roof over heads takes precedence over all else. At its core, sequencing food ahead of freedom is about postponing, not rejecting, democratic capitalism. After all, people in poor countries do understand democracy and why it might matter, and in theory they would love to choose their leaders. But when it comes to the reality of daily life, many people worry a lot less about how the government came to power and a lot more about whether that government can provide jobs, education, and health care.

The debate on whether democracy and market capitalism are prerequisites for economic growth has taken on new urgency now that people around the world see a credible alternative challenging Western economic and political ideology. Across the world, more and more citizens believe democracy and capitalism need not be the answer. Many prefer the economic and political approach of China, a model of state capitalism in which the state steers production and the economy. Democracy is de-emphasized, at least in the short term, as economic rights supersede political rights. This economic and political approach is gathering momentum and increasingly being seen by many across the developing world as the system that can deliver the greatest improvements to the human condition in the fastest period of time.

Several factors place Western economic models at a disadvantage in this scenario. First, China's model has gotten results. China has delivered record economic growth and made a significant dent in poverty. In just one generation, China has moved over three hundred million of its citizens out of poverty—that's roughly equal to the entire population of the United States. And whereas in 1970, Chinese secondary school attendance was at 28 percent, today that figure is at 94 percent. To be sure, the country faces a multitude of challenges—from pollution, environmental concerns, and overpopulation to a corporate debt overhang that many financial market traders worry could derail the economy. But no one can dispute that real strides have been made toward economic prosperity. By some estimates, China now ranks as the largest economy in the world in GDP terms, pumping billions of dollars of capital investment and trade into the global economy. Chinese global investment is estimated to exceed US$1.6 trillion.[2] The United States has been estimated as representing 15.5 percent of world GDP, compared with China at 17.8 and the Eurozone at 11.8 percent. And whereas the United States has a 10.8 percent share of world exports, China has 10.7 percent, and the Eurozone 26.3 percent.[3]

Second, China has shown that it is possible to meaningfully reduce income inequality without changing its economic (or for that matter, political) system. The United States and China, as has been mentioned in previous chapters, have approximately the same Gini coefficient of 0.47, and unlike the United States—where income inequality has been getting worse over time—China has markedly improved. For example, the income distribution plan released by the Chinese State Council in February 2013 explicitly seeks to raise the minimum wage to at least 40 percent of average salaries. It also aims to increase spending on education and affordable housing and requires state-owned enterprises to contribute a greater share of their profits to reducing inequality. The intention of these government-led policies is to ensure that income inequality at best continues to decrease. However, some reports suggest that the results of these efforts is mixed, and progress toward reducing income inequality may have even slowed.

Third, China has delivered a now-legendary infrastructure campaign. Today, China has more paved roads than the United States, having constructed an extensive network of highways in just fifteen years—even going beyond China itself. In Africa, for example, Chinese largesse has paved much of the distance from Cape Town to Cairo. With these types of achievements, it is perhaps no wonder that majorities of people across ten African countries in a 2007 Pew survey believe that the Chinese had at least a fair amount of influence over their countries, with majorities of over 90 percent holding a favorable view of China in some countries. The Heritage Foundation China Investment Tracker shows just how influential China has become—making a mark globally by increasing trade and foreign direct investment across South America,

Africa, and much of the world and becoming an important lender of capital. It is investments and trading opportunities like these monitored by the China Investment Tracker that fund infrastructure, schools, and health care in partnering countries. These considerable investments and prospects for ever closer trading ties are central to why the leaders of many countries are prioritizing stronger connections with the Chinese government. In the last few years the leaders of Argentina, Brazil, India, Russia, Malaysia, and South Africa, to name a few, have all visited China and pledged to forge stronger diplomatic and trade relations. China has also been a significant lender to the US government—the largest lender in decades.

Finally, China is actually following through on providing innovative solutions to age-old social challenges. For example, logistics have long posed a major stumbling block to the eradication of diseases in remote parts of the world. Travel just hours outside Mumbai, Mogadishu, or Mexico City, and you will likely find severe shortages of medicine and health care services. By leveraging the delivery expertise and network of their state-owned companies, China is helping to deliver medicines to some of the world's most far-flung places. In the US system, the delineations among public, private, and NGO sectors are starker, and the opportunity to cross-pollinate in knowledge and expertise is much more limited. By blurring the lines between state control and private industry, the Chinese state capitalist system is legitimately able to resolve some issues that defy the American system.

Under private capitalism, the bedrock of many Western economies, there is generally a clear delineation between public and private sectors. Government is charged with delivering public goods such as education, infrastructure, and national security; providing regulatory oversight; and setting sound economic policies. Businesses are supposed to maximize their profits by selling whatever goods the market demands for more than the cost of production. Under state capitalism as practiced in China, by contrast, the roles of the state and commercial sectors are far more closely aligned, as the government controls much of the domestic economy through an extensive network of state-owned enterprises. In this system, the social and political goals of the government tend to take priority over strictly commercial concerns. Thus, the government can leverage the delivery expertise of a state-owned mining company—for example, by instructing it to transport and distribute medicines in distant areas.

Both paradigms have their costs and benefits. While private capitalism has shown an unmatched ability to create wealth, it also tends to create extreme income inequality and a myopic focus on quarterly results at the expense of long-term growth. In theory, state capitalism gives companies the freedom to invest for the future rather than obsessing about immediate profits. For instance, China has shown that it is willing and able to ride out difficult economic times with trade and investment partners and retain focus on longer-term strategic goals. One example was its ability to resist any temptation to pull out or reduce its commitments to Brazil as recession and political turmoil took hold in 2016.[4] Among the key strategic investors in Brazil are China Three Gorges and China State Grid, a leader in electricity transmission. On the other hand, China's large state-backed enterprises often use their privileged access to capital via state-owned banks to crowd out private competitors that might generate far more value on a level playing field. And although China's state-based model offers useful lessons on how a symbiotic relationship between the public and private sectors can improve the delivery of social goods and services, private capitalism hardly needs to be jettisoned to achieve a higher level of public-private cooperation.

Quite clearly, China has made spectacular progress when viewed within the capital-labor-productivity growth framework. In terms of capital, China has accrued an enormous amount of money (at the time of this writing the Chinese economy boasted foreign exchange reserves of over US$3 trillion—among the highest in the world); in terms of labor, China has invested in quality by focusing on education and leveraging its large population; and in terms of productivity, over the last decade China has recorded the largest increases in the world, including becoming a leader in ideas. The World Intellectual Property Organization recorded large increases in patent filings by China-based innovators in 2015.[5] Between 1999 and 2006, China's total factor productivity (TFP) increased by 4.4 points; between 2007 and 2012, TFP increased by 2 points. Globally during the same time periods, average TFP increased by 1.3 and 0.5 respectively. For many across the globe, China's accomplishments translate into tangible, visible, on-the-ground improvements in people's lives. This visible evidence of economic progress is what prompts many people around the world, and particularly in poorer, emerging countries, to believe China's economic model can transform the arc of their lives in the shortest period of time.

In light of China's meteoric rise, people in emerging economies have grown to doubt the importance of prioritizing democracy in the quest for economic growth. In July 2014, the recently reelected prime minister of Hungary, Viktor Orban, admitted, "the new state that we are constructing in Hungary is an illiberal state, a non-liberal state. It does not reject the fundamental principles of liberalism such as freedom—and I could list a few more—but it does not make this ideology the central element of state organization, but instead includes a different, special, national approach." Hungary is still democratic, in that Orban was elected; he has, however, rejected the "liberal" part of "liberal democracy." Orban cited China, Russia, and Turkey—all illiberal states—as his models and pointed to the 2008 financial crisis as proof that "liberal democratic states cannot remain globally competitive." He is not the only democratically elected leader skeptical that the free market system can deliver sustained growth and reduce poverty. If we look back further in history, we find examples of countries like Chile, Singapore, and Taiwan—not just China—that have made it abundantly clear that democracy is not a prerequisite for economic growth. In fact, overwhelming evidence shows that economic growth is a prerequisite for democracy, not the other way around.

The poorer a country is, the less likely it is to sustain democracy. Economists have found that income is the greatest determinant of how long democracy lasts. In a study entitled "What Makes Democracies Endure," a group of scholars concluded that "poor democracies, particularly those with annual per-capita income of less than $1,000, are extremely fragile. . . . A democracy can be expected to last an average of about 8.5 years in a country with per-capita income under $1,000 per annum, 16 years in one with income between $1,000 and $2,000, 33 years between $2,000 and $4,000, and 100 years between $4,000 and $6,000." It is no wonder therefore that across the world many countries with per capita incomes below the US$6,000 hurdle are plagued by political instability, with Thailand, Argentina, and Nigeria as just a few examples.[6]

A middle class capable of holding government accountable must be created before democracy can take hold and thrive. Prematurely shoehorning democracy into poor countries runs the risk of creating illiberal democracies that can be as bad— or worse—than the authoritarian systems they replaced. This could, in part, explain why it is that although almost 50 percent of the countries in the world can be considered democratic, the majority of them are illiberal. For example, the elections of Egyptian president Morsi in 2012 and Venezuelan president Maduro in 2013 have proven that voters will accept less freedom (for example, worsening press freedoms in Egypt and a hostile media environment in Venezuela) for promises of more security and jobs. Morsi was removed from office in a military coup in 2013, but there is evidence that successful illiberal leaders can last. In Russia, Vladimir Putin retains high approval ratings, having been elected into political office continually since 1999. Turkey's Erdogan has won successive elections since 2003 both as prime minister and as president. Furthermore, the *Financial Times* has reported that public opinion polling reveals that "authoritarian leaders are seen as far more trustworthy than politicians in more openly democratic countries across the emerging world."[7]

These cases are in line with broader statistics indicating that freedoms have declined over the past decade. Seventy percent of the world's democracies have become so illiberal that they're indistinguishable from authoritarian regimes, according to a 2015 Freedom House report that described global freedom as being in decline for the ninth consecutive year. "Nearly twice as many countries suffered declines as registered gains—61 to 33—with the number of gains hitting its lowest point since the nine-year erosion began."[8] These trends tell us one of two things: either the majority of people are willing to live without these freedoms, or the authoritarian governments are able to satiate pressing economic needs that their citizens value more than the political freedoms they are losing.

There are rational reasons behind doubts and skepticism toward liberal democracy and free market capitalism. Over the past decade, those living in emerging markets point to increased geopolitical uncertainty (Brexit, the election of Trump) and economic volatility (the 2008 financial crisis) as both coming from the West. Moreover, structural problems such as slowing economic growth and worsening income inequality serve to highlight fundamental weaknesses with Western democracy and market capitalism that are deemed unappealing and unacceptable. Therefore, as discontent stretches across the world, middle-class citizens in countries like Pakistan and Taiwan, traditional supporters of reform, have turned against democracy. The governments in Hungary and the Czech Republic have cracked down on political freedoms. Countries like Honduras, Thailand, and Fiji have undergone military coups, while the quality of democracy has deteriorated in Russia, Kenya, Argentina, and Nigeria, among others.[9] Prime Minister Orban of Hungary is part of a trend of a political form of recidivism, whereby citizens through democratic process are freely choosing to elect authoritarian leaders and regimes. There is increasing anecdotal evidence from academics and journalists in Eastern Europe that many people in the region feel that they were better off under the pre-1989 regimes, which they regard as having provided security and progress through industrialization. Free citizens are going so far as to vote for politicians who are antithetical to market values—for example, candidates affiliated with Hamas in Palestine and Syriza in Greece.

Meanwhile, there is a growing acceptance that when it comes to economic progress, market precepts only go so far toward making a nation prosperous. In many countries, policymakers bemoan how, despite concerted market-oriented efforts in the preceding thirty years, the economic situation has markedly deteriorated over time. In 2013, South Korea's Park Geun-hye was sworn in as president, having won her mandate on a platform of greater state intervention and increasing welfare support, seen as a move away from South Korea's previous policy stance. (She would be impeached in 2016 on allegations of corruption and charges of excessive meddling that enabled her associates to commit extortion.) A similar pattern of doubt exists in places as disparate as Malaysia, South Africa, and Brazil. Despite early progress after adopting market doctrine, Malaysia is battling entrenched pockets of poverty unresponsive to market interventions. Meanwhile in South Africa, over twenty years into the postapartheid era, market policies like trade liberalization and capital market integration have done virtually nothing to alter the grim unemployment picture in the country. And twenty years after Brazil's thirty-fourth president, Fernando Henrique Cardoso, the architect of the country's economic turnaround, instituted free market reforms, there are real questions about how much economic success free markets can deliver, and increasing doubts about whether such policies can create economic well-being across all segments of Brazil.

These countries, along with many other emerging economies, are grappling with stubbornly high unemployment especially among the young, pockets of poverty, and regressing economic growth, all adding up to worsening living standards. The emerging world is, of course, an incredibly dynamic place, each nation possessing vastly different cultures and unique local challenges. But even taking into consideration the diversity of problems each nation faces on its own, there are uncanny similarities across countries and continents. Throughout the emerging world, the pattern is striking: larger economies like Brazil, South Africa, and Argentina—with populations of around fifty million and higher—face stubborn poverty, stagnant wages, debilitating income inequality, and intractable unemployment. Emerging economies like South Africa and Brazil are not only growing weary and wary of free markets but actively turning toward the Chinese economic model, in which state policies become more interventionist and China becomes a preferred economic partner. The challenges are exacerbated by the global headwinds outlined in Chapter 3, all of which serve to further worsen the global economic growth picture.

AT THE SAME TIME THAT state-led capitalism is enjoying a surge in credibility in emerging markets, governments in developed countries have also dramatically expanded the state's role in the economy in the quest to restore growth. The German chancellor Angela Merkel is known to cite three numbers: 7, 25, 50. These numbers reflect the fact that Europe is roughly 7 percent of the world population, has 25 percent of world GDP, and represents 50 percent of world welfare payments (government social spending). The United States and Europe together account for roughly 12 percent of the world population, approximately 55 percent of world GDP, and 90 percent of world welfare payments. Not only is the welfare commitment growing across democratic capitalist states, but so too is the role of government in the broader economy. In Britain, for example, roughly 60 to 70 percent of average household spending on housing, education, health care, and transportation is subsidized by the government. Both of these developments pose potentially dangerous consequences for growth.[10]

Today, seven of the ten largest employers in the world are governments. The US military employs approximately 3.2 million personnel, closely followed by the Chinese army, with roughly 2.3 million workers. The British National Health Services, China NPC, State Grid Corp., and Indian Railways follow closely behind with 1.7 million, 1.6 million, 1.5 million, and 1.4 million, respectively. The highest-ranked private-sector company is Walmart, the US retailer, which comes in third overall, with approximately 2 million employees worldwide.

The burgeoning size of government across the world raises grave concerns, particularly as government debt burdens appear increasingly unsustainable. Moreover, it is the private sector, and not the government, that is the engine of growth, job creation, and improvements in living wages. In 2010, the UK Department of Business, Innovation and Skills expressed concern in a white paper evaluating the economy since 2000 that "too many parts of the country became over dependent on the public sector." Of course, the question of the ideal size of the state is an age-old debate. However, the argument of big government versus small government is somewhat of a distraction, as in practice the key issue is a government's level of effectiveness.

In fact, according to the Millennium Challenge Corporation (MCC), "countries with more effective governments tend to achieve higher levels of economic growth by obtaining better credit ratings and attracting more investment, offering higher quality public services and encouraging higher levels of human capital accumulation . . . accelerating technological innovation, and increasing the productivity of government spending." Moreover, the MCC finds that "on average, countries with more effective governments have better educational systems and more efficient health care." Crucially, this reflects how government's effectiveness, and not political freedom or democracy, ultimately determines economic growth.[11]

Central to the government's effectiveness is its discipline to resist reaching beyond its core remit. At a very basic level, government has three roles: providing public goods (such as education, national security, health care, and infrastructure), enforcing and regulating laws, and acting as financier of last resort that steps in when the markets fail (for example, in the government bailouts around the financial crisis of 2008). When government reaches beyond these roles, it is inimical to a country's long-term economic growth.

The state is expected to deliver a suite of (quality) public goods—including national security, infrastructure (such as physical roads and electricity), education, and health care. Of course, the most effective governments are able to deliver public goods in such a way that their debt burden remains sustainable. Where government takes the lead in setting out these public goods, the private sector will follow, forming the basis for job creation and economic growth. In the United States, for example, the government has jump-started private-sector investment in at least four noteworthy areas: the Manhattan Project of 1942–1946, which led to a massive wave of scientific innovation; the US interstate highway system, which created a road network crucial for commerce and communication in the country; the NASA-led Apollo landings; and the development of the Internet, which evolved from the US Defense Advanced Research Projects Agency (under the Department of Defense), responsible for the development of emerging technologies for military use.

Second, government enforces the nation's laws, regulates the economy and society, and metes out punishment when the legislature and judicial system deem it warranted. This role, inasmuch as it relates to business and the economy, has reached fever pitch in the wake of the financial crisis, with governments under pressure to support their banking systems and stave off longer-lasting recessions.

Finally, government is expected to act in times of crisis. At a minimum, the state will act if a crisis is of sufficient scale to disrupt the normal workings of the economy and poses a systemic risk. No other entity (for example, the private sector) can step in to remedy the situation if markets fail to clear— that is, if buyers struggle to find people to sell to, and vice versa. Catastrophic situations, whether they take the form of disease epidemics, natural disasters, or financial crises, warrant state redress. For example, the Brazilian government had to contend with lost incomes and the threat to farmers' livelihoods when, as the *Independent* described it in July 1994, "the price of coffee soared by 25 percent after a second frost damaged Brazilian coffee plants and led to fears that as much as half of the crop could be destroyed."[12] More recently, in the 2008 global financial crisis, governments had to step in to stabilize the financial system and the wider economy by buying financial institutions and automotive companies. Even with such aggressive involvement, global GDP slumped by 3.4 percent (according to IMF estimates), and the recovery nearly ten years on is lackluster. Global GDP contracted 1.1 percent from 2008 to 2009, which "masks the shocking depth of the crisis in the winter of 2008–09, when GDP was contracting at an annual rate over 6 percent."[13]

Trouble arises when government policy steps outside these boundaries, however. For example, the "Housing for All" policy in the United States transformed the government from merely an overseer of the financial markets into an active market participant—as an investment adviser that not only encouraged but also incentivized American households to tie their wealth into housing and real estate rather than stocks, bonds, commodities, cash, and so forth. Through Fannie Mae and Freddie Mac, the government became a de facto mortgage lender, providing inexpensive mortgages that made housing investments look artificially cheap when compared to other asset classes. Worse still, this intervention ensured that many people borrowed in excess, owning property when ostensibly they should not have. This was the kernel of what would become the 2008 financial crisis leading to the Great Recession. As of 2014, Fannie Mae ($3.25 trillion of assets) and Freddie Mac ($1.9 trillion) had between them more than $5 trillion of assets—nearly 30 percent of US GDP. In short, the US government's overreach (in financing private-sector housing) contributed to its own burgeoning debt burden as well as to the broader financial crisis.

To take stock thus far, the world is heading in a direction of greater government control and intervention. China's state-led model has a growing appeal and following across developing markets, and Western economies are themselves adopting more state interventionist tendencies. What is clear is that any shift toward an expanding role for the state in an economy poses a risk to government effectiveness and ultimately the prospects for economic growth.

As a practical matter around the world, countries have different views and traditions on where and how a state should intervene. In the United Kingdom, for example, its national health system contrasts with that of the United States, where medicine is largely—even after the Affordable Care Act (which may yet be repealed)—in the purview of the private sector. The Russian government controls protected strategic sectors such as oil and banking, while Canada protects its mining sector (the government blocked a foreign investment into its potash sector in 2010). And despite its commitment to free market values, even the United States places constraints on outside investment in key sectors. Through CFIUS, which reviews and vetoes foreign investment, the United States vetoed a Chinese investment in a lighting technology company in 2016, and the Dubai Ports investment in a US ports facility was scrapped in 2006.

As developed countries are becoming more interventionist in their economies, one has to wonder if they, too, are drawing on the success of the Chinese model, or at least trying to compete with it. Whatever the case, emerging countries in particular should heed this warning: the China model has its limitations and is not necessarily replicable. In the face of an unquestionably impressive track record in China, there are several important reasons to question the viability of the Chinese model when applied to the emerging world and beyond. It is not only difficult for other countries to adopt China's model but also undesirable.

China's economic system contains significant structural inefficiencies of a kind that are baked into any system that dislocates markets. A state-centric system, in which the government is the arbiter of an economy's factors of production, creates mispricing of assets—from goods and real estate to the key inputs necessary for long-term, sustained economic growth such as capital and labor. This can create supply and demand imbalances, in turn leading to inflation rates so high they are inimical to economic growth, development, and living standards. Inflation is less of a threat amid the current economic malaise, but at the height of China's growth phase, and just before the financial crisis, when oil prices were close to US$140 a barrel, this was a real challenge. Moreover, such policy approaches can distort prices and interest rates, increasing the cost of doing business. This can be seen in instances when state-owned enterprises suck up capital and crowd out private-sector capital and investment.

What is more, the Chinese model simply is not viable for many emerging markets. Driven largely by exports to markets in the West, the Chinese economy has little in common with emerging markets that primarily produce and depend on agriculture commodities. As it happens, the United States and Europe have practically prohibited importation of these precise commodities through subsidies for domestic producers. And while state-centric policies may yield artificial employment in the short term, state-centric inefficiencies create enormous dead-weight losses in the longer term that can be so deeply entrenched as to undermine economic progress and prosperity.

Indeed, China itself is now grappling with massive debt problems that are plaguing the financial sector, a property bubble that market actors fear could burst at any time, and pollution that acts as a drag on GDP growth. All of these raise the possibility that a more severe economic slowdown in China could turn out to be inevitable. Whether China's political class will overcome these challenges—whether its system of economics ever can—is still an open question.

Nevertheless, as China moves past the United States to become the world's largest economy in GDP terms—something that experts such as the IMF now predict will happen as soon as 2022—the Chinese model will only continue to gain admirers. The momentum toward state-led capitalism should prompt calm reflection on the future of democratic capitalism and, ultimately, the need for reform. US Supreme Court justice Stephen Breyer's book, *Making Our Democracy Work*, reminds us it took nearly 170 years from the signing of the US Constitution to establishing equal education under the law (this was enshrined in the landmark 1954 Supreme Court case *Brown v. Board of Education*). It would take another eleven years for the Voting Rights Act of 1965 to guarantee universal suffrage for all United States citizens.

If it took the United States over a century and a half to embed free and democratic rights for all its citizens, should China not be afforded similar consideration with respect to the evolution of its own political and economic system? We should perhaps find reassurance in the fact that the Chinese political and economic model is not static but rather in a constant state of flux toward improvement. Its imperfections are not reason for quickly tossing it aside.

Against the backdrop of failing economic growth, leaders across the emerging world are making policy based on daily practical realities rather than ideology. In this regard, the spread of the Western model should come from its appeal, not from strong-arming developing countries into falling in line. Leaders and citizens everywhere should feel that liberal systems will help solve their immediate (economic) problems. Put another way, rather than force people to embrace liberal democracy and free market capitalism, the way to get them to adopt it is to demonstrate that it can work, create growth, and end poverty in an equitable fashion. What could be more compelling for the rest of the world than an economic system seen to create sustainable economic growth and lift people out of poverty and despair?

At its best, the Western model speaks for itself. This is the approach that put food, refrigerators, and televisions in millions of homes. It has fostered and nurtured the innovative spirit that won the space race and put a man on the moon. These are the kinds of concrete, tangible results people want: what they saw, what they envied, and what they believed in. But in this generation, concrete, tangible results are what they are getting from China and are certainly no longer guaranteed from liberal democracy and market capitalism.

IN LATE 2013, KATERYNA ZHEMCHUZHNYKOVA, a twenty-five-year-old journalist leading protests in eastern Ukraine, was asked why she had taken to the streets. "I want to live in a country where the law is not just a word in the dictionary," she explained, but in a country "where people are free to tell what they think; to do what they want; to go where they dream."[14]

Until recently, the world has been on a path that assumed that liberal democracy and free market capitalism were the only real path to economic prosperity. The rise of China has led many to revisit these assumptions. What if Zhemchuzhnykova's dream, a dream shared by many, is not achievable along the paths of liberal democracy and free market capitalism? After all, there are other political and economic policy routes to establishing a middle class, a precursor to a democracy, and a market economic system that lasts. As the twentieth century gives way to a world of slower economic growth, ideology takes a backseat. The world is shifting from pursuing the ideals of freedom to grappling with the reality of earning a living.

International institutions such as the World Bank—purveyors of the famed Washington Consensus that argued that a suite of free market policies were the enlightened path to free markets and free peoples—are changing their tune. Jim Yong Kim, the president of the World Bank, appeared to give a nod to more state-led systems when he proclaimed, "There is more than one path to shared prosperity. One path is through increased opportunities driven by greater economic growth. Another is through a stable social contract, which focuses on raising the living standards of the poor and the disadvantaged."[15] It has been estimated that by 2025 over 80 percent of the world's poor people will be in fragile, mainly low-income states. This emerging backdrop underscores the urgency of getting the economic and political approach right.[16]

Twenty-five years after Francis Fukuyama argued in *The End of History and the Last Man* that democracy and capitalism had emerged victorious over any other form of government, the picture looks quite different. In the United States, our democracy has been unable to address critical problems, including infrastructure, immigration, tax reform, education, and entitlements. Democratically elected leaders in Russia, Turkey, and elsewhere have perverted the system and become autocratic leaders determined to maintain power at all cost. The Panama Papers exposed how many democratic leaders have used the system for personal financial gain.

What went wrong? Is democracy still the best form of government? Can it be salvaged, or have we reached the end of the road? There is certainly a debate to be had as to whether, in a highly globalized world with frictionless communication, the nation-state is becoming obsolete as a way of organizing government. There is a more fundamental question, however, about the behavior of those in power: namely, whether political leaders, particularly in liberal democracies, are capable of looking beyond the short term in order to create long-run economic and social progress.

6

THE PERILS OF POLITICAL MYOPIA

Speaking before the British House of Commons on November 12, 1936, just three years before the start of World War II, Winston Churchill lamented of the ruling government: "So they go on in strange paradox, decided only to be undecided, resolved to be irresolute, adamant for drift, solid for fluidity, all-powerful to be impotent."

Churchill was speaking specifically to a pressing current issue, criticizing the Baldwin government for failing to rearm as Germany was investing heavily in its air force. But his skepticism regarding government's ability to be efficient and even trustworthy transcends time.

According to the 2017 Edelman Trust Survey, only 41 percent of a general global population trusts the government. Meanwhile a 2015 Pew Research Center survey reported that "the public's trust in the federal government continues to be at historically low levels. Only 19 percent of Americans today say they can trust the government in Washington to do what is right 'just about always' (3 percent) or 'most of the time' (16 percent)." The same study found that the share of Americans that trust the government in Washington to do the right thing nearly always or most of the time reached an all-time high of 77 percent in 1964 and has declined ever since.[1] Together with the evidence that citizens in emerging markets see authoritarian leaders as more trustworthy than democratic politicians, it seems that people across the globe are skeptical of the ability of democratic governments to act effectively—including as good custodians of the economy.

The root cause of this skepticism about democracy is also the crux of the forces that have brought us to the edge of chaos: we have embedded in both business and the democratic political system a predilection for short-termism. And as we shall see in the chapters that follow, myopia in business and especially in politics is singularly detrimental to economic success—a key drag on the prospects of long-term economic growth. It is vital that policymakers and politicians act to address it before it grows still worse. Correcting just this one problem would do much to address virtually all of the specific challenges to economic growth that we confront today.

Short-termism is at the heart of liberal democracy—in its design and in practice. By design, Western politicians have relatively short political horizons: they are often in office for terms of fewer than five years. So they find their duties regularly interrupted by elections that distract from the job of addressing long-term policy challenges. As a result, politicians are naturally and rationally drawn to focus their efforts on seducing their electorates with short-term sweeteners—including economic policies designed to quickly produce favorable monthly inflation, unemployment, and GDP numbers. This approach takes focus away from the more insidious structural corrosion of the economy and the policies that might mitigate it. In order to achieve sustainable economic growth we need better-quality decision making by political and business leaders, as well as policy that prioritizes long-term prosperity over short-term political point scoring. Assessing the many facets of our system that we might reform to achieve such a shift is the task of this chapter.

THERE IS A DIRECT LINK between the individuals voters elect and the economic decisions that elected officials make. Voters choose politicians to do their bidding (such as increase pension payments or reduce their taxes) so that when poor economic consequences result and economic growth suffers in the long term, it is most often a matter not of politicians defying the voters' will but rather of their enacting it. In a liberal democratic system, at the heart of virtually all voting decisions are economic choices. While it is true that purely social questions make their way onto the ballot, even many issues that are viewed mostly through the lens of social policy, such as health care or immigration, end up having an economic impact. Economic choices are at the core of politics.

In 1820, the economist David Ricardo came up with a hypothesis that consumers are forward-looking. While Ricardo's assertion was ascribed to consumers, his thinking can be extended to voters, who are essentially the same group of people. Known in economics literature as the Ricardian equivalence proposition, this hypothesis claims that voters internalize the government's budgetary constraints when making their consumption decisions. Essentially, even if the government grants the voters a tax break today, they recognize that today's tax cut will need to be funded by a tax hike tomorrow in order to balance the government's books, and therefore they do not spend the windfall from today's tax cut. Both Ricardo and others, in numerous empirical studies, have found that in practice the Ricardian theory did not hold, and contrary to Ricardo's assumption, consumers were in fact short-term thinkers. This orientation on the part of voters rewards short-term decision making by politicians, effectively pitting generations against each other. Voters will generally favor policies that enhance their own well-being with little consideration for that of future generations or for long-term outcomes. Today, for instance, the demographic shifts that have led to a large group of retiring baby boomers have had enormous economic implications not only because of capital asset allocation shifts (as seen in the move from equities to bonds) and changes in the real estate market (as aging citizens tend to downsize from large homes to smaller apartments and gain an equity release), but also because of this generation's support for the unsustainable funding of retirees by future economic growth.

In short, politicians are rewarded for pandering to voters' immediate demands and desires, to the detriment of growth over the long term. Because democratic systems encourage short-termism in this way, we are unlikely to solve many seemingly intractable structural problems responsible for our global growth lull without an overhaul of democracy.

Shortsightedness infects the body politic. According to a McKinsey Global Institute report, the average tenure of a political leader in the G20 plus Nigeria is at a record low, declining during the postwar era from 6 years in 1946 to a record low of 3.7 years today.[2] The consequences have become increasingly evident. The myopia embedded in the democratic process creates a mismatch between short-term electoral incentives and the long-term economic challenges that need to be addressed. Worse still, this short-termism exacerbates the headwinds that are already dampening economic growth. This political myopia that regularly pits short-horizon politicians against far-seeing civil servants is evident in such policies as tariffs and quotas that limit trade liberalization. Some politicians find the near-term positive effects irresistible—especially if they protect the jobs of a vital constituency and thus ensure reelection. However, the short-term appeal of protecting jobs that are at risk because of competition from imports is offset by the long-term damage to growth.

The frequency of elections entrenches public-sector short-sightedness, which contributes to heightened policy uncertainty and political volatility. This is particularly true in parliamentary systems if a government is unable to complete its term as a result of a no-confidence vote or if the victorious party fails to form a government, thus triggering an additional election. Such was the case in Spain in 2015 and 2016, for example, when voters delivered two inconclusive electoral results, leading to ten months of political impasse. But these problems are not restricted to parliamentary democracies.

During the Obama years, gridlock in the United States between warring political factions, forced to contest elections every two years, led to outright stasis in some major policy areas such as infrastructure and even to government shutdowns.

Political myopia is the central obstacle on the path of growth in advanced economies. The electoral cycles embedded in democratic systems taint policymaking, as politicians, driven by the rational desire to win elections, opt for short-term quick fixes that have the tendency to undermine long-term growth. Meanwhile, they neglect to address more entrenched, longer-term economic challenges, such as worsening education standards, the imminent pension crisis, and deteriorating physical infrastructure, that don't promise immediate political rewards. This is not to say that politicians don't perceive these challenges: poorly educated, unemployable, and disaffected young people; retirees worried about pensions and health care. But short-term electoral considerations tempt politicians to use costly and unsustainable government welfare programs to address these issues and win over these voters; these too weigh on the prospects of long-term growth. Technocratic policymakers are able to take an unbiased view of the economy, which can put them at odds with politicians who are beholden to the short-term electoral cycles.

There is hard evidence of politicians offering welfare promises in order to win public favor. For example, in the 2015 UK election, then–Prime Minister David Cameron courted votes among the pensioner age group, which traditionally has had the highest voter turnout, by promising to increase Britain's state pension by at least £1,000 per person (from just over £6,000 in 2015 to £7,000 in 2020). In the lead-up to the June

2016 referendum for Britain's membership in the European Union, the Brexiteers—those in favor of leaving the Union—pledged, if they won, to redirect £350 million per week paid into the EU coffers toward the National Health System. So crucial to the Brexit campaign was this controversial promise that this message was emblazoned across their campaign bus in the months before the election. Once the election result for Brexit was confirmed, leaders of the "Leave" campaign quickly distanced themselves from the promise, claiming that they had never made the pledge and that the promise was a mistake in the first place. By September 2016, leaders of the pro-Brexit campaign dropped the pledge altogether.

But it is not only the frequency of elections that encourages short-term thinking in many liberal democracies. The poor design of the US government has left the system conducive to brinkmanship where budgetary matters are concerned. In 2013, for example, the United States suffered a prolonged crisis when it reached a debt ceiling of $16.4 trillion, which had been set by the federal Budget Control Act in 2011. This created a political logjam (one that remains unresolved and continues to occur) in which the government had to take emergency measures, including acquiring approvals from Congress to allow it to continue to borrow in order to continue to function, culminating in a two-week government shutdown. More generally, the annual budgeting and appropriations process in the United States allows political differences in the short term to hamper important decisions that are key to long-term economic success.

The crucial point is this: political short-termism makes the economic headwinds we face worse, and it makes the challenges we confront harder to solve. Some of this is due to bad policies implemented for short-term gain. But in many cases policymakers today are guilty of policy omission rather than commission, in that they have opted to do nothing. They choose not to implement good but complex policies (such as a more robust form of globalization), instead preferring half measures or inaction that is less politically risky. For example, doing something about changing demographics, new technologies of automation, and declining productivity has long been on policymakers' agenda. The fact that these challenges remain largely unaddressed even to this day reflects a lack of action for decades. Debt is another prime example. Politicians can be easily persuaded to load up on sovereign debt with little consideration of long-term repayment, especially since borrowing more today enables them to fund policies that might win votes. Reducing debt, on the other hand, may require them to make unpopular cuts to services, placing their reelection at risk. Thus, debt goes up but rarely down. In a similar vein, tackling demographic headwinds by raising the retirement age is a decision that, in hindsight, ought to have been made decades ago to help escape the pension crisis. After all, since the 1990s, economists have been warning of unsustainable pension deficits resulting from a shrinking working population and people living longer. But because this would be unpalatable to retirees, who vote in large numbers, the decision has been deferred.

Today, short-termism has spread beyond the halls of government into the power centers of finance and business. Here, too, it is a drag on economic growth. The tenure of CEOs is growing ever shorter, from an average of 10 years in 1990 to

6.6 years in 2011 to 4.4 years now.[3] Meanwhile, according to Yale executive-in-residence Richard Foster, the average life-span of an S&P 500 company in 1935 was 60 years; in 2011, it was 18 years. And while the average length of time a stock in the New York Stock Exchange is held in a portfolio was 5 years and 3 months in 1970, in 2011 it was just 7 months. The *Financial Times* reports that researchers at Stanford University have found that "pressure to meet quarterly earnings targets may be reducing research and development spending and cutting U.S. growth by 0.1 percentage points a year." On the other hand, private companies have been found to invest at nearly 2.5 times the rate of comparable public companies, perhaps reflecting the fact that they fear failing to meet the short-term demands of shareholders. By persistently investing at a lower rate, America's largest companies may be cutting 0.2 percentage points from US growth yearly. As the investment horizon grows shorter, businesses are less likely to invest in infrastructure and other longer-term propositions.[4]

CEO compensation is symptomatic of a cultural shift toward short-term thinking. According to the same report, "74 percent of remuneration is paid in cash, and tied to outperforming an annual stock market benchmark." There is growing concern that managers today are incentivized to focus on short-term results, such as the next quarter, rather than the next five to ten years, thereby shifting and shortening the investment horizon. In response, there has been considerable effort by corporations to better match senior executive compensation with longer-term company performance.

Such trends are a manifestation of shortening strategic and investment horizons. According to research by WPP, a global communications firm, among companies listed on the S&P 500, share buybacks and dividends have exceeded retained earnings (that is, profits withheld by companies and generally earmarked for investment) in five of the six quarters to June 2016. Moreover, the ratio of payouts and buybacks to earnings rose from around 60 percent in 2009 to over 130 percent in the first quarter of 2016. Companies are choosing to scale back rather than grow, and to return money to shareholders instead of making capital investments, such as building new factories or increasing R&D, to lay foundations for future growth. These are troubling signs of growing risk aversion. Meanwhile pension funds—even public pension funds—are pivoting toward shorter-term investment in hedge funds and private equity. Even a medium-term investment of three to seven years, such as in private equity, is unlikely to flow to infrastructure, thus hurting economic growth.

The damaging way in which capital is being allocated in the economy is also stifling economic growth. This misallocation takes two forms: first, global stock markets are shrinking because investors are reducing the amount of money they allocate to them, as the appetite to sponsor productivity and growth by global investors wanes; second, the aging global population creates an investor class that seeks income today rather than capital returns tomorrow. Underpinning these shifts is investor behavior, driven by their shorter-term horizons.

Amid slowing growth, investors are increasingly pursuing stable income from their investments. This means committing ever greater proportions of their capital to safe, established companies and projects rather than backing smaller, riskier investments in more innovative firms. Small businesses are thus starved for capital, finding it hard to attract investment or borrow, even though they play a critical role in economies and job creation. In the United States, firms with fewer than 500 workers employed 48.5 percent of private-sector payrolls. Small firms have accounted for 63 percent of the net new jobs created in the last twenty years (14.3 million of the 22.9 million jobs created between 1993 and mid-2013). Moreover, since the recession, small firms accounted for 60 percent of the net new jobs, with firms with fewer than 500 employees leading job creation. In the United Kingdom, small and medium enterprises have proven equally important, with small firms accounting for 99.3 percent of all private-sector businesses and 60 percent (15.7 million people) of private-sector employment. Nevertheless, the scale and often short track record of many small businesses tend to make them more risky bets as compared to larger, more established enterprises.

The allocation of capital across portfolios around the world, but particularly in developed countries, is undergoing significant transformations that have implications for economic growth. There is notable evidence that global stock markets, including in the United States, are shrinking. According to *Bloomberg*, in 2015 the number of listed tradable stocks on US bourses was down almost by half, from a peak of 7,322 to 3,700.[5] Inasmuch as the stock markets represent a path for businesses to fund investment and job creation, this "de-equitization" trend is worrisome and could destabilize global debt and equity capital markets.

In addition to the investor behavior outlined above, there are short-term, tactical factors driving this de-equitization trend. Short-termism manifests itself not just by the behavior of investors in the stock markets but also by the behavior of managers of the companies themselves. For example, during 2015 and 2016, the notable mispricing between fixed income and stocks presented an opportunity for arbitrage—that is, opportunities to make short-term trading profits. When compared against historically low interest rates, the return on equities was markedly higher. Thus, the equity risk premium—that is, the excess return that investing in the stock markets offers over the risk-free rate—made a compelling argument for companies to borrow money cheaply and buy back the company stock. In essence, from a company financing perspective, companies are incentivized to buy back stock—the relatively expensive equity financing—and replace it with cheaper financing in the form of debt.

It is not just stock buybacks but also increasing dividend payments that suggest a company's management does not see positive-value projects worth investing in (as opposed to negative-value projects that lose money). In a world characterized by greater uncertainty (low global growth prospects, ever changing regulation and tax environment, no discernible goods inflation), rather than reinvesting free cash flows into the business or having cash sit in the bank earning low interest rates, business managers are returning capital to their shareholders.

Essentially, every dollar used to either buy back company stock or pay out dividends is a dollar not used by the company to invest in long-term projects that could stimulate growth in the economy. As a consequence, capital earmarked for equity investments is taken out of stocks and the stock market, to be

directed to low-yielding, safer fixed-income, or bond instruments. The trend of less money chasing the equity markets,
and more money chasing bonds, diverts funds from equity
risk investments and hurts productivity, reducing the capacity for innovation and damaging growth.

While these equity market gyrations may be short-term,
reversible phenomena, a more structural and long-term factor in the inability of the stock markets to support growth is
the aging global population. As the population ages, savers
and risk-taking investors are transforming into rentiers. An
increasingly large proportion of the economy relies on a stable, regular, and predictable income derived from past investments. In this sense, the baby boomer generation increasingly
favors bond-like instruments and is structurally moving their
portfolios away from stocks. According to the Willis Towers
Watson global pension fund, assets under management in the
nineteen major markets total US$36 trillion, equivalent to
nearly half of global GDP. And in the seven largest markets,
bond allocations (30.6 percent) were close to those of equities (42.3 percent), and there is a discernible trend away from
other investments and toward bonds. This shift to bonds suggests that investors are seeking stable cash flows and pay dividends, looking for companies that harvest cash flows today
rather than invest in companies to grow tomorrow.

In the US context, the class of aging investors who are
no longer investing for the long term hold the lion's share of
savings. Although rational, their decision to collect dividends
and safe, small returns could have significant deleterious consequences for the appetite for equities and thus constrain the
ability of companies to invest and grow.

The trends of less money chasing the equity markets and more money chasing bonds have at least two effects. First, they hurt productivity, which is propelled by innovation and equity risk investments. This is particularly worrisome at a time when global productivity continues to stall. Second, these trends may not be all bad, in that they do present opportunities and more attractive returns for growth investors who are willing to tolerate a longer investment horizon. At the highest level, investors—so crucial to driving capital into infrastructure, innovation, and businesses that drive economic growth—are choosing income today over longer-term investment, to the detriment of growth tomorrow. Short-termism is built into the structure of both governments in liberal democracies and the private sector, with ill effects for long-term economic growth.

THE EXAMPLE OF INFRASTRUCTURE ENCAPSULATES the problem of both public and private myopia. Infrastructure remains woefully inadequate in the United States. Any modern economy needs, as its foundation, a solid infrastructure base: ports, roads, electricity, airports, telecommunications, and railways. While this might appear self-evident, the state of infrastructure in the United States suggests otherwise. A 2017 report by the American Society of Civil Engineers (ASCE) gave the country a grade of D+ for overall infrastructure, citing 2,170 high-hazard dams, 56,007 structurally deficient bridges (9.1 percent of the nation's total), and $1 trillion in needed upgrades to drinking water systems over the next twenty-five years. The report card highlighted the urgent need for substantial funds earmarked for new infrastructure projects and maintenance of existing infrastructure. At a minimum the ASCE suggests that a $2 trillion investment is needed by 2020 to address the significant backlog of overdue maintenance and the pressing need for modernization. Without this much-needed investment, the US economy will certainly see a further erosion in growth.

There are second-order effects of the failure to invest in infrastructure. State and local pension funds, along with insurers and mutual funds, which together manage around $30 trillion, are starved for long-duration assets to match their long-term obligations—the latter mainly in the form of payments to be made to pensioners at future dates. Infrastructure investments are characteristically long dated; they can offer pension funds and insurers an ideal investment opportunity, reducing the risk that the amount of pensions owed in the future is considerably higher than the fund's total assets. The need for investible long-duration infrastructure projects has become more acute in recent years, as the persistent low-interest-rates environment substantially raises future liability obligations on a discounted basis. The asset-liability gap, and ultimately the future pensioners who will depend on the incomes from investments made today, would be helped considerably by a large-scale program of infrastructure rehabilitation and improvement.

The effects of increased infrastructure investment on the prospects of low-skilled labor could also be substantial. With the US unemployment and labor participation rates still of concern, and underemployment over 10 percent (and close to 12.6 percent for recent college graduates), a public commitment to a sizable infrastructure program could meaningfully transform the prospects of the American worker.[6]

Despite these many benefits, political short-termism is contributing to underinvestment in infrastructure in that politicians tend to focus on short-term metrics such as unemployment, growth, and inflation and prefer to postpone longer-term infrastructure decisions. Investing in infrastructure would have all sorts of benefits, but the prevailing democratic political system discourages the sort of long-term thinking necessary to do so.

As a case in point, the former UK chancellor of the Exchequer George Osborne has overtly linked political short-termism and underinvestment in infrastructure in a 2013 government treasury report. In describing how Britain had fallen behind in infrastructure investment, he said, "it's been the result of a collective national mindset that has privileged the short-term over the long-term, and has postponed difficult decisions." Osborne pointed to congested roads, overcrowded trains, and a shortage of affordable housing as evidence of the infrastructure consequences of political short-termism.[7]

Clearly there have been periods in the past when governments have chosen to undertake large infrastructure projects without succumbing to political myopia. In the United States, for example, the federal government drove the rollout of the Work Projects Administration (WPA). Launched under President Roosevelt's New Deal to help address America's chronic unemployment, the WPA was created in 1933 (as the Works Progress Administration, and renamed in 1939), and was America's largest and most ambitious project dedicated to constructing public buildings, roads, bridges, schools, and courthouses. It was possible because short-term political incentives aligned with a long-term agenda of building and expanding infrastructure. Ironically, one of the most successful infrastructure programs in history was fueled by a desire to secure a shorter-term political goal of reducing unemployment. The key rationale for the politicians that set up the WPA was the creation of jobs. The enduring contribution to the nation's infrastructure was simply a by-product of this policy approach, and the WPA was shut down in 1943, when there was a worker shortage in the economy. At that point workers were able to secure jobs mainly in war-related industries.

Nevertheless, despite the complex histories of programs like the WPA, there is a fundamental question that must be addressed: What has occurred to make endemic short-termism a greater problem in liberal democracy today? After all, liberal democracy has not itself changed radically from times of more robust economic growth in the past. Yet there are good reasons why America's democratic politicians—even as late as the 1950s and 1960s—were able to implement large infrastructure projects without engaging in the extensive overhaul of the democratic process that this book will propose. Since then, three significant shifts have occurred that have changed the way in which Western democracies function: first, changes in economic ideology from largely state-centric to a more laissez-faire capitalism; second, the rise of the twenty-four-hour news cycle as well as the advent of social media; and third, a power shift away from the state and toward nonstate actors such as corporations and wealthy philanthropists that are increasingly taking on the role of government (including underwriting public goods), weakening the state in the process. These shifts are closely linked to the broader problem of why democratic governments of today have become less effective at delivering sustained, long-term growth.

First, there has been a fundamental shift from the government interventionism that prevailed as late as the 1950s and 1960s to a more private-sector-centered, smaller-government ideology that became dominant beginning in the early 1980s. Policymakers prior to the 1980s were guided by Keynesian economic thinking. In the wake of the Great Depression and World War II, it was understood that government's actions powered the economy through the creation of jobs and the allocation of capital. This changed in the 1980s with a shift toward greater free enterprise, a more dominant role for the private sector in driving growth, and a diminishing interventionist role for government. Private-sector investment in infrastructure replaced the grand postwar infrastructure programs that were driven by governments. However, momentum in infrastructure investment appears to have been lost as the private sector, seeking profits, replaced the public sector in leading the initiative. The ensuing slowdown in infrastructure investment underscores the view that a successful infrastructure build-out requires leadership from a long-term-oriented government.

A second change since the mid-twentieth century is the growth of media, including the development of the twenty-four-hour news cycle and the emergence of social media. These have intensified short-termism in both the public and private sectors. Politicians find themselves subject to constant short-term media scrutiny, and lured into a perpetual cycle of news and commentary at the expense of a focus on long-term policymaking. For business and political leaders alike, this constant media attention has led to decisions that emphasize the next quarter over the future in a way that was not previously the case.

Finally, the rise in the wealth and influence of private-sector corporations and wealthy individuals has undermined the state. By minimizing their tax obligations, nonstate actors (for example, charitable foundations that receive tax breaks) diminish government tax revenues. Moreover, by assuming many aspects of the roles traditionally ascribed to governments—such as the provision of public goods (education, health care, and so on)—nonstate actors have run roughshod over traditional public policy agendas, answerable to no one and able to change their areas of interest and focus at a whim with little to no recourse. Essentially the charitable foundations take the reins from government in the delivery of public services but are unaccountable for whether and how they actually deliver them. In this regard, the government cedes some power in long-term agenda setting in the delivery of public goods.

The short-termism among US policymakers has meant that the gains from globalization have been misallocated in a way that frustrated millions of Americans and spurred the populist reaction witnessed in 2016. As Alibaba founder Jack Ma pointed out at the Economic Forum in 2017, by choosing to spend $14.2 trillion fighting thirteen wars over three decades, rather than investing in America's infrastructure, industry, and jobs, policymakers misallocated the wins from globalization. What was clear is that even thirty years ago, industrial jobs in the United States were already on the decline and exposing the economy to greater competition inherent in open international trade, further harming the American worker. The outcome was a missed opportunity to distribute the gains of globalization more widely (and in particular to America's Rust Belt) and to fund a longer-term infrastructure investment strategy to galvanize the US economy.

The question of how much the public sector should be involved in the delivery of infrastructure and the creation of jobs is hotly debated across the political aisle, pitting those who maintain that government should largely stay out of job creation against those who believe that it is incumbent on the public sector, and central governments in particular, to put underutilized human resources to work. But the fact that the US dollar remains the world's reserve currency, and the US public sector is capable of financing an enormous infrastructure program at absurdly low interest rates, makes a strong case for a publicly instituted infrastructure rollout today. So long as policymakers remain hamstrung by ideological squabbling on the costs and consequences of deficit financing, the US economy will continue to suffer.

As a practical matter, and given the urgency and significance of the infrastructure challenge to the US economy, the federal government should create a bipartisan infrastructure commission to bypass the political strictures and logjam. This sort of commission would not be a Band-Aid solution to manage today's political schisms but a permanent feature of the government to keep it focused on a long-term infrastructure agenda. Much like the bipartisan National Commission on Fiscal Responsibility and Reform, established in 2010 to address the nation's fiscal challenges (though it ultimately did not succeed in getting its recommendations implemented), an infrastructure commission would be mandated to identify policies to improve US infrastructure in the medium term and address the challenges over the long run, while avoiding the sort of political wrangling that stymied Simpson-Bowles.

Ultimately, however, commissions alone will not be sufficient. The inability of governments today to effectively address long-term problems such as infrastructure and sustainable growth indicates the need for radical reforms of the democratic process to tackle myopia, encourage higher-quality political decision making and longer-term thinking, and jump-start long-term and sustainable economic growth.

To be certain, the accomplishments of democratic capitalism are unmistakable. It has proven itself, historically, to be a peerless tool for growth. During the past fifty years, US income levels have risen thirty times, and poverty has fallen by 40 percent; Europe's per capita GDP tripled between 1960 and 2015, while hours worked declined by a third.[8] The global economy as a whole has tripled in size in twenty years, driven as much by the developed world as the developing one.[9] And with that prosperity came peace unprecedented in modern history. Even as we acknowledge the flaws in the current system, it is worth recalling that for every example of democracy being challenged (as, for example, in Russia and Egypt) there is another example of its durability (for instance, in South Korea and the Philippines, where despite scandals affecting their political leaders these democracies are strong and embedded). Nevertheless, the system urgently needs an overhaul if we are to jump-start the global economy. For beyond myopia, there are other substantial problems with democracy as it functions today.

For instance, democracies tend to misallocate assets. Political decisions for allocating assets should vary with a country's level of development. Too often politicians in a system that follows the principles of democratic capitalism choose policies that limit rather than promote growth. The political system should instead direct available assets to the areas of the economy most in need of development and by extension will have the greatest impact on the country's trajectory of economic growth. China and India, for example, needed roads to increase productivity. China built them, but India's infrastructure programs got bogged down in red tape and political wrangling born of political fissures in its democratic system, suggesting that India's democratic processes stifled decisions that could help drive economic growth. A veteran observer of India, John Elliott, notes that "democracy is also a drag on development [in India] because, while it has rightly opened the way for dissent and opposition to changes in land use and environmental concerns, no effort has been made to curb its misuse by vested interests who corruptly manipulate not only policies but their implementation. This has contributed to India becoming an increasingly unpredictable, unreliable, uncompetitive and difficult place to live and do business."[10]

As a result, India's competitiveness has suffered from historical underinvestment in key infrastructure, including transportation. In 2016 it was ranked 68th of 140 countries for overall infrastructure, well behind China, which was ranked 42nd. India's poor-quality infrastructure directly contributed to its relatively low competitiveness ranking at 39th versus China at 28th. The effects of underinvestment in infrastructure on the economy are real: for India, spending 1 percent of GDP on infrastructure is likely to boost the country's GDP by 2 percent and create as many as 1.4 million jobs.[11]

Interest group lobbying is another feature of liberal democracy that tends to interfere with proper allocation of assets. In 2016, more than $3.15 billion was spent lobbying Congress, roughly double the amount spent in 2000.[12] Across sectors, lobbying by special interest groups has a discernible impact on public policy decisions in ways that negatively affect trade, infrastructure, and ultimately economic growth. For example, environmental groups oppose pipelines and new exploration projects of the oil industry, agricultural interests lobby for farm subsidies, and American trucking interest groups oppose additional tolls earmarked for road maintenance. (This is one possible reason US infrastructure is graded a D+.)

The need to win reelection also impedes the effective allocation of resources by elected officials. Political cycles too often keep politicians beholden to the individuals and corporate interests that help fund their campaigns and to the vagaries of public opinion polling. Little wonder that there are questions about the correlation, and even causality, between liberal democracy and the incentive for people to be productive. In essence, in order to win competitive democratic elections politicians must offer more benefits to voters, such as generous pensions or tax breaks. The electorate becomes conditioned to demand more of the state over time (knowing that they can extract benefits from politicians) and can themselves become less incentivized to be productive.

Another crucial shortcoming of democratic capitalism, despite its vaunted successes, is that in its purer forms it can foster corruption. The scandals of the early 2000s of established, blue-chip US companies such as Enron and WorldCom as well as Italy's Parmalat, along with the global accounting scandals of Arthur Andersen and top-tier investment banks uncovered during subsequent bankruptcy and investigations, proved that the capitalist system was not immune from systematic wrongdoing.

Another problem associated with democratic capitalism is that it does not insure an economy against inequality. To the contrary, in fact: the rich in countries such as the United States (who make large contributions to political campaigns) are gaining more wealth, income, and political influence, thereby widening the gap between them and the rest of society. Because democratic politics rests on political contributions, it widens the inequality between rich and poor. It is the use of wealth to influence political outcomes that helps inequality take root. Until democracies push back on the use of wealth to influence elections and policies, initiatives by governments to address inequality will be blunted. This could explain why both left-leaning and right-leaning democratic governments have failed to counter the persistent widening of income inequality over the past several decades.

Finally, democracy is prone to party duopolies and gridlock. Democratic systems are supposed to encourage competitive elections, but for the most part we see advanced democracies locked into rigidly dogmatic political ideologies. Rather than feature a free-ranging competition that surfaces the best ideas, democratic elections often produce a stale collision between two rigid sets of beliefs. Many Western democracies are little more than duopolies, where two key parties dominate politics, with the United States being a prime example. No third party has come close to challenging the dominance of the Republicans and Democrats. Yet the 2017 French election of Emmanuel Macron's En Marche movement proves that a long-standing and established political duopoly is vulnerable to challenge from a new third party, depending on local circumstances.

Even so, a democratic political process can lead to one-party dominance. The case of Japan is especially instructive. Despite a strong democratic system, it has seen the same party elected and reelected to power for over six decades. The Liberal Democratic Party of Japan (LDP) is a conservative political party, continuously in power since its 1955 creation, with the exception of two brief periods, the first less than a year, the second from 2009 to 2012. In a similar vein, since South Africa's first free and fair elections in 1994, the country has been ruled by the same party, the African National Congress.

In some ways, the electoral process itself occludes deeper flaws in democracy. Voters take comfort in their ability to remove individual politicians when they err, yet this possibility leaves underlying structures largely free from critique, improvement, and enhancement. If anything, we are evangelists for democracy, happy to export it to other countries, content that rotating politicians via the electoral process is enough to sidestep any weaknesses democracy might harbor. Poor economic performance, in this view, can be directly traced to bad policy decisions by individual politicians, leaving aside the question of whether the systems need to evolve. Yet as we saw in the previous chapter, for all their flaws alternate political systems can nevertheless generate meaningful improvements in economic growth and living standards—sometimes precisely because they are unlike mature, liberal democracies. In a world where growth is flagging, it is therefore all the more important for us to acknowledge the weaknesses in the political and economic systems of mature, liberal democracies.

It could be argued that one of democracy's greatest weaknesses is the ability to reform itself. Reform of democracy must, however, be at the heart of a successful plan to improve economic growth and global prosperity.

So far this chapter has detailed how the democratic system inherently contains incentives for policymakers to implement bad policy choices that undermine long-term economic success. Nevertheless, as we seek solutions to remedy democracy's failings, we should acknowledge that politicians in a liberal democracy need not be malicious or even inept to fall prey to short-term thinking. They are wholly rational actors—responding to voters, succumbing to media pressure, and battling to stay in office, even if it means they do so at the expense of the economy's longer-term success.

When democracy works, it delivers economic growth and fundamental freedoms in a way that no other system can. And when it fails, it is rarely, if ever, replaced by a system that can do a better job of delivering for its population. Therefore, creating growth requires that we preserve democratic capitalism's core strengths—freedom, efficient markets, transparency, and correctly constructed incentives—and reform its weaknesses. Something must be done to remedy the political class's severe case of myopia, correcting the mismatch between long-term economic challenges and election cycles, safeguarding independent economic choices from political pressures, and eliminating dysfunction and gridlock.

IN HIS COMMENCEMENT REMARKS AT Virginia's Hampden-Sydney College in 2013, Admiral Eric Olson spoke of how Navy SEAL training has historically graduated only about 20 percent of the physically fit and highly motivated young men who begin the course. A study of the 80 percent who didn't complete training discovered that most of those who quit did so during breakfast or lunch. This "quitting" cohort (who quit in anticipation rather than in the midst of some activity itself) was afraid that the next thing they would be required to do would be too difficult, too cold, too wet, too painful, or too tiring. They quit because they feared that they would fail.

The study also explored factors that contributed to the success of the 20 percent who would actually become Navy SEALs. The research considered age, experience, geographic origin, interests, intelligence, fitness levels, and more. But perhaps more interesting was what the study revealed in the category of "sports and hobbies." The third best indicator of success in SEAL training was being on a water polo team at the high school or collegiate level, and the second best was being on the wrestling team, but the top indicator was a high level of expertise in chess. It is understandable that grueling and physically demanding sports such as water polo and wrestling would figure on the list, but both were outranked by chess.

Chess players are strategic thinkers who see beyond the next move or the next challenge. They were the ones who succeeded in the long, demanding, grueling Navy SEAL program. The winning cohort were not focused on what would happen after breakfast or lunch; they were mentally focused on the days or weeks ahead, already assessing how to be in the best position to overcome a future challenge. Myopia was the challenge for aspiring Navy SEALs, and myopia is the challenge for economic growth as well.

THE REASON TO REFORM DEMOCRACY is to make government more effective and make the state better equipped to address the economic headwinds undermining the global economy. This chapter has detailed how both the democratic political approach and the market capitalist system are beset by short-term thinking, which infects decision making and destroys the prospects for strong, long-term economic growth. The solution to this myopic frame must be for democratic policymakers to better match their approach to long-term economic challenges with political cycles. Crucially, this will first and foremost require the reform of the political system over and above the reform of the market capitalist system, as we must primarily ensure that the state and political leaders are incentivized to set policies for the long term and are dissuaded from myopic thinking.

Eradicating political myopia is necessary, but it is merely a first step. To resolve the growth quandary and combat the fierce headwinds we face today, even more radical reforms will be necessary. Only by fully overhauling and strengthening liberal democracy can we overcome and solve the inherent limitations of capitalism. The next chapter will offer specific proposals that seek to achieve this goal.

Some may be tempted to imagine that these political reforms must be accompanied by a thoroughgoing reimagining of capitalism itself. After all, the surest sign that this system has reached the edge of chaos is the indecision and intellectual exhaustion evident in the leading economists and financial analysts of our time.

The economics profession is frustrated. As the global economy struggles to emerge from the worst financial crisis in over half a century, and citizens reckon with the prospect of a prolonged period of anemic growth and deteriorating standards, the economic orthodoxy of multiple centuries is increasingly viewed with suspicion and derision. Economists failed to predict the 2008 financial crisis and have overseen an unexpectedly slow recovery in which inflation remains low and debt still increases. What went wrong?

Esteemed economists are perplexed, filling professional journals and op-ed pages with attempts to explain the error. One thing is for sure: the canonical models of economics appear increasingly inadequate to the challenge of speeding up economic growth. The toolkit of monetary and fiscal policy that repaired the economic booms and busts of yesteryear seems abruptly impotent. This is partly due to the underlying structural changes in the global economy. Pluses are quickly offset by minuses in the zero-sum game of globalization, which leaves economies everywhere much worse off. Increased trade on the one hand is countered by wider income inequality on the other; increased capital flows beget inflation and debt burdens that drag growth lower.

Complicating matters further are the potentially harmful effects on economic growth emanating from the structural transformations occurring across the global economy: technology advances, demographic shifts, widening income inequality, natural resource scarcity, and the ever-increasing global debt overhang.

That the world's most respected economists are showing some humility is a good thing. But economies do not operate in a vacuum, and neither do markets. Governments manage economies, and politicians make the laws and policies that fuel governments. Economists have shouldered enough blame, and it is time for the political class to face their own responsibility for maintaining the health of their economies and the urgent need for reform—political reform. US politicians love celebrating how "exceptional" the American democratic system is. But that system is showing some wear and tear; major parts need to be retooled or redesigned so that the world's political leaders are better prepared to respond to the demands and volatility of a twenty-first-century global economy. Elections matter. And that is why reform of the democratic system is absolutely necessary.

Economic dogma has taken the place of political compromise, and the chasm between competing schools of thought has widened just when we should be building bridges. In light of this economic paralysis, solutions must be found in political reform.

Thus far, *Edge of Chaos* has elaborated the story of how, in its current guise, the liberal democratic system unwittingly dampens prospects for the economic growth necessary for its continued survival. The pages that follow will seek to reframe and recast the political strictures that govern the world's leading economies. There is enormous scope for improvements in countries guided by liberal democracy. Implicit in the reform agenda offered here is an acknowledgment that the greatest hurdles to economic revival and future success are not economic. They are political. Knocking down political hurdles will require political solutions—and courageous politicians.

At stake is nothing less than economic progress.

7

BLUEPRINT FOR A NEW DEMOCRACY

"GIVE ME LIBERTY OR GIVE me death!"

Uttered in 1775, Patrick Henry's famous words have, over the past two centuries, echoed within political movements around the world, expressing what billions of people have come to believe: that freedom is the most cherished value of all—and should be at the core of every modern political and economic system. Patrick Henry's utterance has so resonated that it appears in national anthems and mottos beyond US borders. Uruguay's anthem, "Orientales, la Patria o la Tumba," includes a similar statement, "¡Libertad o con gloria morir!"—Liberty or with glory to die!—while "Liberty or Death" (Eleftheria i thanatos) is the Greek national motto. It has taken over a century to convince the world of the merits of democratic capitalism and the freedoms these economic and political systems offer. And yet today, skepticism regarding these systems is at a fever pitch at home and abroad, with many now doubtful that these systems can deliver the human progress they once promised.

Over the past decade, Western democracies have been the source of considerable political volatility (with the rise of populism amid disaffected voters), mounting economic uncertainty (emanating from the financial crisis), and worsening prospects for strong economic growth (as the economic headwinds detailed in Chapter 3 gather speed). This unsettling backdrop has brought into sharp focus the urgent need to objectively and critically reassess the limitations of democracy in its current form.

Indeed, the skeptics are right. Democracy must adapt or further decay. With this threat in mind, this chapter presents ten radical reforms intended to revive the quality of political decision making in democracies, enhance civic responsibility and voter engagement, and ultimately forge a democracy where politicians will pursue and voters will support long-term policymaking and fresh approaches to achieving economic growth. The proposals described here will not be easy to implement. Some may find them unpalatable or even downright objectionable. Nevertheless, they map out a path to combating the myopia that plagues democracies around the world.

The proposals offered here fall into two categories. Some are targeted at politicians and political institutions, and others are targeted at voters themselves. They include making it harder to repeal legislation, reducing the frequency of elections, implementing term limits, requiring officeholders to have nonpolitical experience, mandating voter participation, and instituting minimum qualifications for voters.

These recommendations are intended for mature democracies like the United States, the nations of Western Europe, Canada, Japan, and Australia, for these countries have the most to lose if democracy fails. They represent the viability of the democratic system, and their example has persuaded many others around the world to adopt democratic principles and values with great success. As standard-bearers of democracy, they must now demonstrate that it can be resilient, not by remaining unchanged but by adapting so as to once again offer a model of economic success and continual human progress. More generally, countries across the emerging world that adopt and pursue democratic principles should also heed these recommendations as they seek to embed effective democracies for the long term.

These proposals may be met with skepticism from those who believe that whatever the time, whatever the question, the answer is always more freedom, not less. Yet it is important to recognize that unfettered liberty carries with it costs that are weighing down on economic prospects of the world. These proposals would restrict the behavior of politicians, limit the options available to voters, and, indeed, narrow the scope of the electorate itself. But these are necessary constraints at a time when politicians and voters too free to act have acted too often in shortsighted ways.

As WE HAVE SEEN, POLITICAL decision making in liberal democracies has prioritized political outcomes today over economic outcomes tomorrow. What follows are seven proposals aimed at altering the actions of politicians to make them more effective long-term policymakers.

First, policymakers should bind their governments and their successors more firmly to policies. A key problem with government is time inconsistency—the fact that policies committed to and enacted by an incumbent are routinely un-wound, thereby creating policy uncertainty, which in turn hurts investment and ultimately impedes economic growth. Put another way, it is the tendency of the preferences of incumbent politicians to change over time in such a way that today's decision makers' choices become inconsistent with past plans and commitments. Binding the government is a solution to the problem of time inconsistency.

The unraveling of previous commitments to public policy can occur in at least three ways. One problem is structural, wherein one branch of government can override commitments made by another. This can be seen in the tendency of some countries (like the United States) to require the legislature to ratify international agreements already negotiated by the executive. This means that a government can agree to a treaty (like the TPP, say), only to have it shot down by Congress, weakening a state's ability to act on the global stage. A second problem has to do with compliance with existing international agreements. We shall see this phenomenon most clearly in the example of EU members failing to abide by previously agreed levels of debt, in the absence of clear enforcement mechanisms. The third problem is that of policy changeability, when politicians wash their hands of present-day problems created by their predecessors. This can take the form of failing to fund an expensive entitlement program or failing to act on a task force's or commission's urgent recommendations. As shall be seen in the example of the Simpson-Bowles model, this means that even when politicians recognize a problem, they may later avoid the difficult votes necessary to solve it. Solutions to these problems include eliminating additional ratification procedures, ensuring compliance, preventing future repeal, and neutralizing the problem of time inconsistency. All represent methods of binding the government.

The failure of the US Congress to ratify the Trans-Pacific Partnership is a clear example of how a ratification process can reverse a policy decision entered into by the president. Although President Obama signed on to the free trade strategy partnership of twelve countries in February 2016, Congress failed to vote on it. This stalled the agreement until the TPP was ultimately rejected by President Trump in January 2017. A very similar story emerged with the Paris Climate Change Agreement, which President Obama signed on to in December 2015; after another lengthy congressional stonewalling, it was summarily dismissed by President Trump in 2017.

A clear example of lack of compliance can be seen in the impact of the financial crisis, which imposed economic pressure that exposed the high debt levels of many European countries. It became clear that the European Union had allowed several countries to deviate from their commitments to debt and fiscal targets agreed on in the 1992 Maastricht Treaty. Without effective enforcement, future international agreements can fall apart just like Maastricht. A regime for enforcement, complete with costs and consequences, must be established to ensure that such agreements are held in place.

There have been other efforts to rise above political short-termism by establishing superstructures and institutions that work at a national level, independent of party politics, yet even these may fall victim to policy changeability. The United Kingdom's National Infrastructure Commission, established in 2015, is a cross-party, independent body designed to focus on long-term infrastructure needs over the next ten to thirty years. It provides independent advice to ministers and Parliament, and holds policymakers accountable over the long term. Yet though this body was created as a means of looking to the long term and seeking cross-party consensus, its decisions are nonbinding and thus toothless.

In a similar vein, the bipartisan Commission on Fiscal Responsibility and Reform (also known as the Simpson-Bowles Commission) was established in 2010 to address America's fiscal challenges. Here, again, the intent was to free the commission members from the pressures of day-to-day politics and enable them to concentrate on the health of the economy. Specifically, the mandate for the commission was to identify "policies to improve the fiscal situation in the medium term and to achieve fiscal sustainability over the long run." After submitting its recommendations in December 2010, the commission received the bipartisan support of more than 60 percent of its members, but fell short of the required super-majority by fourteen votes. Had this agenda passed, it would have served as a solid basis for setting in motion a strong infrastructure policy push. A revised version was rejected 382 to 38 in the US House of Representatives in March 2012. What the Simpson-Bowles experience highlights is that in practice even bipartisan, widely supported attempts to mold the government can be ignored. The same politicians who support the creation of a task force like Simpson-Bowles may change their minds when it is time to take a difficult vote to change policy. The political mood may change, reforms may languish, and previous policy decisions can be repealed.

International agreements in which governments bind themselves—such as the World Trade Organization (WTO) commitments on trade, environmental treaties such as the Paris Agreement, and security agreements such as NATO—can overcome this problem. By signing these treaties and agreements (some with ten-year commitments and tenures) the hope is that politicians will be insulated from lobbying or voter pressure.

Although in practice governments do renege on these commitments, the European Union provides an example of when governments binding themselves to behave in particular ways can, to a large extent, work. Members of the European Union, with its roots in the 1957 Treaty of Rome, which established the European Community, have largely agreed to stick to their commitments in spirit, if not to the letter. As noted earlier, members of the euro currency have on occasions of economic stress, such as the 2008 financial crisis, breached the debt and deficit limits they bound themselves to in the 1992 Maastricht Treaty. They have failed to adhere to a debt-to-GDP ratio of no more than 60 percent and an annual government deficit of no more than 3 percent. Nevertheless, over the Union's nearly sixty years of history, the breadth and depth of commitments undertaken by its member governments have deepened, and the number of members has swollen to twenty-eight—a notable increase from the original six.

The EU proposition is particularly compelling as an example of different governments reflecting different political persuasions coming together and binding themselves to different areas of trade, economics, and security. By being bound at the international level, national governments have to strike a delicate balance between international agreements and domestic policies as they abide by restrictions on the economic policies they can pursue outside their own borders. In this regard, the national government is accountable to a larger (international) body than just their domestic voters.

In recent years, the political proposition of the European Union has come under increasing scrutiny. Economic stagnation and significant unemployment in the Eurozone has led to skepticism and disillusionment with the Union. With the 2016 Brexit vote, and growing nationalist sentiment across the region (in Austria, France, and the Netherlands, for example), the European Union faces the biggest test in its history. While it has attempted to follow a long-term agenda driven by consensus, tension underpins its dealings with governments, each of which has localized, short-term political pressures. The tradeoff between localized national interests and broader cross-border considerations will always be a sticking point for the viability of group treaties.

The question is whether the resilience of such international commitments can be replicated in the sphere of national, domestic affairs, where day-to-day political pressure is much more acute. As a practical matter, and in certain circumstances, binding future political actors and economic policies can mean ensuring that legislation cannot be repealed at all, or at least for a minimum period. Such legislation ensures that subsequent governments are unable to make changes to laws during a prescribed period. For example, although not directly economic in nature, the Australian government in 2005 introduced new antiterrorism laws, aspects of which would automatically expire ten years later in 2015. In the US context, these would include the federal assault weapons ban, which was passed in 1994 and expired in 2004.

This still requires that the current government take a long-term view of policymaking, forcing politicians to set aside short-term incentives. An infrastructure investment that bears fruit in ten years will rarely help them win votes today. There is also a separate question around what level of crisis the binding should be able to withstand, as there is clear precedent for breaking commitments at times of economic stress and challenge. Such a policy of political binding must be attuned to those economic policies most susceptible to political short-termism.

Binding the government is not a uniformly positive practice. Another type of binding can have deleterious effects if not avoided. As the *Economist* suggested in its powerful essay "What's Gone Wrong with Democracy," government has a "habit of making promises that it cannot fulfil, either by creating entitlements it cannot pay for or by waging wars that it cannot win, such as [the war on] drugs." Governments regularly enter into contracts that are designed to outlast the incumbent's tenure, thereby binding future governments. They order weapons systems in consideration of future installment payments; they accept bids for infrastructure construction projects; they raise debt they commit to repay; and of course they sign up to international treaties and organizations such as NATO, the European Union, the UN, the IMF, the WTO, and NAFTA, binding and committing themselves over multiple generations. To address this problem, "both voters and governments must be persuaded of the merits of accepting restraints on the state's natural tendency to overreach," the *Economist* suggests. "Giving control of monetary policy to independent central banks tamed the rampant inflation of the 1980s, for example. It is time to apply the same principle of limited government to a broader range of policies. Mature democracies, just like nascent ones, require appropriate checks and balances on the power of elected government."[1]

Even the beneficial methods of binding the government are not, in practice, a foolproof strategy for reforming liberal democracy. In many nations, it may not even be possible. For example, common-law countries (United Kingdom, Australia, United States, Canada, India) and civil-law parliamentary republics (Germany, France) generally adhere to the principle of legislative supremacy, also known as parliamentary sovereignty or parliamentary supremacy. This means that no legislature can pass a law that a future session cannot repeal. The notion that no legislature can "bind" a future sitting is a laudable goal, given the detrimental effects of myopic policymaking that we have already seen. Yet, in many respects, there are often existing avenues for addressing a government's failure to abide by its commitments. If, for example, a Canadian defense department bureaucrat fails to process a payment that is properly owed to a contractor in a timely manner, the government can likely be sued for recovery. However, if the Canadian parliament passed a law rescinding all of Canada's agreements to buy fighter jets, there would likely be no legal remedy by Canada's contractual counterparties—at least not in a Canadian court. Thus, formally, none of these countries has the power to tie its own hands or bind itself to some policy commitment; every new sitting of the legislature is autonomous. So while all major democracies sign on to treaties and multinational agreements, those agreements only retain force until a majority of legislators decides they should not.

In these nations, to address time inconsistency and policy changeability, the goal should be to set extremely high hurdles for policy repeal, thereby reducing high policy turnover and short-termism. The crux of the concern here is that multinational agreements and their provisions must remain in force more tenaciously than is currently the case.

Under international law, countries are generally bound to the terms of treaties to which they are signatories. At the same time any sovereign nation can withdraw from a treaty or agreement or international organization anytime it wants to. Governments are free to enter into international agreements, and they should also be free to tell sitting members of their own legislatures that they can never exit the agreement. Substantively, however, the economic stability of these countries' transactions with the private sector depends on the reliability of their contracts. This acts as a deterrent and carries with it reputational risk.

After binding the government, the second major reform has to do with campaign finance. Democracies must implement tighter restrictions on campaign contributions so as to reduce the disproportionate impact of wealthy voters in determining election and policy outcomes. Many democracies already cap the amounts individuals and corporations can contribute to politicians and require transparency regarding where campaign funds come from. However, additional reforms are needed, particularly in the United States, where vast sums of money flow to politicians through campaign contributions by wealthy individuals and businesses. At least $2 billion was raised to support candidates in the 2016 US presidential election, and over $6.8 billion was spent by candidates running for federal offices that year, much of it on television advertising. By comparison, in France, where campaign donations and expenditures are tightly capped, the En Marche campaign surrounding Emmanuel Macron in the 2017 presidential elections received around 9 million euros in donations, from approximately thirty-five thousand individuals, giving an average of 257 euros apiece.[2] Whereas the average cost of a presidential vote in France in 2017 was 2.30 euros (US$2.73), in the 2016 US election each vote for Hillary Clinton cost US$21.64, and each vote for Donald Trump cost US$15.20—over seven times the cost of a French vote.

Whether contribution limits actually yield better policy outcomes may be difficult to pinpoint empirically. Certainly, raising a lot of money via big donors does not guarantee a win, as Hillary Clinton learned in 2016. Likewise, a preponderance of smaller contributions does not preclude a win, as President Obama demonstrated in 2008. However, it is indisputable that relatively unconstrained campaign contributions, and a political system in which money commands political influence, introduce the risk that politicians (very rationally) spend their time courting and catering only to the needs of their wealthy benefactors, rather than to the wishes of all (voting) citizens.

Many democracies already possess stringent campaign finance rules that govern who can contribute and how much. Those that do not should consider similar policies in order to reduce the corruptibility of the political process, protecting and enhancing the integrity of their systems. One possible approach is an outright ban on all forms of private political contributions from individuals and corporations. However, it is also possible that the imperative to solicit such contributions might decline as expensive television advertising becomes less crucial to electoral success and social media enables candidates to spread their message more cheaply and easily. Nevertheless, today's campaign financing remains stubbornly high and suggests that more aggressive restrictions on the flow of funds into politics are warranted. Restricting the amount of money that flows into political campaigns need not only be about capping campaign contributions or limiting campaign expenditures, but could also mean that democracies more tightly restrict and regulate political advertising, or provide all candidates some baseline of publicity for their views. Whatever the precise approach, democracies that do not already do so must take steps to limit the undue influence of the wealthy few in elections and subsequently policy decisions.

Third, in order to improve the quality of lawmaking, officeholders should be paid salaries competitive with those of private-sector leaders, as well as performance bonuses. In the private sector, higher compensation—via higher salaries, bonuses, or other perquisites—is thought to act as an incentive for higher-quality performance. But few nations apply the same principle when it comes to compensating lawmakers and other leaders. An exception is Singapore, where government ministers are among the best paid in the world, and ministers receive bonuses linked to the performance of the economy (including GDP), as well as their own performance. With an annual salary of US$1.7 million, Singapore's prime minister is the highest earner among all world leaders; his compensation exceeds the annual pay of the leaders of Germany, Italy, Japan, and the United Kingdom combined. As of 2016, by comparison, the US president earned US$400,000 per annum, and the leaders of Canada, Germany, the United Kingdom, and Japan earned US$260,000, US$234,400, US$214,800, and US $202,700 per year, respectively. The case of Singapore—admired for its efficient government and economic success—suggests the possible positive effects of revising democratic leaders' pay schedules sharply upward.

The issue of politicians' pay is pertinent to the effectiveness of democracy and its leaders in at least two ways. First, large pay differentials between private and public sectors can lead to the public sector struggling to attract and retain the most talented people, who are instead drawn to higher-paying opportunities in the private sector. The gap between the pay of political leaders and corporate leaders has widened. For example, average CEO pay in the United States rose by a factor of ten, from $1.5 million to $15 million a year, from 1979 to 2013. During roughly the same period, the president's pay merely quadrupled, from $100,000 in 1969 to $400,000 in 2001. Second, a wide pay gap between the private and public sectors can create perverse incentives whereby politicians and policymakers make decisions with one eye toward future, better-compensated employment in the private sector. For instance, government officials might promulgate more diluted and less far-reaching regulations than they would otherwise because they expect to seek work in the regulated industries after their term in office. Raising politicians' salaries to more competitive levels can help address these problems by making continued public service more attractive. The revolving door problem can be further mitigated by restricting politicians from accepting private-sector roles for at least a full electoral term after they leave public office—a "pay them more and shut the revolving door" approach.

Of course, it is one thing to attract people to political office and another to incentivize them to perform effectively in office over the long term. To this end, part of a higher pay package for politicians could be deferred and paid only after a period of several years (or after the end of a term of office). In the case of such deferred pay, and in the case of officeholders' pay more generally, the amount of compensation could be more closely linked to metrics of the country's performance over longer periods, such as education and health care quality or inequality rates. For instance, all members of Congress might receive a bonus in 2020 if GDP has grown (or some other metric of living standards has improved) at a certain rate in the interim.

Some might argue that pay premiums (particularly in the form of bonuses like this one) would encourage politicians to focus on outcomes with relatively little regard for how the results are achieved, thereby encouraging bad behavior. Some claimed that the 2008 financial crisis was the result of excessive risk taking by traders who were focused on generating profits, upon which their bonuses were calculated, without thought of the wider implications of their trades on the broader economy. Similarly, bonuses incentivized mortgage brokers to sell mortgages without sufficient regard for whether buyers could actually afford the mortgages in the first place or for what might happen if they defaulted.

The goal should be to have incentives in place that emphasize long-term rather than short-term achievements and reward the achievement of broader goals (for example, GDP outcomes) rather than narrower profit motives. An annual bonus paid to a trader or mortgage broker does not always incentivize good long-term behavior in the way that the decade-out bonus might.

A combination of increased pay (including bonuses and performance incentives) and more stringent revolving-door rules can help to restore the stature of public-sector work and engender much-needed long-term thinking among public servants. Moreover, a clearer delineation between public- and private-sector work would also mean public policymakers will become less susceptible to lobbying and horse-trading favors on a company-by-company basis. If politicians are adequately compensated, they need not fall prey to the allure of private-sector compensation and will be more at liberty to focus on unbiased and effective long-term policymaking.

A fourth way to discourage politicians' short-term thinking is to alter electoral cycles so as to lengthen politicians' terms in office. The goal of such a change would be to better match political attention spans to longer-term economic challenges, and specifically to match political cycles with the length of the business cycle. According to the National Bureau of Economic Research (NBER), there were eleven business cycles between 1945 and 2009. Each cycle—that is, a period of economic expansion followed by one of contraction—lasted an average of 69 months, or almost six years each. Economic expansions lasted approximately 58.4 months, while contractions lasted around 11.1 months.[3] If politicians' terms in office lasted roughly the same amount of time, policymakers would be incentivized to implement policies that would deliver growth over 5–7 years and beyond, rather than 1–3 years. In this scenario, policymakers would be thinking far enough ahead to know that an economic contraction was inevitably in the offing; they would work to soften its blow rather than, say, take advantage of flush times by enacting a big tax cut or proposing a lot of new spending. Already in a number of countries, politicians hold office for terms that correspond closely to the length of a typical business cycle. In Brazil, for example, federal senators are permitted eight-year terms, and in Mexico and the Philippines, the president is elected for a six-year term. In this respect, the US Senate, with six-year terms, is on the right path, but the US House of Representatives, for which elections are held every two years, is not.

The extension of terms should be accompanied by the imposition of term limits—the fifth crucial reform to mature democracies. In the United States and a handful of other countries, the chief executive is restricted to a limited number of terms in office, and several more impose limits on the number of consecutive terms the executive may serve. But across Europe, the vast majority of heads of government face no set term limits. In Italy, for example, the president may serve an unlimited number of seven-year terms. In the United Kingdom, the prime minister may serve an unlimited number of five-year terms. Meanwhile, there are no limits on the terms served by representatives in the US Congress, and apart from Mexico, the same holds true for national legislators across the mature democracies. US congressman John Dingell from Michigan retired in 2014 after serving fifty-nine years and twenty-one days. Robert Byrd, from West Virginia, served over fifty-seven years total in the House of Representatives and the Senate. The troubling point is that some of the political tenures in democratic states are in line with those in nondemocratic countries. Of course the cases of Dingell and Byrd can be described as outliers in a democratic system (as these are just 2 among 535 members of Congress), but the extraordinary length of their tenures is a product of that system's weaknesses. Any politician granted a position of authority or power for multiple decades risks slipping into complacency and reduced accountability.

A list of the longest-ruling nonroyal national leaders since 1900 amounts to a veritable who's who of authoritarian, illiberal, nondemocratic nation-states. The top three leaders include Cuba's Fidel Castro (52 years, 62 days), China's Chiang Kai-shek (46 years, 82 days, split between mainland China and Taiwan), and North Korea's Kim Il-sung (48 years, 203 days). Tellingly, this is not so dissimilar from the tenure of political leaders in democratic states. The problem in the case of authoritarian states is that they are less subject to checks and challenges on the fate and state of their economies, and in most cases remain in power by military dint rather than by voters' mandates. The underlying premise of "job for life" means these illiberal leaders can survive political office without delivering long-term economic success to their countries.

In a similar vein, a democratic system without term limits runs the risk of engendering this sort of lack of accountability.

Mexico provides an example of how extending but capping terms in elected office can work in practice. In 1910, Francisco I. Madero won the Mexican presidency campaigning under the slogan *"Sufragio Efectivo, No Reelección"*—which translates to "Valid Voting and No Reelection"—defeating Porfirio Díaz, who had been Mexico's president for thirty-five years. Ever since, the Mexican president has been elected to a single six-year term, without possibility of reelection. However, this did not prevent the political party PRI from governing Mexico for over seventy years, enabling the incumbent to handpick his successor. Viewed from the US vantage point, Mexico is not hailed as a paragon of economic success. However, relative to other Latin American countries (such as Brazil, Colombia, Peru, and Ecuador) and starting from a relatively low economic base, Mexico has recorded notable economic success. Moreover, at a Gini coefficient of 0.47, its income inequality is not far off that of the United States; the country enjoys a relatively stable political environment when compared to say, Argentina; and it has a notably high credit rating (Moody's gives it a rating of A3), reflecting its level of economic resilience when compared to other countries in the region—many that are subinvestment grade.

Like Mexico, the world's leading democracies should strongly consider moving toward fewer, longer terms for their elected officials, including presidents, prime ministers, legislators, and members of parliament, with lengths of terms being more than five years and numbers of terms being capped at perhaps two or three. Moving in this direction would insulate politicians from constant campaigning and give leaders the time and space to focus on the nuances of complex long-term economic challenges without engendering the complacency and lack of accountability that come with decades of being in office. Given the high cost of elections, there would also be more immediate economic benefits to reducing their frequency.

However, there are at least two problems with this approach. First, it reduces opportunities to remove ineffectual leaders who fail to move the economy forward quickly. Second, if limited to just one term in office, a politician might feel less accountable to the electorate and thus less constrained in making poor decisions. They can wreak more havoc in a single term, even though they only have one term in which to do it.

Nevertheless, the benefits of giving all politicians more time in which to make better longer-term decisions outweigh the risks that accompany not having the chance to vote out a politician after a few years. It is for this reason that the sixth reform—a more discriminating approach toward who is eligible to run for office—becomes essential. This reform of filtering for quality is designed to exclude those leaders who are narrowly political in their outlook because they lack real-world experience, as well as upgrade the quality of those who occupy political office.

In order to combat career politicians, democracies should set minimum standards for holders of public office, requiring candidates to have work experience outside the political realm—not only in business but in a range of "real-world" jobs, so that politicians collectively bring to their work a greater understanding of the workings of all aspects of the economy and society. In his article "Arise, Novice Leader! The Continuing Rise of the Career Politician in Britain," Philip Cowley notes that, "in late 2010, the leaders of the major British political parties had less experience in the non-political world than any others of the post-war era." Cowley argues this development is "unlikely to be a fluke" as increasingly, over many decades, political parties valued political experience and thus preferred career politicians over those who focused on gaining practical experience before entering the House of Commons.[4] Nearly a decade later, the British political class remains dominated by career politicians.

A 2012 study by the British House of Commons Library sheds further light on the rising trend of professional politicians who have little to no real-world experience. The study finds that since 1983, the number of career politicians in Parliament—insiders who worked in politics in advance of their election—more than quadrupled from twenty to ninety between 1983 and 2010. Over the same period, the number of parliamentary representatives with a background in manual labor has trended in exactly the opposite direction, from more than seventy in 1983 to around twenty-five in 2010. The number of teachers in Parliament halved from 1987 to 2010, and barristers (lawyers) have enjoyed a resurgence as political representatives since a low point of just 60 in 1997, to around 85 in 2010, but still short of the peak in excess of 120 in the 1960s and 1970s.[5]

The British system is now designed to favor those without experience outside politics in two ways: first, those who serve as advisers or aides to politicians are in prime position to replace those politicians in Parliament, and second, once they are in Parliament, officeholders with such backgrounds are in the best position to rise to senior leadership positions, where they have greater decision-making powers. But this professional political class has relatively little real-world experience to inform economic decision making. Its members are arguably more susceptible than most to catering to the whims of the voter at the expense of addressing longer-term economic challenges. It's simply what they have been trained to do. People with real-world experience, on the other hand, are more likely to understand the sorts of policies that are needed in a modern economy than those conditioned on a diet of polls and political tactics.

Democracies should aim to encourage the election of politicians who are not merely political but have nonpolitical experience and who will be more likely to focus on long-term economic outcomes. Of course, asking politicians not to be political at all is a tall order. Reforms must nevertheless aim for a better balance between the pursuit of political objectives and long-term policies, and reducing the politicization of parts of government is a key means of doing so.

A range of initiatives could effect this goal. At a minimum, political parties could simply aim to recruit candidates with relevant experience. Relevant experience encompasses any nonpolitical job that offers a perspective on how the economy functions and how policies might succeed or fail in practice. Alternatively, and much more aggressively, democracies might establish formal eligibility requirements for office holding that mandate a minimum number of years of work experience outside of pure political experience.

The United States, with its minimum age requirements for federal officeholders (thirty-five for a presidential or vice presidential candidate, thirty for a senator, and twenty-five for a representative), already implicitly demands that candidates possess some measure of life experience, though it does not delineate between political and nonpolitical experience. Some might worry that the latter approach embeds age discrimination, as any restrictions related to the minimum age of electability will necessarily favor older candidates. It is fair to say that any and all forms of reforms that may be seen as discriminatory—whether age, education, or occupational—might a priori be unconstitutional. Particularly in the case of the United States, it would be difficult to implement additional restrictions on officeholder experience without an outright constitutional amendment, which would take time and a sustained political campaign.

To achieve the same effect and launch what might potentially become a bipartisan campaign toward improving the caliber of politicians on all sides, political parties might set minimum restrictions on what sort of attributes would be necessary to run on their ticket. In the long run, these minimum standards could be adopted on the state level and eventually nationally.

In addition, some would be concerned that minimum academic requirements would necessarily constrain younger candidates from participating in politics. Schooling mandates would prevent people from quickly beginning work and acquiring the requisite experience for office holding before a certain age. However, in the United Kingdom, where the school-leaving age is eighteen, it is not impossible for a school leaver to acquire a decade of practical business experience and enter Parliament well before their thirtieth birthday.

Another way to increase the chances of higher quality and more motivated politicians taking office is to ensure that elections are competitive and that candidates are responsive to voters with a wide range of political views. Thus, the seventh recommendation for reform would push for democracies to reduce the number of noncontested, or safe, seats in legislative elections.

At its very core, mature liberal democracy reflects a contract between government and its citizens. In the most efficient democracies, governments provide a suite of public goods to their voters in return for tax revenue. If an incumbent officeholder fails to deliver on their promise to help effectively oversee the government's provision of public goods, they are voted out of office. Put another way, driven by individual representatives' desire to stay in office, the government is incentivized to deliver public goods. As discussed earlier, frequent elections can incentivize officeholders to be too responsive to voters today at the expense of making the wisest decisions for the long-term health of the economy. The danger is that the incentive to deliver quality public goods breaks down entirely as politicians favor appealing to voters' immediate demands, such as a tax cut or enhanced welfare benefits. This risk can be mitigated by using longer terms of office to orient policymakers to delivering on long-term goals.

Weaknesses in the democratic process can and do emerge when the elections are no longer closely contested. If a politician knows that there is little chance of losing an election, there is a risk they will make only a minimal effort to court voters and will fail to work vigorously to ensure the provision of public goods. This can undermine the contract between government and governed, diminishing the politician's incentive to be a strong representative and an effective policymaker. A politician in a safe seat might become feckless and ineffective, adversely affecting economic policymaking. Ultimately, what is a grave concern is the inadvertent creation of complacent policymakers, who have little need to fulfill their duty in delivering long-term positive and effective policies.

All mature democracies suffer, to some extent, from uncompetitive elections and could stand to work to further incentivize electoral competition. This is true even in the United Kingdom, which has an independent commission to set constituencies and election boundaries. Uncompetitive elections are particularly a problem in the United States, where district boundaries are often drawn by political incumbents to strengthen their own hand (and in so doing weaken their political opponents) rather than strengthen the political process itself. This sort of gerrymandering means politicians need only persuade their own party faithful, essentially disenfranchising large numbers of voters. According to Pew Research, "since 1992, 93 percent of House members who actually seek re-election have won." For example, in 2014, there were 19 seat switches between the major parties of the 435 contested seats.[6]

The solution is to change electoral boundaries to minimize the number of safe seats. In North Carolina, for example, campaigners for "Fair Maps, Fair Elections" are seeking to reform the election map of their General Assembly, to reduce "bitter partisan divisions and promote public confidence in the political system."[7] Campaigners favor the Iowa model of redistricting boundaries, which ensures "no political influence in the redistricting process" by excluding partisan politicians from decision making regarding electoral boundaries. Instead, the Legislative Services Agency, a nonpartisan body of civil servants, redraws districts after each census without regard to partisan political advantage.

To improve outcomes, electoral boundaries should be redrawn with the aim of encouraging competitive elections and partisan balance. The Iowa approach is one way of pursuing engaged and competitive elections. The purpose should be to maximize competition between different political candidates; there could be scope to move beyond the Iowa model by not just favoring competition within political parties but by actively favoring competition between political parties.

Fully contested elections help to keep incumbent politicians accountable, holding their feet to the fire on the quality of their economic policies and decisions. This would incentivize the elected official to deliver higher-quality economic policymaking that is based on consensus and matches the needs of all residents by appealing to the widest array of voters rather than narrow interest groups. Essentially, the more competitive an election, the greater the pressure there is for the incumbent to deliver on economic promises in order to win the seat.

The debate in political science over the connection between gerrymandering of voting constituencies and political polarization is enormously fraught. Although it seems intuitive that less partisan districts would produce more competitive elections, which, in turn, yield better economic policymaking, it is hard to find empirical evidence that makes a causal link between district boundaries and economic outcomes. In the absence of clear proof of negative economic effects of gerrymandering, legislators create voting districts that favor one party over another. Therefore any effort to counter gerrymandering is a move in the right direction.

To ACHIEVE BETTER ECONOMIC GROWTH outcomes, radical reform of liberal democracies must not stop at overhauling the rules constraining politicians. Voters are ultimately responsible for the politicians they elect and the economic policies those politicians make. We should also reconsider voters' proper role in a smoothly functioning liberal democracy.

One needed reform, and the eighth proposal in my ten-point blueprint, is to address declining voter participation by making voting mandatory. Established democracies, according to the International Institute for Democracy and Electoral Assistance, have seen "a slow but steady decline in turnout since the 1970s."[8] In November 2014, only 36 percent of eligible voters in the United States cast a vote—the lowest turnout in more than seventy years. And while estimates show more than 58 percent of eligible voters voted in the 2016 US presidential election, turnout was down from 2008 (when it was 62 percent). Since 1900, the percentage of voters voting in US presidential elections has scarcely gone above 60 percent.

Many of the world's countries whose turnout rates are highest—including Australia, Singapore, Belgium, and Liechtenstein, where the 93 percent turnout rate is the highest in Western Europe—enforce compulsory voting laws. As of August 2016, of the thirty-five member states of the Organisation for Economic Co-operation and Development (OECD), five had forms of compulsory voting. In those countries, turnout rates were near 100 percent. There are more than twenty countries where voting is compulsory, including Australia, Belgium, Bolivia, Brazil, Democratic Republic of the Congo, Egypt, Mexico, Peru, and Singapore. In Australia, voter turnout is usually around 90 percent. A more direct comparison within the European Union member states reveals remarkable turnouts from states where voting is mandatory, with 89.6 percent in Belgium and 85.6 percent in Luxembourg. For the sake of comparison, voter turnout was only 42.4 percent in France, 43.8 percent in Spain, and a mere 35.6 percent in the United Kingdom.[9]

Most often, compulsory voting is enforced through fines on those who don't vote. Typically these fines are relatively small; in Australia it is AUD 20 the first time you don't vote and have no good reason, and AUD 50 afterward, while it ranges from 10 to 20 pesos in Argentina.[10] Many times, the penalty amounts to little more than a symbolic slap on the wrist. But even the threat of a small fine clearly has an impact, as rates of voter participation in these countries suggest. In some cases, nonvoters do face the threat of imprisonment, but usually for failure to pay the fine, not the underlying failure to vote.

Other penalties for not voting come in the form of restrictions on civil rights or the franchise itself. For example, in Belgium, nonvoters will be disenfranchised for ten years after not voting in at least four elections, and it is difficult to get a job within the public sector if you are a nonvoter. In Singapore, nonvoters must reapply to be included on the voting register, explaining why they did not cast a vote. In Peru, voters receive a stamped card that they must carry for months after the election to prove their participation in the election. This grants them access to certain services and goods from public offices. In Bolivia, voters must show proof of participation in order to receive their salaries from the bank for three months after the election. In Mexico and Italy, no formal sanctions are in place, but failure to vote can lead to informal social sanction. This is called the "innocuous sanction" in Italy, where, if you cannot show evidence that you voted, it may, for example, be difficult to find a child care program for your child.[11]

In countries without mandatory voting, voters' failure to show up at the polls has consequences of a different sort. The variations in voter turnout among different groups can swing elections and skew policy outcomes. According to Lisa Hill, a professor of politics at the University of Adelaide, who writes about the failure to vote by US voters, the "failure to vote is concentrated among groups already experiencing one or more forms of deprivation, namely, the poor, the unemployed, the homeless, indigenous peoples, the isolated, new citizens and the young. . . . This transfers to greater voting power to the well-off and causes policies to be geared disproportionately to the interests of voters (politicians aren't stupid: they know who their customers are). The legitimacy of American democracy is thereby undermined, assuming you agree that political inequality and unrepresentativeness are bad for democracy."[12]

A smaller and narrower electoral base can lead to a more corrupted electoral process. The seventeenth-century *szlachta* in Poland and the early-nineteenth-century "rotten borough" problem in Britain are two historical examples. In the Polish commonwealth, all nobles were initially entitled to vote for the king. Yet over time, elections were monopolized by only the wealthiest and most powerful members of the Polish nobility, thus causing the strength of the Polish crown to wane. "In 1574 the first royal election drew 40,000 szlachta," according to the *Economist*; "by 1674 that number had fallen to 5,000. Low turnout figures were in the interests of powerful noble magnates since they made it easier for them to control elections, but the long-term result was to hollow out the democratic consensus and national strength, ultimately contributing to Poland's partition."[13]

Britain's "rotten borough" problem in the early 1800s is another example of an extreme narrow voter base and its corruptibility. Prior to 1832, many parliamentary constituencies in Britain were described as "rotten boroughs," so named because the borough was found to have decayed to having so few voters that the choice of MP was in the hands of one person or family, whose interests the incumbent inevitably championed. Simply put, the smaller the electorate, the likelier that policies will favor the few.

By creating the broadest possible electoral base, mandatory voting maximizes the quality of democracy, making it more efficient and enhancing economic policy outcomes. But of course democracy dominated by the ill-informed many can also prove hazardous to growth. Countries where voting is mandatory but the population is not well informed can fall prey to populist policies that are inimical to longer-term economic growth and success.

It is imperative to educate the population on the tradeoffs between short-term gains and their costs to future growth. Indeed, democracies should care just as much about the quality of individual voters as they do about the quantity of voter suffrage. Thus, as a ninth reform, democracies must seek to educate voters regarding the impact of policy choices. Voters must be nudged toward the right long-term policy choices, rather than being swayed by personalities and short-term fixes. In its most radical form, this might extend to requiring voters to meet minimum requirements for knowledge of key public policy issues. For instance, voters might be required to pass a government-sanctioned civics test in order to vote (akin to passing a driving test to secure a driver's license) or to pass mandatory civics courses in school before gaining the franchise. The checkered history of civil rights and suffrage means even the suggestion of such tests would be ripe for criticism and if implemented carelessly subject to abuse and discrimination. Moreover, some will object to this proposal—if even just on face value—as reviving the sorts of literary tests once used to disenfranchise racial minorities and the poor in the United States. Yet passing the sorts of civics tests described would ensure that voters made wise economic decisions or took the economic long run into account. The sort of affirmative commitment to voter education proffered by the reforms presented here promises to make a key difference in voter knowledge, their choices, and ultimately policy outcomes.

The notion of restricting citizens' voting powers may seem to fly in the face of democratic values. Because people have died for the right to vote and still to this day campaign for suffrage, many will see the idea of limiting this right as beyond the pale. Nevertheless, there is a valid debate to be had on whether taking steps to ensure a qualified electorate could enhance policymaking outcomes and thereby improve economic growth. What democracies must avoid is lengthening the tenure of elected officials without addressing voter education as well. Otherwise, the risk is that a poorly educated electorate will elect for a long term in office a poor leader or administration that implements poor policies that damage economic growth. Enhancing the quality of voters would further incentivize politicians to make better economic choices—and it would remove another excuse for politicians to focus only on the short term.

In short, democracies should aim both to expand the electorate (as per the eighth reform) and to improve the quality of voter decisions (as per the ninth reform). But a tenth and final reform—weighted voting—would allow them to pursue both in unison. While the ninth reform requires that voters meet a minimum set of standards, the tenth reform has a different objective: enhancing the voting status of highly qualified individuals. Implementing both these reforms (the ninth and tenth) effectively delineates among three tiers of voters: the unqualified, the standard qualified voter, and the highly qualified voter. Some form of weighted voting would boost the influence of the best-informed segment of the electorate, even as that group expanded over time. It thus offers a route to achieving a fully informed and participating electorate. As a practical matter, each society would decide whether voters would be required to sit additional tests to achieve enhanced voter status (as proposed in the tenth reform) or whether a voter would automatically obtain enhanced voter accreditation based on their professional standing or qualifications. This is an example of a reform that would likely require some form of constitutional amendment.

Previous experiments with weighted voting have tended to be rooted in racial or class prejudice, rather than being based on objective or pragmatic assessments of voters' qualifications to influence policy. In ancient Rome, for instance, assemblies provided for weighted voting based on social class and wealth. In the British colony of Southern Rhodesia, under the constitution in effect in the 1960s, a system called "cross-voting" divided voters into two rolls. The A roll was tailored so that it would primarily encompass European-descended citizens, while the B roll largely consisted of indigenous Africans. The votes of those on the A roll had a disproportionate impact on the outcome of elections, amplified by the government's failure to promote registration or turnout of B-roll voters. In the 1969 constitution, this system was replaced by another, in which one roll reserved for Europeans, Coloreds (or the mixed-race populace), and Asians who met higher property and education requirements elected fifty seats, whereas the other roll elected eight seats.

Despite its track record of being deployed for reasons of prejudice, weighting votes by voters' knowledge of civics, age, or professional qualifications might well improve voter quality today. But before considering these potential benefits, it is important to examine the types of weighted voting systems that might be put in place.

According to one proposed vote-weighting proposal, prospective voters might be asked to take a quiz, consisting of "objective, factual questions rather than questions concerning beliefs and convictions." Voters would have to demonstrate knowledge of the structure and broad operations of government as well as key current events and policy debates. Such testing proposals have precedents in the civics tests, which include cultural, historical, and social questions that immigrants must pass in order to earn citizenship rights. If a citizen answers all the questions correctly, their vote would be counted as a whole vote. "If, however, we answer correctly to only three out of ten questions, our vote will be worth three-tenths of a whole vote. In this way, votes from citizens who have kept up with the political debate will be weighted more heavily than votes from citizens who—for one reason or another—gave incorrect answers to the majority of the questions."[14]

An alternative to this approach would be a "voter plus" system, whereby voters would get rewarded for higher attainment. Better performance on the same sort of civics test, for instance, would yield a higher number of votes—a carrot to induce better-informed voting, rather than a stick. Unlike the system described above, everyone qualified to vote would get at least a single vote, but those who performed best would get more.

Age could also be used in a weighted voting scheme. On the one hand, as one progresses through life, gaining work and life experiences, it would seem that one's vote should count more—so that the vote of a novice would count only a fraction of that of a veteran. On the other hand, there is another appealing argument for giving younger people more votes than older ones, on the logic that young people deserve more say in their futures than do older people, who have less time to live. The US health care system is skewed toward serving older Americans—a powerful interest group—rather than young people, who will be driving productivity for decades to come. These intergenerational tradeoffs might change if the votes of the young counted more.

Perhaps most controversially, weighting could also be tied to one's professional qualifications (such as certification as a doctor, teacher, lawyer, and so forth), employment status (such as being an administrator of a hospital, manager, or CEO), and level of educational attainment, on the assumption that excelling in these domains makes one more likely to make well-informed choices in the voting booth. Such weighting might be combined with weighting by age, such that all people under thirty would have influence similar to that of those who are older but possess professional qualifications, or have attained a certain employment status or level of education.

Any type of voter discrimination will no doubt be seen as jarring and antithetical to the principles of democracy. Indeed, the greatest objection to the reform of minimum standards and enhanced voting is that they discriminate against certain citizens. However, it is the very fact that these reforms are discriminatory that holds promise that democracy can be strengthened. Crucially, this form of voter discrimination can only work if it is based on a truly meritocratic system. This means that all citizens should have equal opportunity to become accredited voters and/or enhanced voters.

The system of universal and automatic suffrage that prevails in leading democracies today carries with it the perennial risk that voter apathy and ignorance will allow politicians to sway the electorate with attractive short-term promises they do not follow through on once they are in office. One famous example in the United States is then–presidential candidate George H. W. Bush's famous 1988 pledge, "Read my lips: no new taxes," a promise that likely helped him win the election. Although President Bush opposed the introduction of new taxes when he became president, he eventually agreed to a 1990 budget that saw an increase in several existing taxes. Many voters interpreted this as his going back on his word, and it possibly cost him the next election. A weighted voting system offers a real chance to address this danger by preventing citizens from voting for the wrong reasons and diminishing the influence of the voters most likely to do so. It also reduces the influence of those most likely to be apathetic or disengaged from public policy debates and thus most likely to make poor electoral choices, notwithstanding the fact that the citizen always retains the option to become more knowledgeable and qualified.

Of course, a weighted voting system would not be foolproof. Even highly informed voters will have short-term pain points that will distract them from supporting candidates and policies most conducive to longer-term economic growth. For example, even with the knowledge that a tax hike would improve the chances for better schools tomorrow, voters may be hard-pressed to bring themselves to vote for higher taxes today. But the point is that voters will more clearly understand their decision and the tradeoffs their choices represent regarding the long-term health of the economy.

Overall, what is needed is a new way of understanding voting, its purpose, and participation in the electoral process—not just as a right but rather as a reward to be earned for citizens' fulfillment of their civic duty, reflecting their status as a partner in the democratic process. If the reforms proposed here were pursued in concert, with voting made mandatory while weighting and minimum qualification tests augmented the power of knowledgeable voters, the result would be higher-quality decisions by voters, better policymakers, and policies that maximize an economy's prospects.

It is impossible to propose a credible overhaul of the liberal democratic system without acknowledging the important role of the media. Media, politicians, and voters check and challenge one another in a tripartite structure, thereby ensuring transparent and effective elections. Therefore, as well as the ten reforms proposed above, mature democracies should consider how best to ensure that a free press provides the sort of high-quality, impartial information on which voters rely to make informed decisions.

The media landscape is shifting dramatically. A 2015 Pew Research study found that 61 percent of millennials and 51 percent of those in Generation X use Facebook as their prime resource for news about politics and government. News increasingly reaches voters through social media filters, from like-minded individuals and selective news feeds. News outlets have grown increasingly politicized and ideological, eschewing impartiality.

The proliferation of personalized media diets increasingly means that each voter clings to their own set of facts, assumptions, and beliefs. This creates a weak civic environment, undermining political outcomes. In the context of economic growth, an ideological media imbues and reinforces a culture of short-termism among politicians and political classes though a twenty-four-hour media cycle, as politicians scramble to act and react to an agenda set by the press. This can be a distraction from the longer-term projects and policies necessary for durable economic growth.

In order to address these trends, countries might establish a national journalistic champion mandated to provide impartial information and coverage that voters can use as the basis for informed choices. In the United Kingdom, for example, the BBC was created to address this need. It is certainly true that such institutions are imperfect; incumbent politicians are often tempted to exploit them as propaganda outlets or to attempt to limit the investigations their journalists undertake. On balance, however, they could play an important role in combatting the news media's drift toward partisanship and bias and creating a more informed, engaged electorate. It is ultimately the fundamental reforms to democracy described above that will push politicians and voters toward the wiser policies needed to ensure economic growth, recognizing that the news media has an important part to play in creating a shared understanding of what those policies ought to be.

WITHOUT MEANINGFUL REFORMS LIBERAL DEMOCRACY is at risk. Already, the young are growing more skeptical of the liberal democratic system. The *Guardian* has reported:

A large-scale survey of political attitudes conducted by the Lowy Institute for International Policy in Sydney found that just 42 percent of Australian 18- to 29-year-olds thought democracy was "the most preferable form of government", compared with 65 percent of those aged 30 or above. . . . The twist is that while they disdain democratic institutions, millennials engage in the cut and thrust of democracy with vigor. Alex Oliver, the polling director of the Lowy Institute, points to UK research that shows young Britons are either as or more likely to volunteer, engage with social issues, or "express their political opinions creatively" than earlier generations.

Clearly, young voters are skeptical of liberal democracy as currently constituted, but their enthusiastic participation in all manner of causes suggests they would be eager to take an active role in creating and participating in the sort of reformed approach advocated here. The evidence suggests that the status quo democratic approach might not provide the youth (and voting citizens more generally) the conduit for the progress—political, economic, or otherwise—they seek, and that reform of the current system is a necessary and urgent imperative.[15]

The reform proposals presented here are not simply meant as reactive against rising populism around the world—not merely a "fix" for the problems in democracy that allowed Brexit and election of Trump in 2016 to occur. Rather, they are meant to address the more fundamental structural problem of political myopia, which is leading to economic stagnation. Thus they would be as important even if both Brexit and Trump had been defeated.

The urgent need for democratic reforms transcends the recent backlash against globalization, although the anemic global economic backdrop is an impetus for the overhaul of the liberal political regime. It is true that the prevailing economic malaise and the impotence of traditional public policy tools have exposed weaknesses in the political system and made the need for a reform agenda much more urgent. But the root of the problem undergirding the global economic malaise is political myopia in the democratic system that is leading to the misallocation of resources and making it harder to address long-term intergenerational problems. Even were the trend toward deglobalization to slow or reverse, democratic reform would still be necessary.

This chapter recommends what many will see as uncomfortable alterations to a democratic political system that is viewed as sacrosanct. Nevertheless, the reforms proposed here are critical for achieving economic prosperity and human advancement by addressing political myopia, tackling the headwinds laid out in Chapter 3, and ultimately ensuring long-term sustained economic growth and improved living standards. When this reformed version of democracy begins to delivers attractive outcomes, it will be seen as more attractive across the world.

And as we will see in the next, concluding chapter, the risks of our present democratic stasis and the impact on economic progress are far too great for reform of the political system to be ignored. The ultimate risk is that democracies could be increasingly built on a disillusioned, uninformed electorate and would only produce poor populist leaders who make bad policy that harms growth. In contrast, if the proposals offered here are adopted, the prize is a well-educated, engaged electorate with highly motivated and qualified political leaders driven to deliver the long-term policies best suited for the economic circumstances of their country. With the overhaul of democracy would come a better chance to implement the more flexible and pragmatic approach needed to drive economic growth in the twenty-first century.

The onus for the transformation of democracy falls on the mature democracies of the West, which have promoted the system for centuries. However, emerging democracies should also heed the weaknesses of the democratic process. All democracies should be vigilant against allowing short-termism to undermine political institutions and infect the body politic. Too much is at stake for this danger to be ignored, or for reform to be deferred.

8

RETOOLING FOR TWENTY-FIRST-CENTURY GROWTH

THE PICTURE THAT THIS BOOK has offered thus far is fairly bleak.

Yet positive change in the democratic political realm is possible. After all, change to the democratic political structure has happened before. Economists may never resolve their debate over the origin of the factors engulfing the current global economy, but the fact is the economic malaise warrants intervention—and soon. Democratic reform that tackles political myopia promises the biggest payoff, and arguably it is the only hope to steer for a better economic outcome. This is because democratic reform is a critical prelude for the sorts of long-term economic policies that will reset the global economy's trajectory. Democratic reform will ensure that politicians and policymakers institute long-term think-ing that tackles the long-term challenges currently besetting the global economy, and this will, in turn, drive sustainable economic growth over time. This book thus proposes solving the problem of a lack of economic growth by overhauling our democratic political systems, rather than reforming capital-ism or economic models. While there are barriers to further progress, implementing the reforms described in the previous chapter would allow us to make the policy choices required to avoid the worst economic possibilities.

By many metrics—social, political, and economic—the world has seen remarkably positive changes in the last fifty years. Across the globe, citizens are more connected. The health of the average person has improved. Tens of millions now live without fear of the diseases and high rates of infant mortality that were common in the recent past. People are living longer, and millions enjoy better access to education, potable water, and health care. The fall of the Soviet empire and the end of the Cold War brought liberty to many tens of millions across the globe. Despite recent retrenchment, more people live in countries that are deemed "free," and the prevailing long-term trend worldwide has been toward more democracy, greater press freedom, and improved transpar-ency. According to Freedom House, only 29 percent of all countries in the world were truly free as of 1973.[1] Following the collapse of colonialism, oppressive regimes such as apart-heid in South Africa, and the Iron Curtain, the number now stands at 45 percent free (although global freedom has never-theless declined for eleven consecutive years).[2]

As violence has decreased, more nations and peoples live in security and peace—many decades have passed since the last world war. In *The Better Angels of Our Nature*, Steven Pinker argues that all forms of violence have decreased over time, and to the extent that violence does exist, it has also dissipated in terms of scale and magnitude. These trends, Pinker shows, are true for incidences of violence such as homicide, domestic violence, animal cruelty, and child abuse, as well as for more extreme forms. Genocide and wars, whether international or civil, have been on the decline for many decades. With a few exceptions, such as Russia in Ukraine and Crimea, Syria, and Yemen, wars between states—by far the most destructive of all conflicts—have notably decreased over time.

Economically, too, the world has been transformed for the better, and it is vastly more prosperous today than it was fifty years ago. In the past twenty years, the global economy, measured in GDP, has roughly tripled—from US$43.50 trillion in 1996 to US$77.3 trillion—with developing countries accounting for over 50 percent of that growth. In China alone, astonishing rates of growth have helped move over three hundred million people out of poverty, with millions more across the globe escaping from poverty as a result of China's international trade and foreign direct investment. More than a billion people have escaped from extreme poverty, and the global economy has forged new middle classes across the world.

The past half century has been good for developing and developed country citizens alike. Households in advanced countries have seen their living standards improve as a result of technological innovations and access through globalization to better and cheaper products. Global GDP is higher, GDP per capita is greater, and inequality between countries has lessened as the world's poorest economies have converged to higher levels of income. Despite the many challenges and headwinds this book has enumerated, 70 percent of world GDP (encapsulated in the United States, China, Europe, and Japan) continues to grow economically, even if not at the heady double-digit growth rates of previous years. Moreover, technological innovations are transforming all manner of goods and services with the promise of a future of declining health and energy costs and improving living standards. Although there remain considerable levels of indigence and suffering, today's world is more secure, more prosperous, and freer than it has ever been. By most data-driven accounts, there has never been a better time to be alive.

But past performance is no indicator of the future. Although the world today has made great strides toward security, prosperity, and freedom, it is by no means inevitable that this progress will continue. Press headlines tout bad news virtually every day—Islamic State, Russia and Crimea, Gaza, income inequality, protectionism, disorderly immigration and refugees, nationalism, the populist backlash against globalization, and the resurgence of infectious diseases—and all the while economic growth seems to be trundling down.

Although statistics show the world is more democratic than it has ever been, over 70 percent of these democracies are deemed illiberal. A democracy in which the press is not free and the elections are not fair is ultimately indistinguishable from authoritarian nondemocratic states. Furthermore, although the quantity of newly democratic states has risen over the past thirty years, there are now signs of recidivism; authoritarian capitalism, particularly that of China, continues to have appeal.[3]

The world has enjoyed a notably long period marked by relative peace and security. Nevertheless, the forecasts of increasing fragile states, mounting conflicts born of natural resource scarcity, and the rising risk in the incidence of terrorism around the world all point to an increasingly politically volatile world, one that is worsened by economic uncertainty. The *Horizon 2025: Creative Destruction in the Aid Industry* report cautions that within the next decade more than 80 percent of the world's population will live in fragile states, susceptible to civil wars that could spill into cross-border conflicts.[4] The US National Intelligence Council has published a similarly dire forecast of more clashes in decades to come. While this study focuses largely on the prospect of natural resource conflicts, water especially, it underscores the political vulnerability of many economies. A 2016 report by the Institute for Economics and Peace concludes 2014 was the worst year for terrorism in a decade and a half, with attacks in ninety-three countries resulting in 32,765 people killed; 29,376 people died the year before, making 2013 the second worst year.[5]

To compound these geopolitical challenges, we continue to face a stagnant global economy. At the time of this writing, total global debt stood at $217 trillion (327 percent of global GDP), as unemployment rates across Europe hovered in double digits—higher still for the young. Net capital flows for global emerging markets were negative in 2015, a first since 1988. They have remained volatile ever since, underscoring the feeble global investment environment. In 2016 the WTO registered a fifth consecutive year of trade growth below 3 percent. During the full year of 2016, the United States grew just 1.6 percent. With major emerging economies such as Russia and Brazil in recession in 2016, the global growth picture remains so anemic that the United Nations projects that, lacking a change to the growth trajectory, 35 percent of the population in the least developed countries are likely to remain in extreme poverty by 2030.

Meanwhile, economic depression has left hundreds of millions homeless and jobless, causing more than ten thousand suicides, according to the *British Journal of Psychiatry*. According to the World Health Organization, by 2030 more people will be affected by depression than any other health problem, at which point depression will be the leading contributor to the world's disease burden.[6] Moreover, progress has come at a price. Economic gains have accrued to those with capital, but not laborers. Technology advances are creating a jobless underclass, radical demographic shifts alter both the quality and quantity of labor, natural resource scarcity and widening income inequality contribute to the hollowing out of the middle class in advanced economies, and mounting debt and declining productivity act as a drag on economic growth.

A reasonable person may ask: How is this slow and slowing stagnation in economic growth different from the series of recessions the world economy faced over the last century? And how does the current economic malaise differ from the stagnation and inflation of the 1980s that followed the oil spike of 1973, ushering in a lost economic period in many countries? Chapter 3 addressed these questions by detailing how the scale and strength of the current headwinds to economic growth are unprecedented and how the economic policy tools of global policymakers are proving impotent in the face of these challenges.

Mounting social, political, and economic problems add to the heavy burdens faced by policymakers. To be sure, the global economy has always faced challenges. The problem is that the classical models of economics—the basis of prevailing policymaking—are proving shortsighted, archaic, and inadequate. Nearly ten years after the 2008 financial crisis, the world economy continues to struggle to gain a firm economic footing. There is a broad consensus emerging across the globe that despite arguments about the root of the problems, the global economy is in a precarious situation, facing unprecedented risks.

Across the world, panicked politicians are pivoting to inferior political and economic models: more trade protection, less globalization, more capital controls, fewer capital flows, more siloed corporations, and more state control. These models and policies are leading to a misallocation of resources, notably capital and labor. This in turn is likely to exacerbate military as well as economic conflict over scarce resources—pressuring politicians to make even worse decisions, fomenting a vicious downward cycle. Crucially, these policies are taking nations not only off the path toward democratic capitalism, but also away from solid economic growth. What has emerged is a vicious cycle where a weak, myopic democratic process yields myopic policymaking, which weakens economic growth and creates political vulnerability with dissention and rising populism, which further hurts the democratic process and continues to destroy the prospects for growth. We must break the vicious cycle and create a virtuous cycle, in which a stronger and reformed democracy delivers economic resurgence, which in turn bolsters democracy.

THIS BOOK PRESENTS A CAREFULLY considered package to reform democracy: one that addresses the corrosive short-termism that has beset the democratic process and promises the pursuit of policies that will ultimately deliver more long-term economic growth. Were democracy reformed in the manner recommended in this book, the benefit would be policies less driven by political expedience, short-term promises, partisan bickering, and election cycles, and guided more by long-term considerations and thus more effective. Stripping the short-term polarization and politicization out of the democratic electoral process would allow policymakers to focus on the longer-term issues plaguing the economy. The political imperative would become doing what is in the best interest of the economy over the long term.

The economic policies that would result would prioritize long-term economic challenges and take into account the intergenerational tension between the demands of today's voters for benefits and perks and those of future generations, who face a future debt burden and lower living standards. Unencumbered by myopia and the immediate desire to win votes, politicians more focused on the long term would invest more heavily in sectors that are the backbone of a successful economy, such as infrastructure (including roads, ports, railways) and quality education. These sorts of sustainable investments would raise a country's productivity and significantly improve a country's growth prospects.

Consider how the reformed democratic system described in this book would enhance policy setting in education. As in other aspects of the economy, in education policy there is a tradition of spending itself, rather than outcomes, being cited as a sign of progress. Under a reformed democracy, politicians with a longer-term focus would be dissuaded from courting (and no longer swayed by winning) votes. Instead politicians would be assessed on the basis of how the country performed on education statistics and metrics. Votes would not be earned merely through promises and payments to teachers' unions or advocates of privatization of education. Rather politicians would be judged on their ability to actually deliver efficient, quality public education for all citizens over the long term. A less politicized and more long-term-focused education policy would help circumvent the problem in which the United States ranks among the highest in terms of education spending per capita but in some respects is among the worst in education outcomes when compared against its advanced country peers. Enhancing education policy directly tackles the economic headwinds by addressing the quality of the workforce. This is just one example of how reforms to democracy would deliver forward-looking policy and sustainable long-term investments that would propel the economy in a positive direction.

The best indication of where the world might end up if it continues on its current precarious path is provided by Japan. That country has spent the last decade and a half drawing on old, well-trodden economic interventions (mainly monetary, such as historically low interest rates) to little effect. There is a lesson here for the world's largest advanced economies (and developing countries) about the way tried-and-true policies can eventually cease to deliver and even more so about why the suite of economic policies must be aggressive and not piecemeal if we are to register any economic gains. For instance, Japan has invested enormously in infrastructure, building scores of bridges, tunnels, highways, and trains, as well as new airports. In general, such investments are wise, but poor planning has meant that much of the infrastructure it has built is barely used. Japan has spent a staggering US$6.3 trillion on "construction-related public investment" to little positive effect. Although Japan has shown engineering feats through its infrastructure investments, and some people have remained employed, there is little evidence that Japan's growth has increased. Worse still, the country continues to suffer under a crushing public debt.

ALL OF THE TEN PROPOSED reforms in this book seek to address two central concerns: first, fixing and removing the myopia embedded in the democratic process, and second, improving the effectiveness and quality of policymaking, so as to tackle the headwinds that are threatening the global economy today by enacting long-term policies that drive economic growth. By binding the government, extending political terms, and increasing pay, politicians' outlooks are better aligned to achieving long-term goals, thus addressing the myopia problem. Restricting campaign contributions similarly limits the influence of outside interests that could discourage politicians from taking a longer-term view. Creating minimum standards for voters and politicians alike addresses the need for greater quality in the democratic process. Intensified political competition and fewer safe seats mean more politicians have to demonstrate their quality to their electorate. Minimum voter standards lead to more discerning voters who are better able to parse economic arguments and select the candidate most capable of delivering high-quality policy. Term limits further enhance quality by ensuring politicians avoid complacency and long-term decline. Upending our way of life in the most catastrophic ways and transformational democratic political reform are the only way to halt the erosion and reset the global economy on a firmer footing.

WHO WILL TAKE THE LEAD in advocating for and implementing these political reforms? Myopic politicians are unlikely to take on the challenge. After all, supporting a reform agenda that includes term limits would be tantamount to voting themselves out of a job. Weakened by the rise of non-state actors and reduced budgets resulting from tax breaks for corporations and individuals, politicians are limited in their ability to execute their existing mandate, let alone evolve and change the political system.

Those within the existing political system lack the political courage and strength to take reform on. Therefore, the impetus for democratic reform will have to come from outside the system, rather than within it. Specifically, politically minded individuals and those perhaps with a political leadership pedigree (such as retired politicians) who have been put off by the entrenched divisions of traditional party politics and the complex web of career politicians that has locked them out could lead the reform change. So too could nonpartisan institutions such as think tanks.

The private sector—both wealthy individuals and corporations—also has an important role to play in the renewal of the democratic process. As discussed earlier, the prevailing trend has been for wealth and power to be transferred away from the state and toward nonstate actors like philanthropists. This has not only reduced the amount of cash available to government but also pushed many aspects of the state's mandate to provide public goods such as health care and education into the hands of private individuals. According to Oxfam, if he is not outpaced by Amazon founder Jeff Bezos, Bill Gates is due to become the world's first trillionaire by 2042—essentially a personal fortune greater than the governments of many countries. The World Bank estimates that there are fifty-five countries whose wealth is less than that of Bill Gates.[7] As of 2015, only fifteen countries had GDP in excess of a trillion dollars. His scale of wealth also sets him on the world stage in terms of power, allowing him access to and influence over political leaders around the world.

The point here is that the shift of power and wealth toward wealthy individuals and away from the government weakens the state. In a similar vein, private corporations have seen their wealth and influence grow over time and importance in lobbying and influencing public policy decisions. Their leverage has increased not only because of the vast taxes they pay toward the government purse but also because of the enormous numbers of people they employ and their involvement in the rollout of infrastructure—such as through public-private initiatives.

Moreover, over the past decades, and at the behest of a broader array of stakeholders (government, nongovernmental organizations [NGOs], regulators, broader civil society), corporations have broadened their functions to encompass more than just corporate returns and revenues. They have taken on a whole range of social responsibility initiatives (including education and health), thus again encroaching on what has traditionally been the purview of the state. As in the case of private individuals, this expanding role carries a responsibility to ensure that the political environment in which they operate and make investment decisions is stable and effective over the long term. Corporations rarely take a public lead in political transformations, but nevertheless, given their stature, they should be keen to play an influential role. Many people will be skeptical of the power of citizens and NGOs as a force for political reform, and very likely wary of the idea of corporations making a push to overhaul democracy. Yet an alliance of concerned citizens, NGOs, and corporations could be an important start in the direction toward reform; after all, they all share a common desire to see government operate effectively.

The proposals to overhaul democracy detailed here will undoubtedly face opposition from certain corners. The largest opposing din will likely come from those with the most to lose and the most vested in the current system, including the incumbent politicians who thrive in a myopic, ideological world and enjoy the daily attention of media; career politicians with a lack of work experience; parts of the media, since the short-termism feeds its cycle; political activists who cling to tidbits of the latest news, reaction, and polls to feed their campaigns; and of course, democratic purists, who believe that anyone should be allowed to stand for office and vote regardless of qualifications. For the most part, these objections lack legitimacy in that they serve the narrow interests of the objectors and are not in the broader interest of improving democracy at large.

There should be no doubt that what is being proposed here is a massive overhaul to democracy as we know it now. Implementing any part of the suggested reform agenda would be a big job even if the suggested reforms were not contentious and there was wide agreement that reforms are necessary. That they will be controversial, and that this consensus does not yet exist, will make the task even more challenging.

Nevertheless, it is still worth looking even further ahead. If and when these reforms are enacted, their advocates will need to exercise constant vigilance, monitoring their implementation and ensuring that they are achieving their intended aims.

SOME DEMOCRACIES ALREADY POSSESS SOME version of one or more of the proposals offered here but have nevertheless struggled to successfully navigate the problem of myopia and therefore remain on a precarious economic path. Realizing these reforms' benefits will require avoiding a piecemeal approach and instead committing to at least half of the reform proposals on the menu, drawing from initiatives that tackle managing the politician and the voter so that the vicious cycle becomes a virtuous one. To do one without the other creates an imbalance.

Given the important role of mature democracies in setting the example for liberal democracies across the globe, these societies should endeavor to adopt all the recommendations offered here. Yet, as the table in the appendix shows, none of the major democracies currently score well on their embrace of these reform proposals, with Mexico ranked highest, at five out of ten. The United States only possesses some version of three of these reforms; the United Kingdom possesses only two.

Some may see the reforms proposed here as worthy of consideration in the years ahead but not pressingly urgent. They would do well to take a lesson from our history of complacency in the face of compelling evidence that the world is under threat. In recent decades, from terrorist attacks to the financial crisis, policymakers have shown a predilection to ignore advance warnings of the shifts and the shocks that would alter forever the world as we know it.

IN 1995, VETERAN FBI AGENT and counterterrorist expert John P. O'Neill immersed himself in the operations of international terrorism—investigating, in particular, the 1993 bombing of the World Trade Center. By most accounts, more than anyone else at the FBI, O'Neill was at the forefront of investigating the links between state sponsors of terrorism, Al-Qaeda operatives, and attacks on US interests around the world during the 1990s. In the summer of 1998, two US embassies in Nairobi and Dar es Salaam were attacked simultaneously, and in 2000, the USS *Cole* was bombed while stationed in Yemen.

The more O'Neill investigated the shadowy world of international terrorism, the more he warned anyone in Washington, DC, who would listen that there were major threats to the United States. His cautions went largely unheeded. O'Neill was forced to retire from the FBI, falling prey to what he called a smear campaign by his enemies in the Bureau. He took a job as head of security at the World Trade Center in August 2001. John P. O'Neill was in the north World Trade Center building on September 11, 2001. He never made it out; his body was later found in one of the stair towers of the south building.

In 2005, Raghuram Rajan, the chief economist for the IMF, presented a paper at an annual Federal Reserve meeting held in Jackson Hole, Wyoming, of prominent economists and bankers from around the world. Rajan's paper, "Has Financial Development Made the World Riskier?," charged that financial managers were encouraged to take risks trading complicated, underregulated securities in return for "generous compensation," while their banks were in no position to provide the liquidity that financial markets would need to cover losses should those risks materialize. At a time when investors were enjoying high returns and global financial markets seemed more stable than ever, Rajan was arguing that "the interbank market could freeze up, and one could well have a full-blown financial crisis."[8]

His argument was rebuked. In his own presentation, former secretary of the treasury Lawrence Summers criticized Rajan's premise as "misguided" and dismissed him as a "luddite." Two years later, the prices of those securities went south, triggering the 2008 financial crisis, bringing the global economy to the brink of collapse, and proving that the world's top economists and bankers were not as well guided as they thought.

It is human nature to ignore warnings until it is too late. With that in mind, what does the future look like? In this respect the run-up to and the period through World War II offer a specific analogy to the ways economic policy feeds into global instability. Our choices to avert war and destruction are becoming increasingly limited. The remaining options are quite simple: act now, or we will be forced to react if and when political volatility and economic malaise become considerably worse. The precarious economic and geopolitical situation in which the world finds itself today has many of the disturbing hallmarks of the factors that allowed World War II to occur.

First came policies that hurt the US economy. By undermining and weakening American political strength, they opened the channels for the country's political enemies to rise and trigger the world wars. The US protectionist policies pursued in the 1920s and 1930s under the Smoot-Hawley rubric imposed tariffs on thousands of imported goods, triggered retaliatory trade wars, and worsened the Great Depression by slowing down economic growth and causing a spike in unemployment. On the back of these protectionist and isolationist policies of the 1930s, the weakened economy paved the way for rising enemy powers to start a world war.

In a similar vein, the current path of protectionism and isolationism pursued by the United States and other countries (such as the United Kingdom post-Brexit) spells greater economic and geopolitical volatility and substantially raises the risk of war. The deeper entrenchment of the economic malaise and deglobalization across the world sets the stage for the unraveling of Pax Americana—a state of relative international peace, and the free exchange in trade and capital flows that the US and its allies built after World War II. Moreover, an economically weakened West (and United States in particular) provides a gateway for political upstarts and powers to challenge and undermine the American-led international order.

For well over half a century the United States has supported prosperity and global security, underwriting global public policy such as policing the sea-lanes. America's unsteady economy helped catapult Trump into the US presidency and onto a platform that is destabilizing the global economy and US foreign policy. In this sense, the growing economic and political uncertainty across the globe is today being amplified as much by the Trump administration's foreign policy choices as it is by America's economic fortunes. Virtually every region around the world is vulnerable to security risks because of the economic situation of the United States.

A more isolationist America creates a vacuum at a time when the European Union has grown precarious, facing escalating extremism among the anti-Europe left-wing and right-wing populist parties and the disintegration of the Eurozone. An aggressive Russia (which threatens stability across Eastern Europe and beyond, including Syria and Ukraine), a fractious Middle East (including Turkey, Saudi Arabia, and

Iran), rising terrorism spawned by religion, and the risk of expanding nuclear and cyber-warfare capacities all threaten to worsen as the United States ceases to serve as a stabilizing force. Furthermore, a more isolationist America in effect provides an opening for China to continue to assert its economic and political dominance across Asia, Africa, and Latin America. America's economic and political imprimatur on the globe is under threat, and so too is the global order. The market-oriented regimes of trade liberalization and capital mobility are being unwound in favor of populist, antiglobalization, and protectionist policies that hinder trade, restrict the movement of labor and capital, and act against the deeply interconnected world. As history has shown, these errant economic choices can spill over into political chaos and warfare.

What must be underscored is that the models of economics, fiscal and monetary policy, and politics that dominated the twentieth century are no longer sufficient to address the economic headwinds and growth challenges the world faces. The nature of the role of government has changed with the advent of nonstate actors, and the economic headwinds have become more complex and complicated to resolve within the existing framework of liberal democracy. A world in which democracy is not reformed is grim; more years of unqualified electorates and poor-quality political leaders will lead to worsening poverty and conflict as society becomes more unequal and more deeply split.

All the easy choices are behind us. What is left is messy and hard, and proponents of reform are likely to be pilloried and vilified. Evolving to a new democratic structure will be challenging in the extreme. But reform will help ensure that

Western democracies retain their position as economic leaders and credible vanguards of the democratic process.

Edge of Chaos rings the warning bell regarding the major risks and challenges that the global economy faces and how ill-prepared leaders and policymakers are for the future—in rich countries as well as poor ones. It also lays out in detail what needs to be done to avert a global calamity that will lead to economic impoverishment and chaos. For now, we are woefully unprepared.

This book ensures that, at a minimum, the world has been warned. The hope is, of course, for more: that this book will provoke and frame a much needed discussion about how to restore growth to the global economy and sustain it, so that we can all step back from the edge of chaos.

Appendix

Comparison of Leading Democracies

Key: Shading designates where the recommended democratic reform is not in place. Lack of shading designates where a country has the reform in place.

	Ability to Commit to Long-Term Agreements	Campaign Finance Restrictions	Restrictions on Ability to Take on High-Pay Opportunities	Extended Electoral Cycles (More Than 5 Years)	Term Limits		Minimum Qualifications for Office[1]	Design of Electoral Districts to Incentivize Competition	Mandatory Voting	Minimum Voting Requirements[2]	Weighted Voting System	Number of Reforms in Place (Out of a Possible 10)
					Legislative	Executive						
Australia	No	No	No	No. Maximum terms of 3 and 6 years in the lower and upper houses of Parliament respectively.	No	No	No	No. Districts drawn up by public servants or independent commissions.	Yes	No	No	1
Brazil	No	Yes. Outright ban on corporate contributions, spending caps on campaign outlays.	Cooling-off period, but no permanent ban.	No	No	Yes. Presidents may serve a maximum of two consecutive terms but may serve unlimited nonconsecutive terms.	No	No senators elected per state, other representatives based on party list.	Yes. Ages 18–69; not mandatory for illiterates.	No	No	4
Canada	No	Yes, caps on contributions and expenditures by candidates.	Cooling-off period (5 years).	No. Maximum 5-year term.	No	No	No	No. Districts redrawn to reflect population shifts by independent commissions.	No	No	No	2

| | Ability to Commit to Long-Term Agreements | Campaign Finance Restrictions | Restrictions on Ability to Take on High-Pay Opportunities | Extended Electoral Cycles (More Than 5 Years) | Term Limits | | Minimum Qualifications for Office[1] | Design of Electoral Districts to Incentivize Competition | Mandatory Voting | Minimum Voting Requirements[2] | Weighted Voting System | Number of Reforms in Place (Out of a Possible 10) |
					Legislative	Executive						
France	No	Yes. Monetary caps on donations and expenditures.	Cooling-off period (3 years).	No	No	Yes. Consecutive two-term limit.	No	No. Districts designed on neutral principles by state commission.	No	No	Senate elected by public officials or *grands électeurs*. National Assembly (lower legislative house) elected by direct popular vote.	4
Germany	No	No individual contribution limits.	No	No	No	No	No	No. Half of the Bundestag is elected based on geographical district. The other half is based on national party lists.	No	No	No	0

India	No	Yes. No numerical limits on caps of individuals but total amount that may be contributed by a company to any political party in any financial year shall not exceed 7.5 percent of its average net profits during the 3 immediately preceding financial years.	No	No. Five-year election cycles unless Parliament dissolved earlier on no-confidence vote against president.	No	No	No. Districts redrawn by an independent parliamentary commission every 10 years to reflect census data.	No	No	No	1
Indonesia	No	Yes. Numerical caps on direct contributions by individuals and corporations.	No	No. Election cycles are every 5 years.	Yes. Two terms.	Yes. Believe in one true god; candidates can never have declared bankruptcy; candidates will have at least attended high school or equivalent; physically and mentally healthy.	No. Districts established numerically by province, as set out by law.	No	No	No	3

	Ability to Commit to Long-Term Agreements	Campaign Finance Restrictions	Restrictions on Ability to Take on High-Pay Opportunities	Extended Electoral Cycles (More Than 5 Years)	Term Limits — Legislative	Term Limits — Executive	Minimum Qualifications for Office[1]	Design of Electoral Districts to Incentivize Competition	Mandatory Voting	Minimum Voting Requirements[2]	Weighted Voting System	Number of Reforms in Place (Out of a Possible 10)
Italy	No	Yes. Caps on some monetary donations and all expenditures.	No	No. Maximum of 5-year Parliaments unless dissolved earlier. (Members hold their seat until subsequent Parliament elected and can be held over in times of war.)	No	No	No	No. Districts drawn according to province; delegation size varies depending on population.	No	No	No	1
Japan	No	Yes. Monetary caps on donations and expenditures.	No	No	No, although some political parties impose their own term limits on party leaders.	No	No	No. 300/500 representatives based on geographic district, the 200/500 are elected based on party list.	No	No	No	1
Mexico	No	Yes. Private and corporate contributions banned. Numerical expenditure cap for candidates.	Yes, restrictions on former public officials.	No	Yes. Legislators cannot be elected to consecutive terms. Must sit out a cycle.	Yes. One term only.	No	No. Legislative representation two-pronged: geographic first-past-post, supplemented by a residual party list for well-supported third-place candidates.	Yes	No	No	5

Russia	No	Yes. Upper limits on individual and corporate contributions, calculated as a percentage of maximum campaign expenditures as set out by law.	No	No. Lower house has fixed 5-year terms, upper house serves at the pleasure of regional executives.	No	Yes. Presidents may not serve more than two consecutive terms. Can serve unlimited non-consecutive terms.	No formal requirements; however, in practice many political parties are denied registration.	No. Half of lower house elected based on national party list, half based on fixed geographical districts. Upper house based on federal regions.	No	No	No	2
Singapore	No	No monetary limits on size of donations but transparency and reporting requirements.	Yes, high salaries for public officials.	No	No	No	Yes. Must be at least 45 years old.	No	Yes	No	No	3
United Kingdom	No	Hybrid. No limits on contributions, but limits on expenditures by parties or candidates.	Cooling-off period (2 years for ministers).	No. Maximum of 5 years.	No	No	No	No	No	No	No	2

| | Ability to Commit to Long-Term Agreements | Campaign Finance Restrictions | Restrictions on Ability to Take on High-Pay Opportunities | Extended Electoral Cycles (More Than 5 Years) | Term Limits | | Minimum Qualifications for Office[1] | Design of Electoral Districts to Incentivize Competition | Mandatory Voting | Minimum Voting Requirements[2] | Weighted Voting System | Number of Reforms in Place (Out of a Possible 10) |
					Legislative	Executive						
United States	No	Yes. Limit on direct contributions to campaigns. (No limit on independent spending by outside groups, individuals, and companies on protected political speech.)	Cooling-off period, but no permanent ban.	No. Electoral cycles fixed in the Constitution.	No	Yes. Two terms only.	No	No. Districts are redrawn every 10 years based on census data by state commissions. Mostly partisan. Frequent gerrymandering protects incumbents and favors the party in charge of redistricting.	No	No	No	3

[1]Not including citizenship requirements.

[2]Not including age, citizenship requirements, or past felony convictions.

NOTES

Introduction

1. Greg R. Lawson, "A Thirty Years' War in the Middle East," *National Interest*, April 16, 2014, nationalinterest.org/feature/thirty-years-war-the-middle-east-10266.

2. "Ripe for Rebellion?" *Economist*, November 18, 2013.

3. "Brazil," World Bank, data.worldbank.org/country/brazil (accessed July 29, 2017).

4. "In U.S., 67% Dissatisfied with Income, Wealth Distribution," Gallup, January 20, 2014, www.gallup.com/poll/166904/dissatisfied-income-wealth-distribution.aspx.

5. "Inequality Is a Threat to American Democracy; Who Will Ring the Bell?" Challenges to Democracy, December 17, 2013, www.challengestodemocracy.us/home/inequality-is-a-threat-to-american-democracy-who-will-ring-the-bell/#sthash.EB6SYGib.dpbs.

6. "GDP Ranking," The World Bank, July 1, 2017, data.worldbank.org/data-catalog/GDP-ranking-table.

7. Thom Patterson, "Why Does America Have So Many Hungry Kids?," CNN, June 15, 2017; Alemayehu Bishaw, "Poverty: 2000–2012," US Census Bureau, September 2013.

8. Charles Murray, "Trump's America," *Wall Street Journal,* February 12, 2016.

9. "Reinvention in the Rust Belt," *Economist*, July 11, 2015.

10. "Unemployment Statistics," Eurostat: Statistics Explained, October 2, 2017, ec.europa.eu/eurostat/statistics-explained/index.php/Unemployment_statistics.

11. "The American Middle Class Is Losing Ground," Pew Research Center, December 9, 2015, www.pewsocialtrends.org/2015/12/09/the-american-middle-class-is-losing-ground.

12. Betsy McKay, "Life Expectancy for White Americans Declines," *Wall Street Journal*, April 20, 2016.

13. J. Bradford Delong and Lawrence H. Summers, "Fiscal Policy in a Depressed Economy," Brookings Papers on Economic Activity, Brookings, Spring 2012, www.brookings.edu/wp-content/uploads/2012/03/2012a_delong.pdf; Paul Krugman, "The Simple Analytics of Monetary Impotence," *New York Times*, December 19, 2014.

14. Glenn Kessler, "Trump's Claim That the US Pays the 'Lion's Share' for NATO," *Washington Post* Fact Checker, March 30, 2016, www.washingtonpost.com/news/fact-checker/wp/2016/03/30/trumps-claim-that-the-u-s-pays-the-lions-share-for-nato/?utm_term=.f5bc64e5b8e2.

15. Lawrence H. Summers, "The Age of Secular Stagnation," *Foreign Affairs*, February 15, 2016.

16. "2013 World Population Data Sheet," Population Reference Bureau, 2013, www.prb.org/pdf13/2013-population-data-sheet_eng.pdf.

Chapter 1: The Imperative Is Growth

1. "GINI Index—World Bank Estimate," data.worldbank.org/indicator/SI.POV.GINI (accessed March 4, 2017).

2. David L. Bevan, "Aid, Fiscal Policy, Climate Change, and Growth," WIDER Working Paper 2012/077, UNU-WIDER, Helsinki, 2012.

3. "World Economic Outlook, April 2016," International Monetary Fund, www.imf.org/external/pubs/ft/weo/2016/01 (accessed March 3, 2017).

4. "Small and Medium-Sized Enterprises: Local Strength, Global Reach," Policy Brief, *OECD Observer*, 2000, www.oecd.org/cfe/leed/1918307.pdf.

5. Joseph S. Pete, "U.S. Steel Starts Layoffs of up to 323 Workers at Gary Works," *Northwest Indiana Times*, April 24, 2015.

6. James Manyika, Jonathan Woetzel, Richard Dobbs, Jaana Remes, Eric Labaye, and Andrew Jordan, "Global Growth: Can Productivity

Save the Day in an Aging World?" McKinsey Global Institute, January 2015.

7. Rosemary D. Marcuss and Richard Kane, "U.S. National Income and Product Statistics," Bureau of Economic Analysis, February 2007, www.bea.gov/scb/pdf/2007/02%20February/0207_history_article.pdf.

8. John Helliwell, Richard Layard, and Jeffrey Sachs, eds., *World Happiness Report 2017*, Sustainable Development Solutions Network, 2017, worldhappiness.report/wp-content/uploads/sites/2/2017/03/HR17 .pdf.

9. "Human Development Index," United Nations Development Programme, hdr.undp.org/en/content/human-development-index-hdi (accessed November 15, 2017).

10. Michael E. Porter and Scott Stern, *Social Progress Index 2017 Findings Report*, Social Progress Imperative, 2017, www.socialprogressindex .com/assets/downloads/resources/en/English-2017-Social-Progress -Index-Findings-Report_embargo-d-until-June-21-2017.pdf.

11. "Working Time Required to Buy: Who Works Harder to Buy a Big Mac?" UBS, www.ubs.com/microsites/prices-earnings/edition-2015 .html (accessed March 3, 2017).

Chapter 2: A Brief History of Growth

1. Jared M. Diamond, *Guns, Germs, and Steel: The Fates of Human Societies* (New York: Norton, 1999).

2. "What Dutch Disease Is, and Why It's Bad," *Economist*, November 5, 2014.

3. The Maddison-Project, 2013, www.ggdc.net/maddison/maddison -project/home.htm.

4. Ben Carter, "Is China's Economy Really the Largest in the World?" BBC News, December 16, 2014.

5. American Enterprise Institute, "China Global Investment Tracker," www.aei.org/china-global-investment-tracker (accessed March 4, 2017).

6. "The Demographic Timebomb Crippling Japan's Economy," *National Interest*, March 25, 2015, nationalinterest.org/feature/the -demographic-timebomb-crippling-japans-economy-12479; Danielle Demitriou, "Japan's Population to Shrink by a Third by 2065," *Telegraph*

(London), April 11, 2017; "Population Projections for Japan (2017)," National Institute of Population and Social Security Research, www.ipss.go.jp/pp-zenkoku/e/zenkoku_e2017/g_images_e/pp29gts01e.htm (accessed November 15, 2017).

7. G. P. Thomas, "Argentina: Mining, Minerals, and Fuel Resources," *Azomining*, June 7, 2012, www.azomining.com/Article.aspx?ArticleID=21.

8. "The World Factbook: Argentina," Central Intelligence Agency, October 6, 2017, https://www.cia.gov/library/publications /resources/the-world-factbook/geos/ar.html.

9. David S. Landes, *The Wealth and Poverty of Nations: Why Some Are So Rich and Some So Poor* (New York: Norton, 1998).

10. Niall Ferguson, *Empire: The Rise and Demise of the British World Order and the Lessons for Global Power* (New York: Basic Books, 2004).

11. Dani Rodrik, ed., *In Search of Prosperity: Analytic Narratives on Economic Growth* (Princeton, NJ: Princeton University Press, 2003).

12. Paul Collier and Anke Hoeffler, "Conflicts," in *Global Crises, Global Solutions*, ed. Bjorn Lomborg (Cambridge: Cambridge University Press, 2004).

13. "Rwanda," World Bank, data.worldbank.org/country/rwanda (accessed March 4, 2017).

14. "Global Peace Index 2015," Institute for Economics and Peace, economicsandpeace.org/wp-content/uploads/2015/06/Global-Peace -Index-Report-2015_0.pdf (accessed March 3, 2017).

Chapter 3: Hurricane Headwinds

1. Tom Brokaw, *The Greatest Generation* (New York: Random House, 1998).

2. Richard Dobbs, Susan Lund, Jonathan Woetzel, and Mina Mutafchieva, "Debt and (Not Much) Deleveraging," McKinsey Global Institute, February 2015.

3. "The World Factbook: Country Comparison: World Debt," Central Intelligence Agency, www.cia.gov/library/publications/the-world -factbook/rankorder/2186rank.html (accessed March 3, 2017).

4. "Report on the Municipal Securities Market," US Securities and Exchange Commission, July 31, 2012.

5. Carmen M. Reinhart and Kenneth S. Rogoff, "Growth in a Time of Debt," *American Economic Review: Papers & Proceedings* 100, no. 2 (May 2010): 573–578.

6. Andrea Pescatori, Damiano Sandri, and John Simon, "Debt and Growth: Is There a Magic Threshold?" International Monetary Fund, February 2014, www.imf.org/en/Publications/WP/Issues/2016/12/31/Debt-and-Growth-Is-There-a-Magic-Threshold-41352.

7. Charles Roxburgh et al., "Lions on the Move: The Progress and Potential of African Economies," McKinsey Global Institute, June 2010, www.mckinsey.com/global-themes/middle-east-and-africa/lions-on-the-move.

8. "How Much Water Does It Take to Grow a Hamburger?," USGS Water Science School, water.usgs.gov/edu/activity-watercontent.html (accessed March 3, 2017).

9. "ODNI Releases Global Water Security ICA," Office of the Director of National Intelligence, March 22, 2012, www.dni.gov/index.php/newsroom/press-releases/press-releases-2012/item/529-odni-releases-global-water-security-ica.

10. "Mongolian Government Under Pressure to Resolve Mining Dispute Before End of Year," PGI Intelligence, pgi-intelligence.com/news/getNewsItem/Mongolian-government-under-pressure-to-resolve-mining-dispute-before-end-of-year/499 (accessed March 4, 2017); Terrance Edwards, "Mongolia Votes to Nationalize Former Russian Copper Mine Stake," Reuters, February 16, 2017.

11. Worldometers, www.worldometers.info/world-population (accessed March 4, 2017).

12. Patrick Gerland et al., "World Population Stabilization Unlikely This Century," *Science* 346, no. 6206 (October 2014): 234–237.

13. *The World's Cities in 2016: Data Booklet*, Population Division, Department of Economic and Social Affairs, United Nations, 2016, www.un.org/en/development/desa/population/publications/pdf/urbanization/the_worlds_cities_in_2016_data_booklet.pdf.

14. *Natural Resources in 2020, 2030, and 2040: Implications for the United States*, National Intelligence Council Report, Chatham House for the National Intelligence Council, May 2015, www.dni.gov/files/documents

/NICR%202013-05%20US%20Nat%20Resources%202020,%202030%
202040.pdf.

15. Adam Pasick, "Japan Is Rapidly Losing Population—and Half the World Is About to Join It," *Quartz*, January 2, 2014, qz.com/162788 /japan-is-rapidly-losing-population-and-half-the-world-is-about-to -join-it; "World Population Prospects: The 2015 Revision," Department of Economic and Social Affairs, United Nations, July 29, 2015.

16. *Welfare Trends Report 2016*, Office of Budgetary Responsibility, United Kingdom, October 2016, budgetresponsibility.org.uk/docs/dlm _uploads/Welfare-Trends-Report.pdf.

17. "A Slow-Burning Fuse," *Economist*, June 25, 2009.

18. "Implementing the 2030 Agenda for Sustainable Development," United Nations Research Institute for Social Development, www .unrisd.org/80256B3C005BCCF9%2F%28httpAuxPages%29%2F92 AF5072673F924DC125804C0044F396%2F%24file%2FFlagship2016 _FullReport.pdf (accessed July 13, 2017).

19. *World Population Prospects: The 2015 Revision*, Department of Economic and Social Affairs, United Nations, July 29, 2015, www .un.org/en/development/desa/publications/world-population-prospects -2015-revision.html.

20. *World Employment Social Outlook: Trends for Youth,* 2016, International Labour Organization, 2016, www.ilo.org/wcmsp5/groups /public/---dgreports/---dcomm/---publ/documents/publication/wcms _513739.pdf.

21. Drew DeSilver, "U.S. Students' Academic Achievement Still Lags That of Their Peers in Many Other Countries," Pew Research Center, February 15, 2017, www.pewresearch.org/fact-tank/2017/02/15 /u-s-students-internationally-math-science.

22. Elena Kvochko, "Five Ways Technology Can Help the Economy," World Economic Forum, April 11, 2013, www.weforum.org /agenda/2013/04/five-ways-technology-can-help-the-economy; "What Is the Impact of Mobile Telephony on GDP Growth?," Deloitte, November 2012.

23. Carl Benedikt Frey and Michael A. Osborne, "The Future of Employment: How Susceptible Are Jobs to Computerisation?," *Technological Forecasting and Social Change* 114 (January 2017): 254–280.

24. Joel Lee, "Self Driving Cars Endanger Millions of American Jobs (and That's Okay)," *Make Use Of,* June 19, 2015, www.makeuseof .com/tag/self-driving-cars-endanger-millions-american-jobs-thats-okay; "Reports, Trends & Statistics," American Trucking Association, www .trucking.org/News_and_Information_Reports_Industry_Data.aspx (accessed November 14, 2017).

25. Rex Nutting, "No, 'Truck Driver' Isn't the Most Common Job in Your State," *Market Watch,* February 12, 2015, www.marketwatch.com /story/no-truck-driver-isnt-the-most-common-job-in-your-state-2015-02-12.

26. Carl Benedikt Frey, Michael A. Osborne, Craig Holmes, et al., "Technology at Work v2.0," Oxford Martin School, Citi, January 2016, www .oxfordmartin.ox.ac.uk/downloads/reports/Citi_GPS_Technology _Work_2.pdf.

27. "As Wages Rise, China's Robot Army Set to Swell," *Today Online,* April 11, 2016, www.todayonline.com/chinaindia/china/wages -rise-chinas-robot-army-set-swell; Steven Johnson, "China's Robot Army Set to Surge," *Financial Times,* April 8, 2016.

28. Frey et al., "Technology at Work v2.0."

29. "Digital Disruption: How FinTech Is Forcing Banking to a Tipping Point," Citi GPS, March 2016, ir.citi.com/SEBhgbdvxes 95HWZMmFbjGiU%2FydQ9kbvEbHIruHR%2Fle%2F2Wza4cRvO QUNX8GBWVsV.

30. Brent Neiman, "The Global Decline of the Labor Share," *Quarterly Journal of Economics* 129, no. 1 (2014): 61–103.

31. Darren Acemoglu and David Autor, "Skills, Tasks and Technologies: Implications for Employment and Earnings," chapter 12 in *Handbook of Labor Economics,* vol. 4b (2011): 1075, economics.mit.edu /files/5571.

32. "Cybersecurity: Actions Needed to Strengthen U.S. Capabilities," Government Accountability Office, February 14, 2017, www .gao.gov/assets/690/682756.pdf.

33. Patricia A. Daly, "Agricultural Employment: Has the Decline Ended?," *Monthly Labor Review* (November 1981).

34. Dani Rodrik, "The Past, Present, and Future of Economic Growth," Global Citizen Foundation, June 2013, www.gcf.ch/wp-content /uploads/2013/06/GCF_Rodrik-working-paper-1_-6.17.131.pdf.

35. S. Basu and J. Fernald, "Information and Communications Technology as a General Purpose Technology: Evidence from US Industry Data," *German Economic Review* 8, no. 2 (2007): 146–173.

36. Frey et al., "Technology at Work v2.0."

37. Deborah Hardoon, "Wealth: Having It All and Wanting More," Oxfam International, January 2015; Deborah Hardoon, "An Economy for the 99%: It's Time to Build a Human Economy That Benefits Everyone, Not Just the Privileged Few," Oxfam International, January 2017, www.oxfam.org/en/research/wealth-having-it-all-and-wanting-more.

38. Alan Dunn, "Average America vs the One Percent," *Forbes*, March 21, 2012, www.forbes.com/sites/moneywisewomen/2012/03/21/average-america-vs-the-one-percent/#59ee67212395.

39. Chuck Collins and Josh Hoxie, "Billionaire Bonanza: The Forbes 400 and the Rest of Us," Institute for Policy Studies, December 1, 2015, www.ips-dc.org/billionaire-bonanza.

40. J. A. Cheshire, "Lives on the Line: Mapping Life Expectancy Along the London Tube Network," *Environment and Planning A* 44, no. 7 (2012).

41. Derek Thompson, "Get Rich, Live Longer: The Ultimate Consequence of Income Inequality," *Atlantic*, April 18, 2014.

42. "What's Gone Wrong with Democracy," *Economist*, February 27, 2014, www.economist.com/node/21596796.

43. Nicholas Confessore, Sarah Cohen, and Karen Yourish, "The Families Funding the 2016 Presidential Election," *New York Times*, October 10, 2015.

44. "Productivity Brief 2015," The Conference Board, 2015, www.conference-board.org/retrievefile.cfm?filename=The-Conference-Board-2015-Productivity-Brief.pdf&type=subsite.

45. Edoardo Campanella, "Age and Productivity," *Foreign Affairs*, April 20, 2016.

46. "Productivity Brief 2015."

47. "Labour Productivity: Jan to Mar 2016," Office for National Statistics, United Kingdom, July 2016, www.ons.gov.uk/employmentandlabourmarket/peopleinwork/labourproductivity/bulletins/labourproductivity/jantomar2016.

48. Chris Giles, Ferdinando Giugliano, and Sarah O'Connor, "Professional Services at Heart of UK Productivity Problem," *Financial Times*, April 19, 2015.

49. Jennifer Ryan, "Robots Can't Replace IT Workers, Doctors, Dentists, Haldane Says," *Bloomberg*, December 16, 2015.

50. "The World Factbook," Central Intelligence Agency, www.cia .gov/library/publications/the-world-factbook (accessed March 4, 2017).

51. Adam Szirmai, "Is Manufacturing Still the Main Engine of Growth in Developing Countries?" WiderAngle (blog), United Nations University–Wider, May 2009, www.wider.unu.edu/publication /manufacturing-still-main-engine-growth-developing-countries.

52. Robert J. Gordon, "Is U.S. Economic Growth Over? Faltering Innovation Confronts the Six Headwinds," Working Paper, National Bureau of Economic Research, August 2012.

53. James Manyika, Jonathan Woetzel, Richard Dobbs, Jaana Remes, Eric Labaye, and Andrew Jordan, "Can Long-Term Global Growth Be Saved?," McKinsey Global Institute, January 2015.

Chapter 4: The False Promise of Protectionism

1. John Williamson, ed., *Latin American Adjustment: How Much Has Happened?*, Institute for International Economics, March 1990.

2. "The Battle of Smoot-Hawley," *Economist*, December 18, 2008.

3. Pankaj Ghemawat and Steven A. Altman, *DHL Global Connectedness Index 2014*, DHL, October 2014, www.dhl.com/content/dam /Campaigns/gci2014/downloads/dhl_gci_2014_study_low.pdf.

4. Ibid.

5. "Real Wages in Germany: Numerous Years of Decline," DIW Berlin Weekly Report No. 28/2009, German Institute for Economic Research, October 23, 2009, www.diw.de/sixcms/media.php/73/diw _wr_2009-28.pdf.

6. Elise Gould, "2014 Continues a 35-Year Trend of Broad-Based Wage Stagnation," Economic Policy Institute, February 19, 2015, www .epi.org/publication/stagnant-wages-in-2014.

7. Drew Desilver, "For Most Workers, Real Wages Have Barely Budged for Decades," Pew Research Center, October 9, 2014, www.pewresearch

.org/fact-tank/2014/10/09/for-most-workers-real-wages-have-barely
-budged-for-decades.

8. Shawn Donnan, "Global Trade: Structural Shifts," *Financial Times*, March 2, 2016.

9. John W. Miller and William Mauldin, "U.S. Imposes 266% Duty on Some Chinese Steel Imports," *Wall Street Journal*, March 1, 2016; Shawn Donnan, "US to Hike Duties on Chinese Steel to Over 500%," *Financial Times*, June 22, 2016.

10. "U.S.-China Trade: Eliminating Nonmarket Economy Methodology Would Lower Antidumping Duties for Some Chinese Companies," Government Accountability Office, January 10, 2006, www.gpo.gov/fdsys/pkg/GAOREPORTS-GAO-06-231/html /GAOREPORTS-GAO-06-231.htm; Joshua P. Meltzer, "Deepening the United States–Africa Trade and Investment Relationship," Brookings, January 28, 2016, www.brookings.edu/testimonies/deepening-the -united-states-africa-trade-and-investment-relationship.

11. "October 2015 Capital Flows to Emerging Markets," Institute of International Finance, October 1, 2015.

12. Larry Elliott, "IMF Says Economic Growth May Never Return to Pre-Crisis Levels," *Guardian* (London), October 7, 2014; "Legacies, Clouds, Uncertainties," International Monetary Fund, October 2014, www.imf.org/external/pubs/ft/weo/2014/02.

13. "The Australian Economy and the Global Downturn," Treasury, Government of Australia, www.treasury.gov.au/PublicationsAndMedia /Publications/2011/Economic-Roundup-Issue-2/Report/Part-1-Reasons -for-resilience (accessed July 17, 2017).

14. *Global Employment Trends for Youth* 2015: *Scaling Up Investments in Decent Jobs for Youth*, International Labour Organization, 2015, www .ilo.org/wcmsp5/groups/public/---dgreports/---dcomm/---publ /documents/publication/wcms_412015.pdf.

15. Russell Shorto, "The Way Greeks Live Now," *New York Times Magazine*, February 13, 2012.

16. Shawn Donnan, "Obama Blocks Takeover of Tech Group Aixtron," *Financial Times*, December 2, 2016.

Chapter 5: A Challenge to Democracy's Dominance

1. Maurice Obstfeld, "Global Growth: Too Slow for Too Long," IMFBlog, April 12, 2016, blogs.imf.org/2016/04/12/global-growth-too-slow-for-too-long.

2. China Global Investment Tracker, American Enterprise Institute Database, www.aei.org/china-global-investment-tracker (accessed November 15, 2017).

3. "World Economic Outlook," International Monetary Fund, April 2017, www.imf.org/en/Publications/WEO/Issues/2017/04/04/world-economic-outlook-april-2017.

4. FT Confidential Research, *Financial Times*, May 2016, next.ft.com/content/c33c6854-2351-11e6-aa98-db1e01fabc0c.

5. "Global Patent Applications Rose to 2.9 Million in 2015 on Strong Growth from China," World Intellectual Property Organization, November 23, 2016, www.wipo.int/pressroom/en/articles/2016/article_0017.html.

6. J. A. Cheibub, A. Przeworski, F. P. Limongi Neto, and M. M. Alvarez, "What Makes Democracies Endure?," *Journal of Democracy* 7, no. 1 (1996): 39–55.

7. Steven Johnson, "Strongman Leaders More Trusted Than Democrats in Emerging World," *Financial Times*, October 16, 2016.

8. *Discarding Democracy: A Return to the Iron Fist*, Freedom House, 2015, freedomhouse.org/sites/default/files/01152015_FIW_2015_final.pdf.

9. Joshua Kurlantzick, *Democracy in Retreat: The Revolt of the Middle Class and the Worldwide Decline of Representative Government* (New Haven, CT: Yale University Press, 2013).

10. "World Population," Worldometers, www.worldometers.info/world-population/#region (accessed July 17, 2017); "GDP (Current US$)," World Bank, data.worldbank.org/indicator/NY.GDP.MKTP.CD (accessed July 17, 2017).

11. "Government Effectiveness Indicator," Millennium Challenge Corporation, www.mcc.gov/who-we-fund/indicator/government-effectiveness-indicator (accessed March 4, 2017).

12. Peter Torday, "Coffee Price Soars After Brazilian Frost Damage," *Independent* (London), July 11, 1994.

13. *The Economic Report of the President, 2010*, Cosimo Reports, 2010, 91.

14. David M. Herzsenhorn, "Ukraine in Turmoil After Leaders Reject Major E.U. Deal," *New York Times*, November 26, 2013.

15. "World Bank Group President Jim Yong Kim's Speech at George Washington University: The World Bank Group Strategy: A Path to End Poverty," The World Bank, October 1, 2013, www.worldbank.org /en/news/speech/2013/10/01/world-bank-group-president-jim-yong-kim -speech-at-george-washington-university.

16. Homi Kharas and Andrew Rogerson, *Horizon 2025: Creative Destruction in the Aid Industry*, Overseas Development Institute, July 2012.

Chapter 6: The Perils of Political Myopia

1. "Beyond Distrust: How Americans View Their Government," Pew Research Center, www.people-press.org/2015/11/23/1-trust-in-government -1958-2015 (accessed July 17, 2017).

2. "Turbulence Ahead: Renewing Consensus Amidst Greater Volatility," McKinsey Global Institute, September 2016.

3. Dominic Barton, Presentation at Pi Capital, October 2013.

4. Dominic Barton and Mark Wiseman, "The Cost of Confusing Shareholder Value and Short-Term Profit," *Financial Times*, March 31, 2015.

5. Barry Ritholtz, "Where Have All the Public Companies Gone?" *Bloomberg View*, June 24, 2015.

6. Teresa Kroeger, Tanyell Cooke, and Elisa Gould, "The Class of 2016," Economic Policy Institute, April 21, 2016, www.epi.org /publication/class-of-2016.

7. "Investing in Britain's Future," Her Majesty's Treasury, June 2013, www.gov.uk/government/publications/investing-in-britains-future.

8. "2015 Income and Poverty Census Report," US Census, 2016, documents.latimes.com/2015-income-and-poverty-census-report; "GDP per Capita (Current US$)," The World Bank, data.worldbank.org/indicator /NY.GDP.PCAP.CD?locations=XC (accessed July 17, 2017).

9. "GDP (Current US$)," The World Bank, data.worldbank.org /indicator/NY.GDP.MKTP.CD (accessed July 17, 2017).

10. John Elliott, "Democracy Has Become a Fig Leaf to Cover India's Failures," *Economic Times* (India), March 30, 2014.

11. "Global Infrastructure Investment: Timing Is Everything (and Now Is the Time)," Standard & Poor's Rating Services, January 13, 2015, www.tfreview.com/sites/default/files/SP_Economic%20Research_Global%20Infrastructure%20Investment%20(2).pdf; Klaus Schwab, *Global Competitiveness Report* 2016–2017, World Economic Forum, 2016, www3.weforum.org/docs/GCR2016-2017/05FullReport/TheGlobalCompetitivenessReport2016-2017_FINAL.pdf.

12. "Lobbying Database," Open Secrets, www.opensecrets.org/lobby (accessed November 14, 2017).

Chapter 7: Blueprint for a New Democracy

1. "What's Gone Wrong with Democracy," *Economist*, February 27, 2014, www.economist.com/node/21596796.

2. Andreas Becker, "French Elections: Who Finances the Candidates?" DW, May 5, 2017, www.dw.com/en/french-elections-who-finances-the-candidates/a-38704682.

3. "US Business Cycle Expansions and Contractions," National Bureau of Economic Research, www.nber.org/cycles.html (accessed October 23, 2017).

4. Philip Cowley, "Arise, Novice Leader! The Continuing Rise of the Career Politician in Britain," *Politics* 32, no. 1 (2012): 31–38.

5. Chrysa Lamprinakou, "'The Profession I Chose Was Politics': The New Generation of Political Insiders," Parliamentary Candidates UK, November 27, 2014, parliamentarycandidates.org/news/the-profession-i-chose-was-politics-the-new-generation-of-political-insiders.

6. Drew DeSilver, "House Seats Rarely Flip from One Party to the Other," Pew Research Center, September 7, 2016, www.pewresearch.org/fact-tank/2016/09/07/house-seats-rarely-flip-from-one-party-to-the-other.

7. "End Gerrymandering Now," endgerrymanderingnow.org/why-reform (accessed July 17, 2017).

8. "Global Voter Turnout Declining," press release, International IDEA, archive.idea.int/press/pr20020419.htm (accessed October 23, 2017).

9. "Results of the 2014 European Elections," European Parliament, www.europarl.europa.eu/elections2014-results/en/turnout.html.

10. Costas Panagopoulos, "The Calculus of Voting in Compulsory Voting Systems," *Political Behavior* 30, no. 4 (December 2008): 455–467.

11. Elliot Frankal, "Compulsory Voting Around the World," *Guardian* (London), July 4, 2005.

12. Lisa Hill, "What We've Seen in Australia with Mandatory Voting," *New York Times*, November 7, 2011.

13. "Want to Make Me?" *Economist*, May 20, 2015.

14. Stefan Hansen, "Democracy of the Future—Nothing Less," *Scenario*, May 19, 2011.

15. Michael Safi, "Have Millennials Given Up on Democracy?" *Guardian* (London), March 18, 2016.

Chapter 8: Retooling for Twenty-First-Century Growth

1. "Country Status Distribution, 1972–2016," 2016, Freedom House, freedomhouse.org/report-types/freedom-world.

2. *Freedom in the World 2017*, Freedom House, 2017, freedomhouse .org/sites/default/files/FH_FIW_2017_Report_Final.pdf.

3. Monty G. Marshall, "Polity IV Project: Political Regime Characteristics and Transitions, 1800–2013," Political Instability Task Force, June 5, 2014, www.systemicpeace.org/polity/polity4x.htm.

4. Homi Kharas and Andrew Rogerson, *Horizon 2025: Creative Destruction in the Aid Industry*, Overseas Development Institute, July 2012, www.odi.org/sites/odi.org.uk/files/odi-assets/publications -opinion-files/7723.pdf.

5. "Global Terrorism Index 2016," Institute for Economics and Peace, November 2016, economicsandpeace.org/wp-content/uploads/2016/11 /Global-Terrorism-Index-2016.2.pdf.

6. Aaron Reeves, Martin McKee, and David Stuckler, "Economic Suicides in the Great Recession in Europe and North America," *British Journal of Psychiatry* (June 2014); "Depression: A Global Crisis," World Federation for Mental Health, October 10, 2012, www.who.int/mental _health/management/depression/wfmh_paper_depression_wmhd_2012 .pdf.

7. Chris Weller, "Jeff Bezos Could Be the World's First Trillionaire by 2042," *Business Insider*, July 28, 2017.

8. Raghuram G. Rajan, "Has Financial Development Made the World Riskier?," NBER Working Paper No. 11728, National Bureau of Economic Research, November 2005, www.nber.org/papers/w11728.

BIBLIOGRAPHY

Acemoglu, Darren, and David Autor. "Skills, Tasks and Technologies: Implications for Employment and Earnings." Chapter 12 in *Handbook of Labor Economics*, vol. 4b (2011): 1075. economics.mit.edu /files/5571.

Alpert, Daniel. "Glut: The U.S. Economy and the American Worker in the Age of Oversupply." Third Way. April 4, 2016. www.thirdway .org/report/glut-the-us-economy-and-the-american-worker-in-the -age-of-oversupply.

American Enterprise Institute. "China Global Investment Tracker." www.aei.org/china-global-investment-tracker. Accessed March 4, 2017.

"Are the Rich Getting Richer and the Poor Getting Poorer?" US Census Bureau. September 2015. www.census.gov/topics/income -poverty/income-inequality.html.

"Argentina GDP Growth Rate." Trading Economics. www.tradingeco nomics.com/argentina/gdp-growth. Accessed October 23, 2017.

"As Wages Rise, China's Robot Army Set to Swell." *Today Online*, April 11, 2016. www.todayonline.com/chinaindia/china /wages-rise-chinas-robot-army-set-swell.

"The Australian Economy and the Global Downturn." Treasury, Government of Australia. www.treasury.gov.au/PublicationsAnd Media/Publications/2011/Economic-Roundup-Issue-2/Report /Part-1-Reasons-for-resilience. Accessed July 17, 2017.

Barton, Dominic. Presentation at Pi Capital. October 2013.

Barton, Dominic, and Mark Wiseman. "The Cost of Confusing Shareholder Value and Short-Term Profit." *Financial Times*, March 31, 2015.

"The Battle of Smoot-Hawley." *Economist*, December 18, 2008.

Becker, Andreas. "French Elections: Who Finances the Candidates?" DW. May 5, 2017. www.dw.com/en/french-elections-who-finances-the-candidates/a-38704682.

Bevan, David L. "Aid, Fiscal Policy, Climate Change, and Growth." WIDER Working Paper 2012/077. UNU-WIDER, Helsinki, 2012.

"Beyond Distrust: How Americans View Their Government." Pew Research Center. November 23, 2015. www.people-press.org/2015/11/23/1-trust-in-government-1958-2015.

"The Big Mac Index." *Economist*, July 13, 2017.

Bildt, Carl. "How the West Was Lost." Project Syndicate, May 25, 2016. www.project-syndicate.org/commentary/free-trade-trump-sanders-protectionism-by-carl-bildt-2016-05.

Bishaw, Alemayehu. "Poverty: 2000–2012." US Census Bureau. September 2013.

Bloom, Nicholas, Mirko Draca, and John Van Reenen. "Trade Induced Technical Change? The Impact of Chinese Imports on Innovation, IT and Productivity." National Bureau of Economic Research. January 2011. www.nber.org/papers/w16717.

Brancaccio, David. "From the Richest to Poorest in New York City." Marketplace.org. April 24, 2012. www.marketplace.org/2012/04/24/elections/real-economy/richest-poorest-new-york-city.

Brokaw, Tom. *The Greatest Generation*. New York: Random House, 1998.

Bulletin. Reserve Bank of Australia. June Quarter 2014. www.rba.gov.au/publications/bulletin/2014/jun/pdf/bu-0614.pdf.

Campanella, Edoardo. "Age and Productivity: Do Older Workforces Contribute to Low Economic Growth?" *Foreign Affairs*, April 20, 2016.

Carter, Ben. "Is China's Economy Really the Largest in the World?" BBC News, December 16, 2014.

Caumont, Andrea, and D'Vera Cohn. "10 Demographic Trends That Are Shaping the U.S. and the World." Pew Research Center.

March 31, 2016. www.pewresearch.org/fact-tank/2016/03/31/10
-demographic-trends-that-are-shaping-the-u-s-and-the-world.

Chambers, Elizabeth G., et al. "The War for Talent." *McKinsey Quarterly*, August 29, 2007.

Cheibub, J. A., A. Przeworski, F. P. Limongi Neto, and M. M. Alvarez. "What Makes Democracies Endure?" *Journal of Democracy* 7, no. 1 (1996): 39–55.

Cheshire, J. "Lives on the Line: Mapping Life Expectancy Along the London Tube Network." *Environment and Planning A* 44, no. 7 (2012).

"China Global Investment Tracker." American Enterprise Institute and the Heritage Foundation. www.aei.org/china-global-investment-tracker. Accessed November 15, 2017.

"China Going Global Investment Index." Economist Intelligence Unit. www.eiu.com/public/topical_report.aspx?campaignid=ChinaGoing Global. Accessed November 15, 2017.

Chinn, Menzie D., and Hiro Ito. "A New Measure of Financial Openness." *Journal of Comparative Policy Analysis: Research and Practice* 10, no. 3 (September 2008): 309–322.

Collier, Paul, and Anke Hoeffler. "Conflicts." In *Global Crises, Global Solutions*, edited by Bjorn Lomborg, 129–174. Cambridge: Cambridge University Press, 2004.

Collins, Chuck, and Josh Hoxie. "Billionaire Bonanza: The Forbes 400 and the Rest of Us." Institute for Policy Studies. December 1, 2015. www.ips-dc.org/billionaire-bonanza.

"Coming to an Office Near You." *Economist*, January, 18 2014.

"Compulsory Voting." International Institute for Democracy and Electoral Assistance. www.idea.int/data-tools/data/voter-turnout/compulsory-voting. Accessed November 15, 2017.

Confessore, Nicholas, Sarah Cohen, and Karen Yorish. "2016 Presidential Election Super Pac Donors." *New York Times*, October 11, 2015.

Coolidge, Kelsey, D. Conor Seyle, and Thomas G. Weiss. "The Rise of Non-State Actors in Global Governance Opportunities and Limitations." One Earth Future Foundation. November 2013. acuns.org/wp-content/uploads/2013/11/gg-weiss.pdf.

"Country Status Distribution, 1972–2016." Freedom House. 2016. freedomhouse.org/report-types/freedom-world.

Cowen, Tyler. "Income Inequality Is Not Rising Globally; It's Falling." *New York Times*, July 19, 2014.

Cowley, Philip. "Arise, Novice Leader! The Continuing Rise of the Career Politician in Britain." *Politics* 32 (2012): 31–38.

"Crisis and Recovery in the World Economy." In *2010 Economic Report of the President*. White House. 2010. obamawhitehouse.archives .gov/sites/default/files/microsites/economic-report-president -chapter-3r2.pdf.

"Cyber Crime—A Growing Challenge for Governments." *KPMG International Issues Monitor* 8 (July 2011).

Cybersecurity: Actions Needed to Strengthen U.S. Capabilities. Government Accountability Office. February 14, 2017. www.gao.gov /assets/690/682756.pdf.

Dabla-Norris, Era, Kalpana Kochhar, Nujin Suphaphiphat, Frantisek Ricka, and Evridiki Tsounta. "Causes and Consequences of Income Inequality: A Global Perspective." International Monetary Fund. June 2015. www.imf.org/external/pubs/ft/sdn/2015/sdn1513.pdf.

Daly, Patricia A. "Agricultural Employment: Has the Decline Ended?" *Monthly Labor Review* (November 1981).

"Debt and Growth: Breaking the Threshold." *Economist*, March 1, 2014.

Delong, J. Bradford, and Lawrence H. Summers. *Fiscal Policy in a Depressed Economy*. Brookings Papers on Economic Activity. Brookings. Spring 2012. www.brookings.edu/wp-content /uploads/2012/03/2012a_delong.pdf.

Demitriou, Danielle. "Japan's Population to Shrink by a Third by 2065." *Telegraph* (London), April 11, 2017.

"Democracy in an Age of Anxiety: Democracy Index 2015." Economist Intelligence Unit. www.eiu.com/public/topical_report.aspx? campaignid=DemocracyIndex2015.

"Demographics and Commodities." Evercore ISI Global Demographics. June 2015.

"Demographics of Frontier Economies." Credit Suisse Global Fixed Income Research. April 2016.

"Depression: A Global Crisis." World Health Organization. October 10, 2012.

DeSilver, Drew. "For Most Workers, Real Wages Have Barely Budged for Decades." Pew Research Center. October 9, 2014. www.pewresearch .org/fact-tank/2014/10/09/for-most-workers-real-wages-have-barely -budged-for-decades.

———. "House Seats Rarely Flip from One Party to the Other." Pew Research Center. September 7, 2016. www.pewresearch.org /fact-tank/2016/09/07/house-seats-rarely-flip-from-one-party -to-the-other.

———. "U.S. Students' Academic Achievement Still Lags That of Their Peers in Many Other Countries." Pew Research Center. February 15, 2017. www.pewresearch.org/fact-tank/2017/02 /15/u-s-students-internationally-math-science.

Diamond, Jared. *Guns, Germs, and Steel: The Fates of Human Societies.* New York: Norton, 1997.

"Digital Disruption: How FinTech Is Forcing Banking to a Tipping Point." Citi Global Perspectives & Solutions (GPS). March 2016. ir.citi.com/SEBhgbdvxes95HWZMmFbjGiU%2FydQ9kbvEbHIru HR%2Fle%2F2Wza4cRvOQUNX8GBWVsV.

Discarding Democracy: A Return to the Iron Fist. Freedom House. 2015. freedomhouse.org/sites/default/files/01152015_FIW_2015_final.pdf.

"Disruptive Technologies: Advances That Will Transform Life, Business and Global Economy." McKinsey Global Institute. May 2013. www.mckinsey.com/business-functions/digital-mckinsey/our -insights/disruptive-technologies.

Dobbs, Richard, Tim Koller, Susan Lund, Sree Ramaswamy, Jon Harris, Mekala Krishnan, and Duncan Kauffman. "Why Investors May Need to Lower Their Sights." McKinsey Global Institute. April 2016. www.mckinsey.com/industries/private-equity-and -principal-investors/our-insights/why-investors-may-need-to-lower -their-sights.

Dobbs, Richard, Susan Lund, Jonathan Woetzel, and Mina Mutafchieva. "Debt and (Not Much) Deleveraging." McKinsey Global Institute. February 2015.

Dobbs, Richard, James Manyika, Jonathan Woetzel, Jaana Remes, Jesko Perry, Greg Kelly, Kanaka Pattabiraman, and Hemant Sharma. "Urban World: The Global Consumers to Watch." McKinsey Global Institute. March 2016.

Donnan, Shawn. "Global Trade: Structural Shifts." *Financial Times*, March 2, 2016.

———. "Obama Blocks Takeover of Tech Group Aixtron." *Financial Times*, December 2, 2016.

———. "US to Hike Duties on Chinese Steel to Over 500%." *Financial Times*, June 22, 2016.

Donnan, Shawn, and Joe Leahy. "World Trade Records Biggest Reversal Since Crisis." *Financial Times*, February 25, 2016.

Dreher, Axel. "Does Globalization Affect Growth? Evidence from a New Index of Globalization." *Applied Economics* 38, no. 10 (2006): 1091–1110.

Dunn, Alan. "Average America vs the One Percent." *Forbes*, March 21, 2012.

Dwyer, Paula. "A Basic Income Should Be the Next Big Thing." *Bloomberg*, May 2, 2016.

"The Economic Impact of the Achievement Gap in America's Schools." McKinsey Global Institute. April 2009. mckinseyonsociety.com /the-economic-impact-of-the-achievement-gap-in-americas-schools.

The Economic Report of the President 2010. Cosimo Reports. 2010.

"Economy and Growth." World Bank. data.worldbank.org/topic /economy-and-growth. Accessed November 14, 2017.

Edwards, Terrance. "Mongolia Votes to Nationalize Former Russian Copper Mine Stake." Reuters. February 16, 2017.

Eichengreen, Barry. "What's Holding Back Global Productivity Growth?" World Economic Forum. December 11, 2015.

Elliott, John. "Democracy Has Become a Fig Leaf to Cover India's Failures." *Economic Times*, March 30, 2014.

Elliott, Larry. "IMF Says Economic Growth May Never Return to Pre-Crisis Levels." *Guardian* (London), October 7, 2014.

Ezrati, Milton. "The Demographic Timebomb Crippling Japan's Economy." *National Interest*, March 25, 2015.

FAO Statistical Pocketbook 2015. Food and Agriculture Organization of the United Nations. 2015. www.fao.org/3/a-i4691e.pdf.

Ferguson, Niall. *Empire: The Rise and Demise of the British World Order and the Lessons for Global Power.* New York: Basic Books, 2004.

"Financial Trust Index." University of Chicago Booth School of Business and Northwestern University Kellogg School of Management. www.financialtrustindex.org. Accessed November 15, 2017.

Forttrell, Quentin. "Most Americans Are One Paycheck Away from the Street." *Market Watch*, January 31, 2015. www.marketwatch.com /story/most-americans-are-one-paycheck-away-from-the-street-2015 -01-07.

Fox, Margalit. "Keith Tantlinger, Builder of Cargo Container Dies at 92." *New York Times*, September 6, 2011.

"Fragile States Index: 2015." The Fund for Peace. 2015.

Frankal, Elliot. "Compulsory Voting Around the World." *Guardian* (London), July 4, 2005.

Freedom in the World Report 2012. Freedom House. freedomhouse.org /report/freedom-world/freedom-world-2012.

Freedom in the World Report 2015. Freedom House. freedomhouse.org /report/freedom-world/freedom-world-2015.

Freedom in the World Report 2017. Freedom House. freedomhouse.org/sites /default/files/FH_FIW_2017_Report_Final.pdf.

Frey, Carl Benedikt, and Michael A. Osborne. "The Future of Employment: How Susceptible Are Jobs to Computerisation?" Oxford Martin School. September 17, 2013.

———. "Technology at Work: The Future of Innovation and Employment." Citi Global Perspectives & Solutions (GPS) and Oxford Martin School. February 3, 2015.

Fry, Richard. "Millennials Overtake Baby Boomers as America's Largest Generation." Pew Research Center. April 25, 2016. www.pewresearch .org/fact-tank/2016/04/25/millennials-overtake-baby-boomers.

FT Confidential Research. *Financial Times*, May 2016. next.ft.com /content/c33c6854-2351-11e6-aa98-db1e01fabc0c.

Furceri, Davide, Prakash Loungani, and Jonathan D. Ostry. "Neoliberalism: Oversold?" *International Monetary Fund* 53, no. 2 (June 2016).

"The Future of Jobs." World Economic Forum. January 2016. reports .weforum.org/future-of-jobs-2016.

Gabler, Neal. "The Secret Shame of Middle-Class Americans." *Atlantic* (May 2016).

Gallup. "2015 Gallup World Poll." www.gallup.com/services/170945 /world-poll.aspx. Accessed July 13, 2017.

Gallup-Sharecare. Well-Being Index 2014. www.well-beingindex.com. Accessed July 13, 2017.

Garemo, Nicklas, Martin Hjerpe, and Jan Mischke. "The Infrastructure Conundrum: Improving Productivity." McKinsey & Company. July 2015. www.mckinsey.com/industries/capital-projects -and-infrastructure/our-insights/the-infrastructure-conundrum -improving-productivity.

Gerland, Patrick, et al. "World Population Stabilization Unlikely This Century." *Science* 346, no. 6206 (2014): 234–237.

Ghemawat, Pankaj, and Steven A. Altman. *DHL Global Connectedness Index 2014*. DHL. October 2014. www.dhl.com/content/dam /Campaigns/gci2014/downloads/dhl_gci_2014_study_high.pdf.

Giles, Chris, Ferdinando Giugliano, and Sarah O'Connor. "Professional Services at Heart of UK Productivity Problem." *Financial Times*. www.ft.com/content/3e0082a8-e502-11e4-bb4b-00144feab7de. Accessed March 4, 2017.

"Global Competitiveness Report: 2015–2016." World Economic Forum. reports.weforum.org/global-competitiveness-report-2015-2016. Accessed November 15, 2017.

"Global Economic Outlook, June 2017." Organisation for Economic Co-operation and Development. June 2017. www.oecd.org/eco/outlook /economicoutlook.htm.

Global Employment Trends for Youth 2015: Scaling Up Investments in Decent Jobs for Youth. International Labour Organization. 2015. www.ilo.org/wcmsp5/groups/public/---dgreports/---dcomm/--- publ/documents/publication/wcms_412015.pdf.

"Global GDP Database." World Economics. www.worldeconomics .com/GrossDomesticProduct/GDPByCountry.aspx.

"Global Infrastructure Investment: Timing Is Everything (and Now Is the Time)." Standard & Poor's Rating Services. January 13, 2015.

"Global Patent Applications Rose to 2.9 Million in 2015 on Strong Growth from China." World Intellectual Property Organization. November 23, 2016. www.wipo.int/pressroom/en/articles/2016/article_0017.html.

"Global Peace Index: 2015." Institute for Economics & Peace. June 2015. economicsandpeace.org/wp-content/uploads/2015/06/Global-Peace-Index-Report-2015_0.pdf.

"Global Pension Asset Study 2015." Willis Towers Watson. February 2015. www.towerswatson.com/en-US/Insights/IC-Types/Survey-Research-Results/2015/02/Global-Pensions-Asset-Study-2015.

"Global Terrorism Index 2016." Institute for Economics and Peace. November 2016. economicsandpeace.org/wp-content/uploads/2016/11/Global-Terrorism-Index-2016.2.pdf.

Global Trends: Forced Displacement in 2014. United Nations High Commissioner for Refugees. 2014. www.unhcr.org/en-us/statistics/country/556725e69/unhcr-global-trends-2014.html.

Global Trends 2025: A Transformed World. National Intelligence Council. November 2008. www.dni.gov/files/documents/Newsroom/Reports%20and%20Pubs/2025_Global_Trends_Final_Report.pdf.

"Global Voter Turnout Declining." Press release. International IDEA. archive.idea.int/press/pr20020419.htm. Accessed October 23, 2017.

Glynn-Burke, Tim. "Inequality Is a Threat to American Democracy. Who Will Ring the Bell?" Challenges to Democracy Public Dialogue Series. Ash Center for Democratic Governance and Innovation, Harvard Kennedy School. December 17, 2013. www.challengestodemocracy.us/home/inequality-is-a-threat-to-american-democracy-who-will-ring-the-bell/#sthash.GVLoihqR.vxzITL9k.dpbs.

Gordon, Robert. "Is U.S. Economic Growth Over? Faltering Innovation Confronts the Six Headwinds." National Bureau of Economic Research. August 2012.

Gould, Elise. "2014 Continues a 35-Year Trend of Broad-Based Wage Stagnation." Economic Policy Institute. February 19, 2015. www.epi.org/publication/stagnant-wages-in-2014.

"Government Effectiveness Indicator." Millennium Challenge Corporation. www.mcc.gov/who-we-fund/indicator/government-effectiveness-indicator. Accessed March 4, 2017.

Graham, Carol. "Unhappiness in America." RealClear Politics, May 27, 2016. www.realclearpolitics.com/articles/2016/05/27/unhappiness_in_america_130669.html.

Greenberg, Jon. "47% Say They Lack Ready Cash to Pay a Surprise $400 Bill." *PolitiFact*, June 9, 2015. www.politifact.com/punditfact/statements/2015/jun/09/hunter-schwarz/47-say-they-lack-ready-cash-pay-surprise-400-bill.

Gwartney, James, Robert Lawson, and Joshua Hall. *Economic Freedom of the World: 2015 Annual Report.* Fraser Institute. September 14, 2015. www.fraserinstitute.org/studies/economic-freedom-of-the-world-2015-annual-report.

Haksever, Cengliz, and Barry Render. *Service Management: An Integrated Approach to Supply Chain Management and Operations.* Upper Saddle River, NJ: FT Press/Pearson Education, 2013.

Hansen, Stefan. "Democracy of the Future—Nothing Less." *Scenario*, May 19, 2011.

Hanushek, Eric A. "Economic Growth in Developing Countries: The Role of Human Capital." *Economics of Education Review* 37 (December 2013): 204–212.

Hardoon, Deborah. "An Economy for the 99%: It's Time to Build a Human Economy That Benefits Everyone, Not Just the Privileged Few." Oxfam International. January 2017. www.oxfam.org/en/research/wealth-having-it-all-and-wanting-more.

———. "Wealth: Having It All and Wanting More." Oxfam International. January 2015.

Hatzius, Jan, and Kris Dawsey. "Doing the Sums on Productivity Paradox 2.0." *Goldman Sachs US Economics Analyst* 15, no. 30 (July 2015).

Haub, Carl. "How Many People Have Ever Lived on Earth?" Population Reference Bureau. 2011.

Hausman, Jonathan. "Globalization and Emerging Market Portfolios." Presentation delivered at McGill University. February 2015.

Hedrick-Wong, Yuwa. "Economic Development and Productivity: The Crucial Linkage of Inclusive Growth." MasterCard Center. August 12, 2015, mastercardcenter.org/insights/economic-development-productivity-crucial-linkage-inclusive-growth.

Helliwell, John, Richard Layard, and Jeffrey Sachs, eds. *World Happiness Report 2017.* Sustainable Development Solutions Network. 2017. worldhappiness.report/wp-content/uploads/sites/2/2017/03/HR17.pdf.

"How Much Water Does It Take to Grow a Hamburger?" USGS Water Science School. water.usgs.gov/edu/activity-watercontent.html. Accessed March 3, 2017.

"Human Development Index." United Nations. hdr.undp.org/en/composite/HDI. Accessed November 15, 2017.

"Implementing the 2030 Agenda for Sustainable Development." United Nations Research Institute for Social Development. www.unrisd.org/80256B3C005BCCF9%2F%28httpAuxPages%29%2F92AF5072673F924DC125804C0044F396%2F%24file%2FFlagship2016_FullReport.pdf. Accessed July 13, 2017.

"In It Together: Why Less Inequality Benefits All." Organisation for Economic Co-operation and Development (OECD). May 21, 2015.

"In U.S., 67% Dissatisfied with Income, Wealth Distribution." Gallup. January 20, 2014. www.gallup.com/poll/166904/dissatisfied-income-wealth-distribution.aspx.

"Inequality: What Causes It, Why It Matters, What Can Be Done." *Foreign Affairs* (January/February 2016).

"International Property Rights Index 2017." Property Rights Alliance .internationalpropertyrightsindex.org.

"Investing in Britain's Future." Her Majesty's Treasury. June 2013. www.gov.uk/government/publications/investing-in-britains-future.

Isaksson, Anders, Thiam Hee Ng, and Ghislain Robyn. "Productivity in Developing Countries: Trends and Policies." United Nations International Development Organization. 2005.

Johnson, Steven. "China's Robot Army Set to Surge." *Financial Times*, April 8, 2016.

———. "Strongman Leaders More Trusted Than Democrats in Emerging World." *Financial Times*, October 16, 2016.

Kaplan, Steven N., and Joshua Rauh. "It's the Market: The Broad Based Rise in the Return to Top Talent." *Journal of Economic Perspectives* 27, no. 3 (Summer 2013): 35–56.

Keeley, Brian. "The Gap Between the Rich and the Poor." Organization for Economic Cooperation and Development. December 2015. www.keepeek.com/Digital-Asset-Management/oecd/social-issues -migration-health/income-inequality_9789264246010-en.

Kesler, Stephen E. "Mineral Supply and Demand into the 21st Century." USGS Online Publication Paper 9. 2007. pubs.usgs.gov /circ/2007/1294/reports/paper9.pdf.

Kessler, Glenn. "Trump's Claim That the US Pays the 'Lion's Share' for NATO." *Washington Post*, March 30, 2016.

"Key World Energy Statistics." International Energy Agency. 2016. www.iea.org/publications/freepublications/publication/KeyWorld 2016.pdf.

Keynes, John Maynard. "Economic Possibilities for Our Grandchildren." In *Essays in Persuasion*. New York: Harcourt, Brace, 1932.

Kharas, Homi, and Andrew Rogerson. "Horizon 2025 Report." Overseas Development Institute. July 2012.

Kochhar, Rakesh. "Seven-in-Ten People Globally Live on $10 or Less per Day." Pew Research Center. September 23, 2015. www .pewresearch.org/fact-tank/2015/09/23/seven-in-ten-people-globally -live-on-10-or-less-per-day.

Landes, David S. *The Wealth and Poverty of Nations: Why Some Are So Rich and Some So Poor*. New York: Norton, 1998.

Lawson, Greg R. "A Thirty Years' War in the Middle East." *National Interest*, April 16, 2014. nationalinterest.org/feature/thirty-years -war-the-middle-east-10266.

Lee, Joel. "Self Driving Cars Endanger Millions of American Jobs (and That's Okay)." *Make Use Of*, June 19, 2015. www.makeuseof.com /tag/self-driving-cars-endanger-millions-american-jobs-thats-okay.

"Legacies, Clouds, Uncertainties." International Monetary Fund. October 2014. www.imf.org/external/pubs/ft/weo/2014/02.

Legatum Prosperity Index. Legatum Institute. 2014. www.li.com
/programmes/prosperity-index.

Lipton, David. "Can Globalization Still Deliver? The Challenge of
Convergence in the 21st Century." International Monetary Fund.
May 24, 2016. www.imf.org/en/News/Articles/2015/09/28/04/53
/spo52416a.

"The Little Green Data Book 2016." World Bank Group. openknowledge
.worldbank.org/bitstream/handle/10986/24543/9781464809286
.pdf.

"Lobbying Database." Open Secrets. www.opensecrets.org/lobby. Accessed November 14, 2017.

Machin, Stephen, and John Van Reenen. *Changes in Wage Inequality*.
Centre for Economic Performance. April 2007. cep.lse.ac.uk/pubs
/download/special/cepsp18.pdf.

MacMillan, Margaret. *The War That Ended Peace: The Road to 1914*.
New York: Random House, 2013.

The Maddison-Project. 2013. www.ggdc.net/maddison/maddison-project
/home.htm.

Mahbubani, Kishore, and Lawrence H. Summers. "The Fusion of Civi-
lizations: The Case for Global Optimism." *Foreign Affairs* (May/
June 2016).

Malter, Jordan. "Why Poor People Still Aren't Voting." CNN Money,
August 5, 2015. money.cnn.com/2015/08/05/news/economy/poor
-people-voting-rights/index.html.

Malthus, Thomas Robert. "An Essay on the Principle of Population."
1798. www.esp.org/books/malthus/population/malthus.pdf.

Manyika, James, and Charles Roxburgh. "The Great Transformer:
The Impact of the Internet on Economic Growth and Prosperity."
McKinsey Global Institute. October 2011. www.mckinsey.com
/industries/high-tech/our-insights/the-great-transformer.

Manyika, James, Jonathan Woetzel, Richard Dobbs, Jaana Remes, Eric
Labaye, and Andrew Jordan. "Can Long-Term Global Growth Be
Saved?" McKinsey Global Institute. January 2015. www.mckinsey
.com/global-themes/employment-and-growth/can-long-term
-global-growth-be-saved.

———. *Global Growth: Can Productivity Save the Day in an Aging World?* McKinsey Global Institute. 2015.

Marcuss, Rosemary D., and Richard Kane. "U.S. National Income and Product Statistics." Bureau of Economic Analysis. February 2007. www.bea.gov/scb/pdf/2007/02%20February/0207_history_article .pdf.

Marshall, Monty G. "Polity IV Project: Political Regime Characteristics and Transitions, 1800–2013." Political Instability Task Force. June 5, 2014. www.systemicpeace.org/polity/polity4x.htm.

McKay, Betsy. "Life Expectancy for White Americans Declines." *Wall Street Journal*, April 20, 2016.

Meadows, Donnella H., Dennis L. Meadows, Jorgen Randers, and William W. Behrens III. "Limits to Growth." Club of Rome. 1972.

Meltzer, Joshua P. "Deepening the United States–Africa Trade and Investment Relationship." Brookings. January 28, 2016. www .brookings.edu/testimonies/deepening-the-united-states-africa -trade-and-investment-relationship.

"Millennial Disruption Index." Scratch Viacom Media Networks. 2013. www.millennialdisruptionindex.com.

Miller, John W., and William Mauldin. "U.S. Imposes 266% Duty on Some Chinese Steel Imports." *Wall Street Journal*, March 1, 2016.

Milman, Oliver. "Earth Has Lost a Third of Arable Land in Past 40 Years, Scientists Say." *Guardian* (London), December 2, 2015.

Mishel, Lawrence. "The Wedges Between Productivity and Median Compensation Growth." Economic Policy Institute. April 26, 2012. www.epi.org/publication/ib330-productivity-vs-compensation.

M. S. "Mandatory Voting: Want to Make Me?" *Economist*, May 20, 2015.

Murphy, Kevin M., and Robert H. Topel. "Human Capital Investment, Inequality and Economic Growth." National Bureau of Economic Research. January 2016. www.nber.org/papers/w21841.

Murray, Charles. "Trump's America." *Wall Street Journal*, February 12, 2016.

"National New-Type Urbanization Plan (2014–2020)." Mizuho Bank. March 16, 2014.

Natural Resources in 2020, 2030, and 2040: Implications for the United States. National Intelligence Council Report. Chatham House for the National Intelligence Council. May 2015. www.dni.gov/files /documents/NICR%202013-05%20US%20Nat%20Resources% 202020,%202030%202040.pdf.

Neiman, Brent. "The Global Decline of the Labor Share." *Quarterly Journal of Economics* 129, no. 1 (2014): 61–103.

Nettesheim, Christoph, Lars Faeste, Dinesh Khanna, Bernd Walter-mann, and Peter Ullrich. "Transformation in Emerging Markets: From Growth to Competitiveness." Boston Consulting Group. February 4, 2016. www.bcgperspectives.com/content/articles /globalization-growth-transformation-emerging-markets.

Nutting, Rex. "No, 'Truck Driver' Isn't the Most Common Job in Your State." *Market Watch*, February 12, 2015. www.marketwatch.com /story/no-truck-driver-isnt-the-most-common-job-in-your-state-2015 -02-12.

O'Connor, Sarah. "UK Productivity Falls by Most Since Financial Crisis." *Financial Times*, April 7, 2016.

"October 2015 Capital Flows to Emerging Markets." Institute of International Finance. October 1, 2015.

"October 2015 Stress from Within: EM Capital Flows Chartbook." Institute of International Finance. October 15, 2015. www.iif.com /publication/capital-flows/october-2015-stress-within-em-capital -flows-chartbook.

"ODNI Releases Global Water Security ICA." Office of the Director of National Intelligence. March 22, 2012. www.dni.gov/index .php/newsroom/press-releases/press-releases-2012/item/529-odni -releases-global-water-security-ica.

"OECD Better Life Index." Organisation for Economic Co-operation and Development (OECD). www.oecdbetterlifeindex.org. Accessed November 15, 2017.

"OECD Forum 2015: Income Inequality in Figures." Organisation for Economic Co-operation and Development (OECD). www.oecd .org/forum/issues/oecd-forum-2015-income-inequality-in-figures .htm. Accessed November 15, 2017.

Ortiz, Isabel. *Global Inequality: Beyond the Bottom Billion*. UNICEF. April 2011. www.unicef.org/socialpolicy/files/Global_Inequality .pdf.

Osborne, Hilary. "Rise in Consumer Borrowing Is Fastest Since Pre-crisis Says Bank of England." *Guardian* (London), January 4, 2016.

Panagopoulos, Costas. "The Calculus of Voting in Compulsory Voting Systems." *Political Behavior* 30, no. 4 (December 2008): 455–467.

Pasick, Adam. "Japan Is Rapidly Losing Population—and Half the World Is About to Join It." *Quartz*, January 2, 2014. qz.com/162788/japan-is-rapidly-losing-population-and-half-the -world-is-about-to-join-it.

Patterson, Thom. "Why Does America Have So Many Hungry Kids?" CNN, June 15, 2017. www.cnn.com/2017/06/09/health/champions -for-change-child-hunger-in-america/index.html.

Pescatori, Andrea, Damiano Sandri, and John Simon. "Debt and Growth: Is There a Magic Threshold?" International Monetary Fund. February 2014. www.imf.org/en/Publications/WP /Issues/2016/12/31/Debt-and-Growth-Is-There-a-Magic-Threshold -41352.

Pete, Joseph S. "U.S. Steel Starts Layoffs of Up to 323 Workers at Gary Works." *Northwest Indiana Times*, April 24, 2015.

Peters, Ole. "Developing a Time-Based Economic Formalism." Thinking Ahead Institute. November 11, 2015.

PGI Intelligence. "Mongolian Government Under Pressure to Resolve Mining Dispute Before End of Year." pgi-intelligence.com/news /getNewsItem/Mongolian-government-under-pressure-to-resolve -mining-dispute-before-end-of-year/499. Accessed March 4, 2017.

"PISA 2009 Results: What Students Know and Can Do." Organisation for Economic Co-operation and Development Programme for International Student Assessment. 2009. www.oecd.org/pisa/key findings/pisa2009keyfindings.htm.

"PISA 2012 Results: What Students Know and Can Do." Organisation for Economic Co-operation and Development Programme for International Student Assessment. July 2014. www.oecd.org/pisa /keyfindings/pisa-2012-results.htm.

"Population Projections for Japan (2017)." National Institute of Population and Social Security Research. www.ipss.go.jp/pp-zenkoku/e /zenkoku_e2017/g_images_e/pp29gts01e.htm. Accessed November 15, 2017.

Porter, Michael E., and Scott Stern, with Michael Green. *Social Progress Index 2017 Findings Report.* Social Progress Imperative. 2017. www .socialprogressindex.com/assets/downloads/resources/en/English -2017-Social-Progress-Index-Findings-Report_embargo-d-until -June-21-2017.pdf.

"The Privileged Few: To Those That Have Shall Be Given." Special Report: The World Economy. *Economist*, October 3, 2014.

Productivity Brief 2015. The Conference Board. 2015. www.conference -board.org/retrievefile.cfm?filename=The-Conference-Board-2015 -Productivity-Brief.pdf&type=subsite.

Rajan, Raghuram G. "Has Financial Development Made the World Riskier?" NBER Working Paper No. 11728. National Bureau of Economic Research. November 2005. www.nber.org/papers /w11728.

"Rate of Increase in Indian Population." Medindia. www.medindia.net /patients/calculators/pop_clock.asp. Accessed July 13, 2017.

"Real Wages in Germany: Numerous Years of Decline." DIW Berlin Weekly Report No. 28/2009. German Institute for Economic Research. October 23, 2009. www.diw.de/sixcms/media.php/73/diw _wr_2009-28.pdf.

Reeves, Aaron, Martin McKee, and David Stuckler. "Economic Suicides in the Great Recession in Europe and North America." *British Journal of Psychiatry* (June 2014).

Reinhart, Carmen M., Vincent R. Reinhart, and Kenneth Rogoff. "Public Debt Overhangs: Advanced Economy Episodes Since 1800." *Journal of Economic Perspectives* 26, no. 3 (Summer 2012): 69–86.

Reinhart, Carmen M., and Kenneth Rogoff. "Errata: Growth in a Time of Debt." *American Economic Review* (May 2013). www.carmenreinhart .com/user_uploads/data/36_data.pdf.

———. "Growth in a Time of Debt." *American Economic Review: Papers & Proceedings* 100, no. 2 (May 2010): 573–578. scholar.harvard .edu/files/rogoff/files/growth_in_time_debt_aer.pdf.

"Reinvention in the Rust Belt." *Economist*, July 11, 2015.

"Report Card on International Cooperation: 2015–2016." Council of Councils: An Initiative of the Council on Foreign Relations. www .cfr.org/councilofcouncils/reportcard2016/#!. Accessed July 13, 2017.

"Report on the Economic Well-being of US Households in 2013 (Executive Summary)." Federal Reserve. www.federalreserve.gov /econresdata/2013-report-economic-well-being-us-households-201407 .pdf.

"Report on the Municipal Securities Market." US Securities and Exchange Commission. July 31, 2012.

"Reports, Trends & Statistics." American Trucking Association. www .trucking.org/News_and_Information_Reports_Industry_Data .aspx. Accessed November 14, 2017.

"Results of the 2014 European Elections." European Parliament. 2014. www.europarl.europa.eu/elections2014-results/en/turnout .html.

"Ripe for Rebellion?" *Economist*, November 18, 2013.

Ritholtz, Barry. "Where Have All the Public Companies Gone?" *Bloomberg View*, June 24, 2015.

Roberts, Dexter. "China Wants Its People in the Cities." *Bloomberg*, March 20, 2014.

Rodrik, Dani, ed. *In Search of Prosperity: Analytic Narratives on Economic Growth*. Princeton, NJ: Princeton University Press, 2003.

———. "The Past, Present, and Future of Economic Growth." New York University. June 2013. www.technologyreview.com/s/515926 /how-technology-is-destroying-jobs.

Roser, Max. "Life Expectancy." Our World in Data. 2017. ourworldindata .org/life-expectancy.

Rosling, Hans. "Global Population Growth, Box by Box." TED. June 2010. www.ted.com/talks/hans_rosling_on_global_population _growth.

Rotman, David. "How Technology Is Destroying Jobs." *MIT Technology Review* (June 2013). www.technologyreview.com/s/515926 /how-technology-is-destroying-jobs.

Roxburgh, Charles, et al. "Lions on the Move: The Progress and

Potential of African Economies." McKinsey Global Institute. June 2010. www.mckinsey.com/global-themes/middle-east-and-africa/lions-on-the-move.

Ryan, Jennifer. "Robots Can't Replace IT Workers, Doctors, Dentists, Haldane Says." *Bloomberg*, December 16, 2015.

Safi, Michael. "Have Millennials Given Up on Democracy?" *Guardian* (London), March 18, 2016.

Sala-i-Martin, Xavier. "The Disturbing 'Rise' of Global Income Inequality." Working Paper No. 8904. National Bureau of Economic Research. April 2002. www.nber.org/papers/w8904.

Sandbu, Martin. "Free Lunch: Where Has All the Productivity Gone?: Arithmetic and the Golden Age of Growth." *Financial Times*, May 17, 2016.

Schwab, Klaus. *Global Competitiveness Report 2016–2017*. World Economic Forum. 2016. www3.weforum.org/docs/GCR2016-2017/05FullReport/TheGlobalCompetitivenessReport2016-2017_FINAL.pdf.

Scott, Robert E. "The Manufacturing Footprint and the Importance of U.S. Manufacturing Jobs." Economic Policy Institute. January 22, 2015. www.epi.org/publication/the-manufacturing-footprint-and-the-importance-of-u-s-manufacturing-jobs.

Scully, Gerald W. *Constitutional Environments and Economic Growth*. Princeton, NJ: Princeton University Press, 2014.

Shorto, Russell. "The Way Greeks Live Now." *New York Times Magazine*, February 13, 2012.

"A Slow-Burning Fuse." *Economist*. June 25, 2009.

"Small and Medium-Sized Enterprises: Local Strength, Global Reach." Policy Brief. *OECD Observer*, 2000. www.oecd.org/cfe/leed/1918307.pdf.

Spencer, Ben. "No Antibiotics Unless Doctors Run Tests: Superbugs Tsar Urges Crackdown over Fears Infections 'Will Kill More Than Cancer' by 2050." *Daily Mail* (London), May 18, 2016.

"Spring 2013 Survey." Pew Research Center. May 1, 2013. www.pewglobal.org/2013/05/01/spring-2013-survey.

Standing, Guy. "The Precariat and Class Struggle." *Revista Crítica de Ciências Sociais* 103 (May 2014): 9–24.

Stephanopoulos, Nicholas. "A Feasible Roadmap to Compulsory Voting." *Atlantic*, November 2, 2015.

Summers, Lawrence H. "The Age of Secular Stagnation." *Foreign Affairs*, February 15, 2016.

Sumner, Daniel A. "Recent Commodity Price Movements in Historical Perspective." *American Journal of Agricultural Economics* 91, no. 5, (2009): 1250–1256.

Szirmai, Adam. "Is Manufacturing Still the Main Engine of Growth in Developing Countries?" WiderAngle (blog). United Nations University–Wider. May 2009. www.wider.unu.edu/publication /manufacturing-still-main-engine-growth-developing-countries.

Thomas, G. P. "Argentina: Mining, Minerals, and Fuel Resources." *Azomining*, June 7, 2012. www.azomining.com/Article.aspx? ArticleID=21.

Thompson, Derek. "Get Rich, Live Longer: The Ultimate Consequence of Income Inequality." *Atlantic*, April 18, 2014.

Tontrup, Stephan, and Rebecca Morton. "The Value of the Right to Vote." New York University Public Law and Legal Theory Working Papers 536. 2015. lsr.nellco.org/nyu_plltwp/536.

Torday, Peter. "Coffee Price Soars After Brazilian Frost Damage." *Independent* (London), July 11, 1994.

"Trends in International Mathematics and Science Study (TIMSS)." National Center for Education Statistics. nces.ed.gov/timss. Accessed November 15, 2017.

"Trends in Urbanisation and Urban Policies in OECD Countries: What Lessons for China?" Organisation for Economic Co-operation and Development and China Development Research Foundation. 2009–2010. www.oecd.org/urban/roundtable/45159707.pdf.

"2016 Edelman Trust Barometer: Annual Global Study." 2016. www .edelman.com/insights/intellectual-property/2016-edelman-trust -barometer.

"2016 Index of Economic Freedom." Heritage Foundation. 2016. www .heritage.org/index.

"2017 Social Progress Index." Social Progress Imperative. 2017. www .socialprogressimperative.org/global-index.

"UBS Wealth Management Research Adjusted Big Mac Index 2014–2015." UBS. 2015. www.ubs.com/microsites/prices-earnings/edition-2015.html.

"Unemployment Statistics." Eurostat: Statistics Explained. October 2, 2017. ec.europa.eu/eurostat/statistics-explained/index.php/Unemployment_statistics.

"Universal Declaration of Human Rights." United Nations. 1948. www.un.org/en/universal-declaration-human-rights.

"U.S.-China Trade: Eliminating Nonmarket Economy Methodology Would Lower Antidumping Duties for Some Chinese Companies." Government Accountability Office. January 10, 2006. www.gpo.gov/fdsys/pkg/GAOREPORTS-GAO-06-231/html/GAOREPORTS-GAO-06-231.htm.

Van Reenen, John. "Wage, Inequality, Technology and Trade: 21st Century Evidence." *Labour Economics* 18, no. 6 (December 2011): 730–741.

Vina, Gonzalo. "UK Graduates Leave University with More Debt Than US Peers." *Financial Times*, April 28, 2016.

Vlieghe, Gertjan. "Debt, Demographics and the Distribution of Income: New Challenges for Monetary Policy." London School of Economics. January 18, 2016.

"Want to Make Me?" *Economist*, May 20, 2015.

Ward, John. "The Services Sector: How Best to Measure It." International Trade Administration. October 2010. trade.gov/publications/ita-newsletter/1010/services-sector-how-best-to-measure-it.asp.

Welfare Trends Report 2016. Office for Budget Responsibility, United Kingdom. October 2016. budgetresponsibility.org.uk/docs/dlm_uploads/Welfare-Trends-Report.pdf.

Weller, Chris. "Jeff Bezos Could Be the World's First Trillionaire by 2042." *Business Insider*, July 28, 2017.

Wharton, Knowledge. "Will Common Ground Between the U.S. and China Strengthen Their Bond?" Value Walk, April 11, 2016. www.valuewalk.com/2016/04/common-ground-u-s-china-vs-war.

"What Dutch Disease Is, and Why It's Bad." *Economist*, November 5, 2014.

"What Is the Impact of Mobile Telephony on GDP Growth?" Deloitte. November 2012.

"What's Gone Wrong with Democracy." *Economist*, February 27, 2014. www.economist.com/node/21596796.

Williamson, John, ed. *Latin American Adjustment: How Much Has Happened?* Institute for International Economics. March 1990.

Wilson, Dominic, and Roopa Purushothaman. "Dreaming with BRICs: The Path to 2050." Global Economics Paper No. 99. Goldman Sachs. October 1, 2003. www.goldmansachs.com/our-thinking /archive/archive-pdfs/brics-dream.pdf.

Woetzel, Jonathan, Anu Madgavkar, Kweilin Ellingrud, Eric Labaye, Sandrine Devillard, Eric Kutcher, James Manyika, Richard Dobbs, and Mekala Krishnan. "The Power of Parity: How Advancing Women's Equality Can Add $12 Trillion to Global Growth." McKinsey Global Institute. September 2015. www.mckinsey.com /global-themes/employment-and-growth/how-advancing-womens -equality-can-add-12-trillion-to-global-growth.

"Working Time Required to Buy: Who Works Harder to Buy a Big Mac?" UBS. www.ubs.com/microsites/prices-earnings/edition-2015 .html. Accessed March 3, 2017.

"World Bank Group President Jim Yong Kim's Speech at George Washington University—The World Bank Group Strategy: A Path to End Poverty." The World Bank. October 1, 2013.

"World Economic Outlook." International Monetary Fund. April 2017. www.imf.org/en/Publications/WEO/Issues/2017/04/04 /world-economic-outlook-april-2017.

"World Economic Outlook." International Monetary Fund. April 2016. www.imf.org/external/pubs/ft/weo/2016/01. Accessed March 3, 2017.

"World Economic Outlook: Legacies, Clouds, Uncertainties." International Monetary Fund. October 2014. www.imf.org/en /Publications/WEO/Issues/2016/12/31/World-Economic-Outlook -October-2014-Legacies-Clouds-Uncertainties-41632.

"World Economic Outlook Update: Subdued Demand, Diminished Prospects." International Monetary Fund. January 2016. www.imf .org/external/pubs/ft/weo/2016/update/01.

World Employment Social Outlook: Trends for Youth, 2016. International Labour Organization. 2016. www.ilo.org/wcmsp5/groups /public/---dgreports/---dcomm/---publ/documents/publication /wcms_513739.pdf.

"World GDP." *Economist*, May 20, 2014.

World Population Prospects: The 2015 Revision. Department of Economic and Social Affairs, United Nations. July 29, 2015. www.un.org/en /development/desa/publications/world-population-prospects-2015 -revision.html.

"World Urbanization Prospects." Population Division, Department of Economic and Social Affairs, United Nations. 2014. esa.un.org /unpd/wup.

Worldometers. www.worldometers.info/world-population. Accessed March 4, 2017.

"The World's Biggest Employers [Infographic]." *Forbes* (June 2015).

The World's Cities in 2016: Data Booklet. Population Division, Department of Economic and Social Affairs, United Nations. 2016. www.un.org /en/development/desa/population/publications/pdf/urbanization /the_worlds_cities_in_2016_data_booklet.pdf.

Zhu, Xiaodong. "Understanding China's Growth: Past, Present, and Future." *Journal of Economic Perspectives* 26, no. 4 (Fall 2012): 103–124.

Zingales, Luigi. "Capitalism After the Crisis." *National Affairs* (Fall 2009). nationalaffairs.com/publications/detail/capitalism-after-the -crisis.

———. "What Future for Capitalism?" Presentation. March 2010.

INDEX

Page numbers in italics refer to appendix table.

Dambisa Moyo is a prizewinning economist. The author of *New York Times* best sellers *Winner Take All* and *Dead Aid*, she was named one of the "100 Most Influential People in the World" by *Time*. Moyo is a regular contributor to the *Wall Street Journal* and *Financial Times*. She lives in New York City.

Photo credit: © Helen Trueman, Pink Orange Photography